Basing his argument on a wealth of historical and contemporary support, Jacobs makes a strong case for his argument that deference by federal courts to the political branches of government through their political question and standing doctrines is unconstitutional and denies individuals access to the courts to address violations of their most fundamental human and constitutional rights. Using the Juliana case as his primary example, Jacobs convincingly argues that we have reached a point to where only monied interests have effective access to the courts. His solution points to a difficult process of uniting the diverse voices of the American populace. An important and inspiring book for anyone interested in reclaiming fundamental human rights for the American people.

Lance N. Long
Professor of Law
Stetson University College of Law

Many writers have explored the negative impact of monied, special interests on American government, but Jacobs provides a unique perspective by focusing on the judicial branch and how it has become overly deferential to its political counterparts in recent decades. As evidenced by Jacobs' ample historical support, that deference means the courts no longer function how the founders intended – as a check on the branches more susceptible to special interests. Highlighting contemporary cases such as Juliana, Jacobs explores specifically how deference through the standing and political question doctrines denies ordinary citizens access to the courts, and how failure to review harmful political actions by acquiescing to those doctrines could likely be in itself unconstitutional. Refusing to accept the status quo, Jacobs proposes a return to proper judicial review as means to protect individual rights and ensure America is no longer a Dem— ~acy of Dollars moving forward.

ghey
Law
022

St_   ._ule Member
Stetson Democrats | Secretary

Let me congratulate you on a most complete, concise reporting of an incredible range of subjects and problems which have evolved in our system of governing since our forefathers set this great idea in motion. From your insightful look at partisan gerrymandering to the chaotic results of shadow lobbyists and administrative agencies run amuck, you have managed to enlighten, encourage and certainly interest not only the legal field, I'm sure, but additionally clarified such events and circumstances even to a lay person like me. Many thanks for your incredible efforts.

Joyce Beltz, retired

The Democracy of Dollars describes and decries the transformation of the US government into one in which the separation of powers provided by the Constitution has become amalgamated and corrupted: Influence peddling has strengthened special interests to the disadvantage of citizens, the Congress has abdicated its legislative duties, the Supreme Court no longer calls the balls and strikes with regard to clear Constitutional issues before it, the imperial presidency is unbound, and the unelected administrative state is accountable to no one. A fascinating read which ends with a plea to the reader to get involved, become informed, demand change. For only through the concerted will of the people will our democracy be restored.

Martha Lockhart, retired

Mandatory reading if you care about America!

John Cole, Attorney

First Edition

We thank Black's Law Dictionary, Bryan Garner, Editor, for the definitions used in this book that are identified [BLD] in its Definitions Appendix.

ISBN 978-1-64456-176-8
Library of Congress Control Number: 202094326

INDIES UNITED PUBLISHING HOUSE, LLC
P.O. BOX 3071
QUINCY, IL 62305-3071
http://www.indiesunited.net/

Dedicated to Our Children's Trust, and those gutsy kids and their pro bono attorneys, who have sued governments, state and federal, to protect children's inherent Natural and Constitutional Rights, which are being trampled by America's Democracy of Dollars.

DEMOCRACY
OF DOLLARS

**WHERE NATURAL AND CONSTITUTIONAL RIGHTS
GO TO THE HIGHEST BIDDER**

RICHARD JACOBS

INDIES UNITED PUBLISHING HOUSE, LLC

The Constitution of the United States is a carefully balanced document. It is designed to provide for a national government sufficiently strong and flexible to meet the needs of the republic, yet sufficiently limited and just to protect the guaranteed rights of citizens; it permits a balance between society's need for order and the individual's right to freedom.

About the Supreme Court
www.SupremeCourt.gov

I agree to this Constitution with all its faults.... I believe, further, that this is likely to be well administered for a course of years, and can only end in despotism, as other forms have done before it, when the people shall be so corrupted as to need a despotic government, being incapable of any other.

Benjamin Franklin
Constitutional Convention 1787

You are where you are today because you stand on somebody's shoulders. And wherever you are heading, you cannot get there by yourself. If you stand on the shoulders of others, you have a reciprocal responsibility to live your life so that others may stand on your shoulders. It's the quid pro quo of life. We exist temporarily through what we take, but we live forever through what we give.

Vernon E. Jordan, Jr.
Attorney, Civil Rights Activist
Circa 1990

Table of Contents

Foreword

It is the year 2021 and we live at the intersection of so many critical tipping points. The climate crisis. Racial injustice. A global health pandemic. Social media and the [mis]information age. Politicizing the Supreme Court. These tipping points tell us that our entire democracy is at risk. Will we be a true constitutional democracy for the sake of our children, or to a democracy sold to the highest bidder and the most influential interest groups?

These tipping points are interrelated and interdependent. As Dick Jacobs so insightfully explains in the pages to follow, the red tide of money's power in our constitutional democracy has become the lifeblood oxygenating these crises. While the arc of justice may be long and the pendulum will naturally swing along that arc, the scales of justice that live within any form of government can and do come crashing down when the systems no longer serve the people and those in power don't reform the systems.

What I love about *Democracy of Dollars*, and the incredible citizen behind it, is its historical, practical, and gracious optimism about what can yet be done to tip our nation back toward a healthy, sustainable constitutional democracy. Dick Jacobs never just lays down a problem and throws up his hands. He implores you to learn, question, explore, and then act, as he himself continues to faithfully do now in his ninth decade on our planet.

Dick Jacobs found me through his journeys around the world. A lawyer turned photographer and writer turned constitutional scholar and climate guardian. Dick first uncovered the climate crisis through his camera. He amplified Our Children's Trust and our most well-known case, *Juliana v. United States*, through his passion to see the planet protected from the utter failings of our majoritarian politics and the

1

ensuing climate destruction his journeys showed him. Dick Jacobs is an ethical caretaker and ally to future generations, the best kind of living ancestor, the kind I want my children to be one day.

The need for the stories contained in this book to make their way into the minds of Americans could not be more pressing or timely, and they will be relevant whether a Republican or a Democrat sits in the White House for these crises did not originate only under one party's power.

If we are living at the intersection of tipping points, then our courts are at its fulcrum. Central to Dick's plea to us to save our nation is for us to revive our third branch of our federal government to its vital role of calling balls and strikes in a way to provide each of us with the benefits of our democracy. As *Democracy of Dollars* shows us, if we really want to avoid revolution, we need to re-learn the lesson from James Madison: "A dependence on the people is, no doubt, the primary control on the government; *but experience has taught mankind the necessity of auxiliary precautions.*" Too often today, our courts fail to be that auxiliary precaution and shut their doors on the politically powerless minority, the interests that don't come monetized and who can't afford the price of admission to be heard.

Even the process of nominating and confirming our federal judges to their lifetime appointments has lost its precautionary nature. In the 2017 Seventh Circuit Court of Appeals confirmation hearing for Amy Coney Barrett (later confirmed to the Supreme Court by the Senate October 31, 2020, to replace Justice Ginsburg), Senator Sheldon Whitehouse said the judicial confirmation process had become preposterous. Whitehouse too has long warned of the monetization of democracy: "I look out at a very significant machinery of influence that is designed, that has as its purpose, to bring the will of ideological and commercial interests into our courts in ways that will follow the wishes of those ideological and commercial interests. And then I see nominees who have the support of that President with his litmus tests and with his disregard for the rule of law who've been cleared by those very ideological and commercial interests for policymaking on our courts."

And yet, despite these many daunting tipping points, weighted heavily with dollars, I believe, like Dick, that we can reclaim our children's inalienable rights, their equal protection of the law, and be good ancestors for Our Posterity. We can reclaim our courts and rescue our democracy through good lawyering, good judging, and good citizenship. Justice Ginsburg wrote in *U.S. v. VMI*: "A prime part of the history of our Constitution ... is the story of the extension of constitutional rights and protections to people once ignored or excluded ... as our comprehension of 'We the People' expanded." It starts with waking up and ends with never giving up.

The book that follows is a culmination of a lifetime of learning and of love, for our laws, our land, and our legacy. It is an honor and a gift to know Dick Jacobs. We are all better off for his many contributions to our country and our planet. I hope this book inspires others, as it did me, to keep striving for justice and fighting for the survival of our constitutional democracy from the pinnacle of that proverbial – and, for our planet, literal - melting iceberg on which it rests. Read on and join us as a difference maker.

Julia A. Olson
Chief legal counsel, Our Children's Trust
Lead counsel, *Juliana v. United States*

Preface

In 1919, Supreme Court Justice Oliver Wendell Holmes, in a famous dissent, wrote that our Constitution is an "experiment, as all of life is an experiment." The experiential history of our Constitution is a continuum of course corrections, as we so often stumble in our attempts to retain a founding purpose. We fail from time to time to keep our world on track, often bringing American institutions and people to the precipice of crisis and failure.

Democracy of Dollars creates a narrative that exposes and examines the systemic threat to 21st Century America. This threat has grown exponentially in recent times, suppressing the Democracy of People the Framers of our Constitution provided for themselves and for us as their posterity.

Although I am an attorney, *Democracy of Dollars* is not speaking primarily to an audience of lawyers. Nor is *Democracy of Dollars* a political book. Political authors implicitly choose sides and sooner rather than later begin filtering the issues through a partisan or factional lens. That filtering is a kind of censorship that has become the *weltanschauung* of today's discourse, which limits enlightenment, rather than facilitates it. However, in the interests of currency, the elemental examples provided in this book are set in today's reality – the reality provided us during the Presidency of Donald J. Trump. Although the Democracy of Dollars, and the issues we present, did not originate during Trump's Presidency, Trump's ramp up provides us with current examples useful in our analyses.

But the underlying issues will not disappear simply because a successor administration leads our nation. Until we have the courage to rid ourselves of the Democracy of Dollars infliction, the potential harm of the underlying issues will continue to fester and harm us whether Republicans or Democrats are in charge. The harm will occur until we reestablish our Democracy of People.

Democracy of Dollars is about context, not theory. It is an examination of today's context in which the interplay of our three branches of government – the legislative, executive, and judiciary – reveal themselves as far different institutions than those in 1789, when our Constitution was adopted. Although our Constitution's Framers had remarkable insight, they never contemplated America as it exists today.

General Colin Powell once said that understanding context in military preparation is everything. Similarly, in our course-correcting as we live the American experiment, context is the guiding light in our making good decisions. A decision that was made, or a theory that was promulgated, decades or centuries ago under different circumstances may not work in our times.

What is the context of our times, here in America?

As a society we have morphed from a Democracy of People into a Democracy of Dollars, described in detail in the chapters that follow. Consequently, the two political branches of our federal government, the legislative and the executive branches, designed to protect and serve all Americans, have become willing resources to special interests who, in today's pricy politics, can buy their way to the head of the line.

Besides our two political branches of government, fortunately, our national government has a co-equal third institution, the judicial branch, the federal judiciary headed by the Supreme Court. The federal judiciary, with its lifetime appointment of judges, is intended by our Constitution's Framers to function as nonpolitical and independent. And, most importantly, the judiciary is intended to provide a constitutional check over the other two branches. Supreme Court Chief Justice Roberts said in his 2005 confirmation hearing, "Judges are like umpires.... They make sure everybody plays by the rules."

The "everybody" includes our two political branches of government, and the Court itself.

Unfortunately, the Court has grown overly dependent on its

judge-made rules of deference to those political branches. By so doing, it has too frequently discarded its important judicial review function of their actions and inactions. Thus, the Court has become their unwitting handmaiden, allowing the political branches to operate outside the four corners of our Constitution. Unchaperoned by constitutional checks and balances, the political branches too frequently fail to operate by the rules.

To use a metaphor neither we nor the Court should overlook, the 21st Century sandlot in which our government plays its game today is not the same as the 18th Century sandlot when the Constitution was adopted. The game of government is not played the same way. The equipment is different. The ground rules are different. The price of admission is different. The Court's challenge in fulfilling its umpire role is dramatically different.

It may seem counterintuitive that I, an attorney, would argue that the Supreme Court should be more sensitive to context and less bogged down by its judge-made rules. However, in today's Democracy of Dollars, the rights of individuals are too often subordinated by a political branch of government aligning itself with special interests and their lobbies. When that happens, the judicial branch's deference to the political branch fails the American people. A consequence, as I see it, is that our Supreme Court must reassert its umpire role in an independent, nonpolitical way, providing the checks and balances over our two political branches of government with the objective of protecting the unalienable rights of the people.

Rights-protection is what Thomas Jefferson wrote about in 1776 in our Declaration of Independence. It is what people seek when they form their government. The checks and balances must operate successfully in the context of each successive generation. To reach our constitutional destiny, and accomplish its mission in protecting our rights, the 21st Century Supreme Court must follow the lead of the Supreme Court at the early beginnings of our country.

The prime role model was provided by Chief Justice John Marshall, appointed by our second President, John Adams. During the 34 years of John Marshall's leadership, the Marshall Court did more than call balls and strikes. Through its role as umpire, it shaped the responsibilities of the Supreme Court for all time. The Marshall Court defined the role of the federal judiciary and architected judicial solutions needed to deal with constitutional ambiguities or omissions. The Marshall Court was a solution-oriented judiciary. It created legal precedents – stare decisis — courts follow as authority to this day.

The 21st Century Supreme Court must be of a similar mindset when it comes to its use of its judge-made rules of deference created in another time, when special interests and lobbies were less influential. Today's Court must revamp its judge-made rules of deference, rules we discuss in this book. Rather than negate its judicial authority through deference to the political branches, the Court must reassert its constitutional responsibility. In particular, the Court must provide judicial reviews of cases and controversies when natural and constitutional rights of persons are at stake. Because the Supreme Court decisions bind lower federal and state courts, the judicial system falls into sync with an engaged Supreme Court.

Now, what does all this have to do with us in 21st Century America?

This question brings me to a central thesis of my narrative. In today's complexity it is impossible to totally change the over-all way our government operates, primarily through administrative agencies within the executive branch – a method of operation that by its very nature enhances the influence of special interests. Constitutional amendments might create a structure for change. But that kind of change is difficult, expensive, time consuming, and unlikely to provide the solutions we need. Amendments must originate through Congress and the state legislatures, which in too many instances today are the source of the problems the amendments must address.

What we and the Court need to hear is a strong voice that

originates from the people. A strong, persistent voice will catch the attention of the Court. Ultimately, the Court will recognize that its Deference Doctrines yielding to the two political branches is in fact abandonment of its constitutional status as a coequal branch of government. The Court's Deference Doctrines, which negate judicial review, invite influence and power from special interests and their lobbies into our government. This book calls for this void in the Court's performance to be corrected.

Over time, public influence can have a dynamic and positive effect on the Court. David Cole, national legal director of the ACLU, wrote in the 2016 *Engines of Liberty:* "The reality is that the formal mechanisms of constitutional law – the separation of powers, a Bill of Rights, federalism, and judicial review – are not enough to sustain liberty. Citizen engagement on the side of liberty is essential to the defense, and the evolution, of the nation's fundamental values." Effective citizen engagement takes sustained action. It takes dedication over the "long haul." Without meaningful citizen engagement, as Judge Learned Hand said in 1944 in a talk with political immigrants, liberty can die and "no court can save it." To reignite our Democracy of Dollars, we cannot remain silent on the sidelines. As important as voting is, it is not enough.

But with citizen engagement, public influence can guide the Court in perceiving and understanding the systemic threats to our survival as a nation that can otherwise overwhelm and destroy us. Public influence can guide the Court to understand that its deference to the political branches defeats the Court's responsibility to protect the people and has the unintended effect of empowering special interests to our detriment.

The Court has fulfilled this responsibility in the past. In response to public outcries, our Supreme Court has reacted to fill unmet human needs. It has recognized new forms of cruel and unusual punishment. It has guaranteed that people charged with serious crimes must have appointed counsel. And perhaps, in its most shining hour, it has recognized that "separate but equal" education violates the 14th Amendment's equal protection guarantee to all children regardless of race.

The Court also had no timidity in America's Gilded Age, the late 1800s, the period of great economic expansion as America moved from coast to coast. In 1886, the Court decided that corporations were "persons" within the meaning of the 14th Amendment. Thus, corporations are entitled access to federal courts and a bevy of constitutional rights intended by the Founders exclusively for individuals. Furthermore, the Court did not hesitate to opine in a series of cases, collectively known since 2010 as *Citizens United,* that unlimited amounts of money contributed in political campaigns is a form of constitutionally protected "free speech." However, those sorts of decisions by the Court represent the musings of an activist court, stretching the Constitution beyond its four corners and underlying intent to reach a political goal. The Court's political activism represented by those decisions has contributed to the diminution of our Democracy of People and its replacement by a Democracy of Dollars. Thom Hartmann concludes in his 2019 *The Hidden History of The Supreme Court and the Betrayal of America* that by those decisions the Court "essentially handed our elections over to the highest bidders."

Clearly, a course correction by the Court is needed if we are to return to our Democracy of People.

Fulfilling the Court's responsibility, as this book advocates, does not make the Court an activist court, moving us outside the frame of the Constitution. Rather, when fulfilling its responsibility, the Court is an engaged Court. An engaged Court is fully attuned to the challenges of the 21st Century, bringing the political branches back within the intent and meaning of the Constitution. In doing so, the Court shines as the bastion of American democracy and the protector of our rights. That is its role as envisioned by our nation's Founders in the Declaration of Independence and Constitution. Reaching this goal will require the encouragement by the strong voice of the people.

Perhaps most illustrative of the role of a strong public voice is the way the Supreme Court listened to the public during the Great Depression in the 1930s. The Court's record evolved from opining that Franklin Roosevelt's New Deal legislation was unconstitutional to the Court's supporting it.

In her 1958 American Heritage article, "F.D.R. Vs. The Supreme Court," Merlo Pusey wrote, "The great struggle between the President and the Supreme Court in 1937 stirred the national emotions to unusual depths because it brought Franklin D. Roosevelt's crusade against depression into collision with one of our most hallowed traditions.... [I]t remains high on the list of the most dramatic contests in our constitutional history."

William Leuchtenburg wrote in his 2005 article for the Smithsonian, "When Franklin Roosevelt Clashed with the Supreme Court and Lost," that the early Supreme Court decisions holding the offerings of Roosevelt's New Deal legislation unconstitutional "drew biting criticism, from inside and outside the court.... On the night following [the Court's] opinion, a passerby in Ames, Iowa, discovered life-size effigies of the six majority justices hanged by the side of the road." Disgusted with the Court's holding New York's minimum wage law unconstitutional, Secretary of the Interior Harold Ickes said, "If this decision does not outrage the moral sense of the country then nothing will."

The monumental public fight between Roosevelt and the Court was described by Leuchtenburg as the fight for the Court's need for independence versus the fact that "a few judges appointed for life would be able to ignore the popular will, destroy programs vital to the welfare of the people...." A frustrated Roosevelt proposed legislation to solve the problem: he would pack the Court with new judges. His court-packing proposal failed to gain support from Congress or the people – on that point he lost. But after a few initial setbacks, the Supreme Court never again held any other of Roosevelt's New Deal legislation unconstitutional. Among the results: we have Social Security and a minimum wage.

Pusey concludes her American Heritage article with: "The net effect of the 1935-37 ferment over constitutional issues was to confirm their insistence that the judges must take into account changed social and economic conditions as well as past legal precedents.... The principle for which they struggled was continued independent judgment on the part of the court [stood firm]."

This question needs to be asked. Has our Court – have we – forgotten the lessons from that struggle?

This book illustrates how our democracy and many of our unalienable rights have suffered as a result of the forgotten lessons. The public voices so important in championing our rights in the past have grown too silent.

After introducing *The Problem*, Part I and its three chapters provide us with a background about our Constitution.

In Chapter 4, we focus on the Supreme Court's indifference to Congress's delegation of its exclusive legislative power to the executive branch's administrative agencies. The outcome is to increase the political power and influence of special interests on our government.

In Chapter 5, we focus on the Supreme Court's deference through judge-made rules of "standing" and "redressability" that deny judicial review to aggrieved persons whose rights have been injured by a political branch of government. These Deference Doctrines leave the injured without effective remedies.

Chapter 6 focuses on the plight of individuals whose voting effectiveness is diluted by partisan gerrymandering, through a judge-made "political question" rule. This Deference Doctrine destroys the Constitution's mandate that the vote of each person is equally effective.

Chapter 7 looks closely at the chaotic effect of our legislative branch's sweeping delegation of legislative and judicial powers to the executive branch. The result has been the unfettered growth of our "fourth branch" of government. That administrative state has created the 21st Century's "Era of Presidential Administration" as our government's modus operandi, driven by lobbies and special interests and not the will of the people.

Chapter 8 focuses on our natural rights, rights not written into the Constitution's Bill of Rights, but protected by Article 9 of the Bill of Rights. Natural rights have their roots deep within the history of humankind, predating the Constitution. These rights include life, liberty and the pursuit of happiness championed in the Declaration of Independence. Too many of these unenumerated rights — particularly those rights that provide for a healthy environment, clean air, and clean water – are being badly damaged by our political branches of governments' devotion to special interests. However, the little-used Article 9 of the Bill of Rights, which provides, "The enumeration in the Constitution of certain rights, shall not be construed to deny or disparage others retained by the people," confirms for us that, although these fundamental human rights are not constitutional rights, our Constitution protects them from manipulation or interference by the political branches of government.

These examples are not exclusive, they are illustrative. And they lead us to an important conclusion, expressed in an old saw attributed to Michael Moore:

"Democracy is not a spectator sport, it's a participatory event. If we don't participate in it, it ceases to be a democracy."

An engaged Court and the importance of the voice of the people are the subjects of the final section of this book. America needs us to become involved. The Epilogue provides us with five takeaways from the 2020 presidential election, and the insurrection and failed coup d'état that followed. These takeaways confirm that we must be an informed and active citizenry if we are to reestablish our Democracy of People.

In our discussion, certain key legal terms are used. Legal terms are defined in the Definitions appendix and in appropriate chapters.

Please read on.

Dick Jacobs
Tierra Verde, Florida
March 2021

We are all Republicans; we are all Federalists.

President Thomas Jefferson
First Inaugural Address, March 4, 1801

Prologue

I am writing this *Prologue* in late 2020, at a time when the most contentious presidential political campaign and election of my lifetime refuses to draw to a harmonious close. The contention has deep roots within our political culture and has been growing for years.

The inability of competing political parties to talk to and work with each other, along with the growing inability for people to determine the truthfulness of the news and what our government tells us, has been too much. The American people have lost faith in our institutions and our political leadership.

In July 2020, the Associated Press-NORC Center for Public Affairs Research reported that three-quarters of Americans believe our country is headed in the wrong direction.

Trust in our government's political institutions could hardly be lower.

A January 2020 Pew Research Center thirty-three country international poll concluded that only 29% of the people in those countries trusted our President. In February 2020, Pew found that "just 15% of U.S. adults say they like the way he conducts himself as President." In June 2020, Gallup determined that just 25% of Americans trusted Congress.

Pew's poll in July 2019 reported two-thirds of Americans said they find it hard to tell when elected officials are telling the truth. Political parties are factious and rarely agree. They hardly speak to each other. The growing political divide between political parties and the eroding public trust in our political institutions and elected officials represents a serious handicap in our nation's abilities to solve its pressing problems.

In 1952, when I was a student at the University of Wisconsin, I cast my first presidential vote, for Eisenhower as President. During his two terms, Pew reported in a 2015 study, that trust in the federal government to do the right thing most of the time exceeded 70%. Trust reached an all-time high, 77% in 1964, the year Lyndon Johnson defeated Barry Goldwater.

Pew also reported in the same study that in the decade after Johnson's election, "a period that included the Vietnam War, civil rights legislation, civil unrest and Nixon's Watergate Scandal," public trust fell to 36%. "By the end of the 1970s, only about a quarter of Americans felt they could trust the government at least most of the time." There were ups and downs in the 1980s and 1990s, with trust never exceeding 50% until the 9/11 attacks in 2001 when trust rose to 60%. But Trust fell in the "summer of 2002 to the 20-25% range, essentially where it has remained."

Pew's 2015 study also concluded that the lack of trust in government "has been mirrored by the steep decline in the belief that the government is run for the benefit of all Americans."

As contentious as our times may be, they pale in comparison to the election of 1800 and the political conflicts which led up to it. Alfred J. Mapp, Jr., wrote in his 1987 *Thomas Jefferson, a Strange Case of Mistaken Identity*, those were times when our young nation suffered through its "Struggle of Titans." Mapp refers to the battle of our Founders, the Framers of our Constitution, who couldn't agree on the kind of government the Constitution they wrote and just adopted was meant to give us.

George Washington, our first President, was unanimously elected to two terms by the electoral college. His first term began April 30, 1789. During his presidency, as Washington and his cabinet wrestled with problems, both domestic and international, differing views about the role our federal government should play developed.

There were sharply contrasting opinions about the Constitution's implied but unstated meanings, as new and unforeseen problems and opportunities faced our young nation. For example, Washington established the first "cabinet" under the Constitution's implied meaning. The Constitution does not provide for an executive branch cabinet. Washington also issued the first eight presidential executive orders, also not specifically authorized by the Constitution.

Some of Washington's cabinet members saw America as a nation of commerce with a need for international alliances and taxes to build our infrastructure. They were led by Alexander Hamilton, Washington's Secretary of Treasury, and favored a strong central government. Hamilton had an ally in John Adams, Washington's Vice President. This faction ultimately formed the Federalist Party (later replaced by the Republican Party).

Other cabinet members saw America as primarily a nation of small farmers with low taxes. Those favored a decentralized government and were led by Thomas Jefferson, Washington's Secretary of State, who picked up an ally in James Madison. That faction became the Republican Party (initially referred to as the Democratic-Republican Party, and ultimately given the name of the Democratic Party).

When Washington declined to serve a third term, he retired. His Vice President, John Adams, became our second President in the election of 1796, winning the electoral college by three votes. Adams' opponent, Thomas Jefferson, came in second in voting. Under the checks and balances in our original Constitution (amended by the 12th Amendment in 1804), Jefferson became Adams' Vice President. During that period, it became apparent that political parties were necessary to channel conflicting views among the American people on the role of government.

Washington opposed political parties and when he died during Adams' term, our nation lost his leadership, and its cohesiveness.

For the first time, with the election of 1800, political parties nominated candidates. Each party nominated two, with the idea that the candidate with the most votes would be President and the runner up would be Vice President. Each member of the electoral college could cast two votes.

The 1800 election pitted the Federalist candidates, Adams, seeking his second term, and Charles Pinckney, against the Republicans' Jefferson and Aaron Burr. The campaigns, however, were very contentious and failed to produce the expected result. Jefferson and Burr, not Jefferson and Adams, tied for the lead.

Among the issues, New Englanders favored the Federalists and sought a return to a closer relationship between religion and government. They did not trust Jefferson and labeled him an atheist. Some New Englanders feared they would have to hide their Bibles from Jefferson if he were elected. The political differences between New Englanders and the rest of the 13 states were so strong that New England thought about leaving the union.

It took 36 ballots in the House of Representatives – and Hamilton's efforts to influence Federalists to vote for Jefferson – before the deadlock between Jefferson and Burr was broken. Jefferson only then became our third President, Burr his Vice President.

After being sworn into office by Supreme Court Chief Justice John Marshall, Jefferson delivered his first inaugural address. It was a masterful speech, set on healing the factions that had built in our nation. Jefferson began with recognition that America was a "rising nation, spread over a wide and fruitful land, traversing all the seas with rich productions of their industry, engaged with commerce with nations who feel power and forget right…" followed by: "During the contest of opinion through which we have passed, the animation of discussions and of exertions has sometimes worn an aspect which might impose on strangers unused to think freely, and to speak and write as they think; but this being now decided by the voice of the nation…. [The differences] will of course arrange themselves under the rule of law and unite in common efforts for the common good…. Let us then, fellow citizens unite with one heart and one mind, let us restore to social intercourse that harmony and affection without which liberty, and even life itself, are but dreary things.... We are all republicans: we are all federalists."

As our young nation settled into its new form of government as a democratic republic, factions and differing views about the independence of each of the three branches of government surfaced. Which branch had the ultimate authority regarding the Constitution's mandate of checks and balances was far from resolved. It was in Jefferson's first term of office that Chief Justice John Marshall, a Federalist appointed by President Adams, took charge, and resolved the question.

The Marshall Court defined the role of the Supreme Court as the final arbiter to determine whether Congress's laws were constitutional. Marshall rejected the Jeffersonian idea that the Constitution was merely a platform on which Congress could stand to build on with later laws.

Marshall's 1803 *Marbury v. Madison* Opinion, which we discuss in Chapter 5, asserted that Congress did not have the power to modify the Constitution by passing laws. Rather, the Constitution, being a grant of power, provides the full expression of the authority for Congress's legislative powers. The Supreme Court, Marshall opined, has "emphatically the duty to say what the law is" and, as to the President and other officers, "no high [executive] officer is above the law."

The *Marbury* opinion solidified the Court's role as including constitutional checks and balances over both the legislative and executive branches through its judicial review. That role is the most important responsibility the Supreme Court and the federal judiciary have.

But, as I argue in this book, it is an essential role from which the Supreme Court too frequently strays in our time. During these fractious times, when our Democracy of People has morphed into a Democracy of Dollars driven by special interests, the Court's check and balance role must be reestablished.

We started this *Prologue* with context provided by Pew's

research on the attitude of the American people about our government's direction and the lack of confidence we have in our political branches of government, the legislative and executive branches.

Of prime importance to our discussion is the Pew 2015 study concluding that our lack of trust in government "has been mirrored by the steep decline in the belief that the government is run for the benefit of all Americans." That uneasy feeling each of us has is a result of our Democracy of People morphing over time into today's Democracy of Dollars. Lack of trust is primarily the result of our two political branches of government, the legislative and executive branches, operating as an oligarchy, the government of the few for the benefit of a privileged few, driven by dollars and not the will of the people.

Of our three institutions, legislative, executive, and judicial, public confidence in the Supreme Court and its judicial branch remains highest. A September 2020 Pew Research Center Survey, reported by Hannah Hartig in "Before Ginsburg's death, a majority of Americans viewed the Supreme Court as 'middle of the road,'" concluded that 70% of Americans viewed the Supreme Court favorably.

We argue in the *Preface,* and throughout this book, that an independent, engaged Supreme Court providing constitutional checks and balances is, along with a strong voice of the people, necessary for us to return to a Democracy of People.

However, a May 2019 Quinnipiac University poll warned that there is a growing understanding among Americans that Supreme Court appointments have become too political. To the poll's question, "In general do you think that the Supreme Court is mainly motivated by politics or mainly motivated by the law?" 55% chose "politics."

For years, Senatorial confirmations of the federal judiciary were subject to its filibuster rule. It takes a vote of sixty percent of the Senators to waive a Senator's right to filibuster a vote. That rule was revoked, first by the Democrats in 2013 for judicial appointments other than the Supreme Court, and then by the Republicans in 2017 for Supreme Court appointments. Since compromise is no longer necessary, politicization of the appointment and confirmation process intensified.

With the October 2020 confirmation of Amy Coney Barrett as Ginsburg's successor, six of the current nine judges have been appointed by Republican presidents. Unlike past judicial appointments, which followed Senatorial discussion and compromise necessary to earn 60 votes, the most recent three appointments confirmed by the Republican Senate majority (Gorsuch, Kavanaugh and Barrett) were made without meaningful input or vote from Democrat Senators.

In contrast, in 1986, with the filibuster rule in place, when President Reagan nominated conservative justice Antonin Scalia, he was confirmed 98-0. When President Clinton nominated liberal justice Ruth Bader Ginsburg, she was confirmed 96-3. Republican Presidents have appointed 15 out of the last 19 Supreme Court judges. Appointments before Gorsuch's appointment in 2017 required confirmation votes from Democrats.

Without the guidance of the filibuster rule, the contentious factions our Framers were sure would be minimized by our Constitution have been extended to the lifetime appointments of the judiciary. In the future, Democratic appointments could likewise be confirmed without Republican input. The result would be the continuation of the politicization of the confirmation process. The extension thwarts the Framers' intent that the judiciary be independent and nonpolitical — capable of fulfilling their umpire role for the benefit of all Americans. A balanced, middle of the road Court sought by the American people has become further out of reach, to the detriment of us all. Thus, concerns of Americans that our government doesn't represent all of us are perpetuated.

Throughout this book, we focus on underlying issues that have grown over decades, regardless of the political party in power. Our failure to solve these issues has produced today's Democracy of Dollars. That failure should be a concern to each of us regardless of our political affiliation.

The November 3, 2020 election results reflect the broad divide we have in this country. Reporting on the election in the November 16, 2020 issue of *Time Magazine*, David French writes in "Polarization Prevailed, Again," that "[T]he nation's politics look like a version of trench warfare… [T]he reality of American politics and culture remain the same. Our nation is deeply divided, our partisans are very angry, and there is no immediate prospect for change."

That divide is exacerbated by America's Democracy of Dollars. We repeat:

> "Our factiousness will not subside until we reinstate the Democracy of People our Constitution's Framers sought to provide for us as their 'Posterity.'"

A Democracy of Dollars speaks for a few, with no regard for the many. A Democracy of People speaks for the many, but with regard for the few.

Democracy of Dollars is driven by money, not principle. A Democracy of People is driven by principle, not money.

A Democracy of People confirms that our government is run for the benefit of us all.

The confidence of the American people in our government and its institutions must be restored. Contributing to that objective is the mission of this book.

Throughout this book, we stress our need for a Supreme Court that provides us with constitutional checks and balances over the two political branches of government. We point out course corrections the Court must make.

We advocate for a strong *Voice of the People,* so necessary to influence the result we all seek: a return to our Democracy of People. A return to our cherishing the "We." The *We* in *We the People*, the opening stanza of our Constitution.

The essence of democracy is that the right to make law rests in the people and flows to the government, not the other way around. Freedom resides first in the people without need of a grant from government.

Justice Anthony Kennedy, dissent
Hollingsworth v. Perry, 2013

The Problem

Lincoln's Apple of Gold

We Americans are uncommonly lucky. Thomas Jefferson, James Madison, and the other Founding Fathers who shaped our country were not simply gun-slinging revolutionaries; they were men anchored in worldly philosophies. The Age of Enlightenment was their *Weltanschauung* – their worldview, their political "ground of being."

Our Founding Fathers' thinking was not short term, concerned only about the here and now. The Founders understood the awesome responsibility for future generations they had assumed. Their sense of history and purpose underlies their heroic conduct.

John Locke's writings in his *Second Treatise on Government* were important for Jefferson, the author of our Declaration of Independence. Jefferson considered Locke, along with Bacon and Newton, as the three most influential men in history. It was Locke who wrote in 1690 that all men have natural rights to life and liberty. He also wrote that in the state of nature, men's rationality led them to behave socially. Locke concluded, however, that the self-interest of some men leads them to violate the natural rights of others. It is to protect individuals' rights that governments are formed.

After his Presidency, in a letter to James Madison, Jefferson proposed that Locke's work, along with the Federalist Papers, be mandatory readings in Virginia's law school.

But times change. Our study of the past and its meaning for today has become shallow or nonexistent not only in our law schools, but also in all our schools.

Seventy years ago, in 1950, sociologists David Riesman and his co-authors wrote in *The Lonely Crowd* that from those days of the Age of Enlightenment, our American society gradually changed from a people who were "inner-directed" to a people who become "other-directed." Relationships in other-directed societies tend to be shallow and mass media driven. Advertisers tell us what we should be like, what we should wear, what we should value, and what we should do from childhood throughout our lives. Marketing has become the prevailing source of judgment and measure of success.

Thus, when challenges come to us, there is no deeply imbedded ground of being. There is no internal guidance system providing us with a source of judgment to measure proper actions or reactions. Short-term behavior – selfish and fickle – becomes the norm. Without internal grounding, people become narcissistic, shifting blame to others, grabbing what they can at the expense of anyone in their way.

Ironically, a decade after Jefferson wrote our Declaration of Independence, as James Madison architected our Constitution, he considered those issues in his 1787 *Federalist Papers #10*. Madison's concern was about factions – citizens actuated by passion or interest averse to the rights of others or of the community. He concluded that democracy inherently cannot control factions, for the "overbearing" tyranny of the majority prevails. Although he could not foresee the concentration of today's wealth and it's distorting political influence, he recognized that the unequal distribution of property was one of the greatest causes of factions.

Madison recognized that factions reside deep within the nature of man. Thus, neither moral nor religious motives can provide enough control to benefit either man or society. Madison also understood enlightened statesmen will not always be at the helm. And he concluded that factions could not be eliminated without destroying liberty.

Since the causes of factions can't be removed, the effects of factions must be controlled by the structure of government. Representative government is a necessity. Elected representatives, Madison wrote, provide the people with a "public voice." But he recognized that representatives can also corrupt their public trust. When factions are in control, they can be tyrannical, even when they represent the majority. Thus, the "structure" of government must be such that it protects the rights of people. The republican democracy architected in our Constitution by Madison, with its three branches, is structured to provide balance. Factions within a state may "kindle a flame," he wrote, but balance comes from competing factions in other states and by the independence of the federal branches.

As we reflect on the sacred writings of our Founders – our Declaration of Independence and our Constitution, the first written by Jefferson, the latter by Madison a decade later – we could easily read them as unconnected documents. The Declaration is a writing of motivating philosophy, written to start a revolution. The Constitution, a thoughtfully crafted working document of delegated powers and reserved rights, was written to establish the principles for a new government, a constitutional democracy. But is there a central principal, a necessary relationship between the two?

We start our inquiry with two sets of questions:

- Is the Declaration of Independence nothing more than Jefferson's philosophizing about the "oughts" of human existence? If so, was the late Justice Antonin Scalia, a right-leaning Supreme Court judge and champion of originalism, correct when he wrote in his 1998 *A Matter of Interpretation* that "there is no philosophizing in the Constitution"? Or is the Declaration essential "context" for our understanding our Constitution? In 1825, the year before his death, in a letter to his friend

Henry Lee, Jefferson wrote that the Declaration was "intended to be an expression of the American mind.... All its authority rests then on the harmonizing sentiments of the day, whether expressed in conversation, in letters, printed essays, or in the elementary books of public right, as Aristotle, Cicero, Locke, Sidney, etc."

- Is Justice Scalia's theory of democracy correct? In a 1996 speech in Rome at the Gregorian University he said, "The whole theory of democracy ... is that the majority rules; that is the whole theory of it. You protect minorities only because the majority determines that there are certain minority positions that deserve protection." Or was Jefferson correct that fundamental human rights are not grants from a generous governing majority, but that governments are formed to secure our preexisting, unalienable rights? Jefferson wrote in the Declaration of Independence: *"We hold these truths to be self-evident, that all Men are created equal, that they are endowed by their Creator with certain unalienable Rights, that among those are Life, Liberty, and the Pursuit of Happiness. That to secure those rights, Governments are instituted among Men, deriving their just Powers from the Consent of the Governed."*

As we think these questions through, consider the Eighth Amendment to the Constitution. It provides that no "cruel and unusual punishments be inflicted." George Will, in his provocative work of 2019, *The Conservative Sensibility*, points out "pillorying, whipping, and mutilating of criminals" bodies had been standard punishments in the original colonies, and these lurid displays of community disapproval were performed in public for the purpose of "overawing and deterring the spectators." These forms of punishment were neither cruel nor unusual when the Constitution was written. There was no wrong-doer rehabilitation. That was considered too sentimental. When the idea of cruel and unusual punishment came before the Warren Court in 1958 in *Trop v. Dulles*, Supreme Court Chief Justice Earl Warren (Republican governor of California, appointed to the Court by Eisenhower) wrote that the meaning of the Eighth Amendment "must draw its meaning from the evolving standards of decency that mark the progress of a maturing society."

Consider the Supreme Court's right to privacy decision in *Griswold v. Connecticut* in an opinion written by Justice William O. Douglas. The Court opined that individuals have a constitutional right to privacy on which our state and federal governments may not intrude. Douglas wrote that this unstated right exists in the "penumbra" surrounding our Constitution's Bill of Rights, not in its written words.

Douglas wrote in his 1961 *The Right of the People*: "Governments exist for man, not man for government. The aim of government is security for the individual and freedom for the development of his talents. The individual needs protection from the government itself – from the executive branch, from the legislative branch, and even from the tyranny of judges."

Does the recognition of evolving standards and the existence of rights not specifically stated in the Constitution lead us to conclude the Constitution has no fixed meaning? Or that the rights of the minority of us are only those rights the controlling majority graciously decide we minorities can have?

The Conservative Sensibility, written in 2019 by political commentator George Will, provides us with insight: "[T]he fixed meaning of the Constitution is to be found in its mission to protect natural rights and liberty in changing – unfixed – circumstances. Fidelity to the text requires fidelity to some things that were, in a sense, prior to the text – the political and social principles and goals for which the text was written."

As to Justice Scalia's comments on philosophizing, Will writes that there is "no philosophizing," until we read the Constitution through the eyes of Lincoln. Will concludes that

Lincoln understood that the Constitution is "dedicated to a proposition that Scalia dismisses as philosophizing." That proposition, all men are created equal and possess natural rights, was expressed by Jefferson in the Declaration of Independence. Will concludes with the words of constitutional scholar Walter Berns: "'[T]he Constitution is related to the Declaration as effect is related to cause.'"

This discussion leads us to Lincoln and his *Apple of Gold*.

After his death, Abraham Lincoln's 1861 writing, *Fragment on the Constitution and the Union,* was found among his private papers. Lincoln wrote:

> "All this is not the result of accident. It has a philosophical cause.... That something, is the principle of 'Liberty to all'.... The expression of that principle, in our Declaration of Independence, was most happy, and fortunate. The principle clears the path for all — gives hope to all — and, by consequences, enterprise and industry to all.

> "Without this, as well as with it, we could have declared our independence of Great Britain; but without it, we could not, I think, have secured our free government, and consequent prosperity. No oppressed, people will fight, and endure, as our fathers did, without the promise of something better, than a mere change of masters. The assertion of that principle at that time was the word, 'fitly spoken' which has proved an 'apple of gold' to us. The Union and the Constitution are the picture of silver, subsequently framed around it.

> "The picture was made, not to conceal, or destroy the apple; but to adorn, and preserve it. The picture was made for the apple–not the apple for the picture."

Today, we are torn by political factions every bit as divisive as James Madison imagined.

Today, we are torn by a tyranny of elected representatives who act because they can, not because they should. Rather than representing the people, our representatives tie themselves to factions and their lobbyists. Their prime objective is to chase political dollars to assure their perpetuation in office in ways that Madison and the other Founders could never have foreseen.

Today we are disadvantaged by a Supreme Court that has become too indifferent to the context of our time, granting deference to the two political branches of government instead of exercising its responsibility to provide checks and balances regarding the offerings of the political branches of government.

The Problem

Simply put:

> We have lost sight of the purpose of our Constitution as contemplated by its Framers. The purpose is expressed in Jefferson's words in the Declaration of Independence. Our government was formed to protect our unalienable rights, Lincoln's *Apple of Gold*.

As a result, we have morphed from a republic established as a "Democracy of People" to a despotic government operating as a "Democracy of Dollars." How did this happen? Over the 230 plus years since the Constitution was adopted, our three branches of government, the legislative, executive, and judicial, have strayed far from the Constitution – not only from the four corners of its written words, but from principles that underlie its purpose and meaning.

Speaking at the Constitutional Convention in 1787, as if predicting our 21st Century's Democracy of Dollars, Benjamin Franklin said:

> "I agree to this Constitution with all its faults.

> ... I believe, further, that this is likely to be well administered for a course of years, and can only end in despotism, as other forms have done before it, when the people shall be so corrupted as to need a despotic government, being incapable of any other."

Are we on the edge of despotism? Are we where we want to be? Polls cited in the *Prologue* clearly indicate to the contrary – as a community of people we are not pleased with the direction of our country. Consider the roads we have traveled over the past 230 years: Our morph from a Democracy of People to a Democracy of Dollars has been shaped by the choices made, which include:

1) Congress's excessive delegation of its exclusive law-making power to the executive branch. In the Democracy of Dollars, through its administrative agencies, the executive branch has become our prime lawgiver, law interpreter, and law enforcer. This unfettered delegation from the legislative to the executive violates the Constitution's separation of powers requirement. Furthermore, Congress has been hampered by presidential vetoes from revoking any misguided or ineffective delegated authority.

2) Congress's delegation to the executive branch has also dramatically increased the influence of special interests and their lobbies over our government. Congress's delegation invites lobbyists and their clients to concentrate more of their efforts to influence government on the executive branch and its agencies. Their influence shapes executive branch administrative agency regulations and operations to further the desires of special interests, not the needs of the people.

3) The Supreme Court's recent approval of partisan gerrymandering, which favors the political party in power and dilutes the power of individual voters who are not members of the favored political party.

The problem is exacerbated by the Supreme Court's failure to provide meaningful constitutional checks and balances on the two political branches of government, primarily through judicial reviews. The Court's failure to provide necessary checks and balances on the political branches of government is a result of:

1) The Court's deference to Congress's too routine delegation of legislative authority to the executive branch. The Court does this through judge-made rules justifying deference. The result is that the executive branch's administrative agencies have become our unelected, powerful "fourth branch" of government, our primary lawgiver.

2) The Court's deference to the executive branch's administrative agencies regarding their interpretations of ambiguities in the statues that regulate them and in their own rules and regulations. The agencies are not only the creator of their regulations that have the force of law but are their own judge and jury as to their meaning and their enforcement. Furthermore, when administrations change, prior interpretations of rules are skewed. Old rules are revoked. New rules are adopted to fit the political views of the new party in power, frequently uninhibited by judicial review or legislative negotiation and compromise.

3) The Court's failure to provide judicial review for individuals aggrieved by one or both

political branches of government is a blatant disregard and abuse of individuals' natural and constitutional rights. Political branch disregard or abuse is frequently related to a political branch favoring special interests that conflict with infringed rights. The Court's failure occurs when the Court relies on its judge-made deference rules that deny judicial review, such as its Standing Doctrine and Political Question Doctrine. These Deferential Doctrines shift responsibility for providing judicial solutions from the Court to the political branches, frequently to the branch causing the harm. The result is the injured individuals have no solution.

The Court's deference is like Farmer Brown telling his hens whose henhouse has been invaded by the Fox that he is sorry, but if the hens want protection, they will have to work it out with the Fox.

Judicial review is the essential tool in the Court's arsenal of tools, by which it discharges its constitutional obligations to provide checks and balances against the two political branches of government. Failure to provide judicial review violates the Constitution's separation of powers requirements. The Court's failure to provide judicial review also invites special interests and political factions to assert their influence with impunity. The result is that the executive branch functions as an oligarchy, not a coordinated, constitutional cog in our democracy.

As pointed out, our government now operates primarily through the executive branch of government and its administrative agencies, which have become our fourth branch of government. We live in the "Era of Presidential Administration," a subject to which we direct our attention in this book.

There are dozens, if not hundreds, of administrative agencies now in existence, with tens of thousands of people employed by those agencies. We are dependent on these agencies for governmental services and for regulating industry. Thus, a substantial change in the way we operate our government is highly unlikely in today's complexity. The fourth branch of government and the Era of Presidential Administration are here to stay.

What We Need

We may not be able to change the way our government operates, but we can mitigate *The Problem*.

How?

The Supreme Court could reconstruct its oversight in ways that follow the model of the Marshall Court. For 34 years, beginning in 1801, the Marshall Court gave definition and shape to the role of the Supreme Court and the federal judiciary. The 21st Century Court can reimagine its role so it can transition away from the Democracy of Dollars it has created, returning us to the Democracy of People our Framers sought to provide and we so desperately need.

The mandate of the 21st Century Supreme Court can easily become the rediscovery of the goals Madison set forth in the Constitution and explained in the Federalist Papers, particularly in number 10.

Madison said that factions are with us forever, and he and the Framers designed the Constitution with its separation of powers to mitigate their harm. Similarly, the Court must redesign its judge-made rules of deference to mitigate the harm of today's Democracy of Dollars. Deference is not mitigation; it is an exacerbation of the problem.

When the Court accepts that an important value of its check and balancing role is mitigation of the harm special interests inflict through their influence on the political branches, it will have enhanced its constitutional role, particularly where the rights of the people are abused by a political branch.

The Court's checks and balances, carefully implemented with judicial review, and when appropriate, reshaped judge-made rules, will not evolve into the Court usurping constitutional responsibilities of the two political branches. Rather, the Court's checks and balances will minimize the legislative and executive branches straying outside the Constitution's grant of authority as they are doing today.

The above conclusions in no way remove the responsibilities for us to be informed, active and concerned citizens. Madison wrote in 1788, Federalist Papers #51:

"A dependence on the people is, no doubt, the primary control on the government; but experience has taught mankind the necessity of auxiliary precautions."

Yes, as Madison and political philosophers have pointed out, democracy is dependent on the people. But experience has taught us there is a need for more. The "more" is a Supreme Court that fulfills its constitutional responsibilities. That obligation includes judicial reviews of legislative delegation to the executive branch and executive branch actions and inactions that marginalize rights of individuals. We return to this point in the final section of this book.

Part I

Background

RICHARD JACOBS

*The Constitution does not provide for
first-class and second-class citizens.*

Wendell Willkie
Republican Presidential Candidate
1940

Chapter 1 - Democracy of Dollar versus Democracy of People

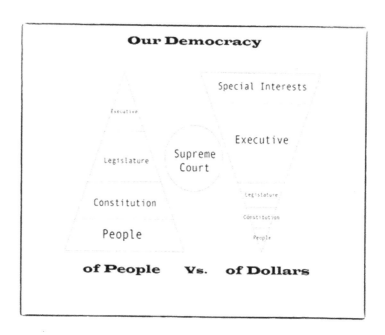

What the Diagram Tells Us

Democracy of People Triangle

The Democracy of People triangle on the left rests on a solid base, the will of the American people, the people having an effective voice, as Madison and the Framers contemplated. The Constitution provides the framework, stating the principles governing the actions and decisions of our constitutional democracy. The legislature makes the laws. The executive branch manages our government under constitutional mandates and in accordance with the legislature's determinations. The Constitution's Bill of Rights secures the rights of the people from intrusive governmental interference.

The Declaration of Independence provides the context – the protection of our unalienable rights – under which the Constitution is to be interpreted and is to operate.

Initially, our Constitution was a compromise, and it began as a Democracy of White Males. (Women's rights? Abigale Adams tried to influence her husband John Adams at the Constitutional Convention regarding giving rights to white women, but she was rejected.) Since then, the Civil War, constitutional amendments, civil rights legislation, and a maturing voice of the people, ultimately accomplished much of what could not be accomplished in 1789, except by compromise.

Judiciary and the Democracy of People

The Supreme Court and the rest of the federal judiciary sit outside the triangle. The judiciary is the people's compliance officer. When people's grievances about the laws passed by the legislature or the actions or inactions of the executive branch come before the judiciary, the claims are evaluated, and the judiciary opines on the peoples' rights. The judiciary also decides whether the legislature's and the executive branch's performance for, and responsibilities to, the people meet the requirements of our Constitution.

Democracy of Dollars Triangle

The Democracy of Dollars triangle on the right is an unstable, poorly grounded, upside-down-triangle. The people don't fit into the small, pointed, unstable base layer. The focus of government is no longer on the people, crunched at the bottom of the triangle. Government's focus is on satisfying the demands of special interests occupying the top layer of the triangle. Special interests weigh heavily on those areas of the triangle under it with their demands.

The Constitution no longer fits into its layer on the triangle. It is frequently ignored.

The legislature fits within its layer on the triangle, but it occupies smaller territory, with a less significant purpose because of its delegation to the executive branch.

The executive branch's share of the triangle is expanded to monarchial proportions and near absolute authority. Government now functions primarily through administrative agencies in the executive branch and its many agencies – the fourth branch of government.

Executive branch judicial checks and balances envisioned by our Constitution's Framers are minimized through judicial deference. Administrative agencies are neither elected by the people nor directly responsible to the people. In fact, when people challenge the actions or omissions of the fourth branch, the federal judiciary frequently determine that the challengers don't have "standing" – the right to have their concerns heard by any federal court.

Executive branch administrative agencies make their rules and regulations, having the force of law with little input from the people. But the agencies receive much input from regulated special interests. It is the lobbies of special interests that substantially influence and direct the rule-making process, as a result of the swinging door of personnel moving from the regulated private sector to government agencies and then back again to the regulated private sector. Agencies write rules that too often favor special interests.

The President also issues executive orders on issues beyond presidential constitutional authority. As Trump did,

Presidents can appoint "acting heads" of agencies not approved by the Senate in accordance with the Constitution's mandates, thus bypassing the constitutional oversight afforded by Senate approval.

Technically, people have a voice by their right to participate in administrative hearings, which they can learn about if they have access to the Federal Register, the skills to read and understand its thousands of pages, and the money to travel to hearings held in Washington, D.C., or other far-away places selected by the government. The practical effect is that the Democracy of Dollars muffles the voice of the people at the triangle's bottom.

(Professor Christopher Stone wrote in his 2010 *Should Trees Have Standing?* that our lives are now so directed by corporations – corporations that are legal fictions created by law, which have the status of *persons* for much of American law – that "It is more and more the individual human being, with his consciousness, that is the legal fiction.")

The co-opting of responsibilities, contemplated by the Constitution to be provided by the judicial and legislative branches, into the executive branch, results in legislative instability, inefficiency, unnecessary costs, and lack of public awareness. The result occurs because elections provide us with a new President every 4 or 8 years. Typically, each newly elected President:

1) fires and replaces administrative agencies' leadership, frequently with inexperienced political appointees often selected from regulated entities,

2) revokes some old rules and adopts new rules,

3) revokes some old executive orders and issues new executive orders, and

4) decides which laws and rules the executive branch will enforce.

These actions and inactions have minimal oversight from

the judicial branch and little, if any, voice from Congress, particularly if the President is from the political party controlling Congress. If Congress attempts to stand up to the President by passing legislation limiting presidential authority, the President simply exercises his veto power. Once power is delegated by Congress to the executive branch, it is difficult for Congress to redeem.

The prime beneficiaries of the government under the Democracy of Dollars are the special interests – frequently the regulated – occupying the top layer, shaping our laws to their purpose. Instead of being regulated in ways that are protective of the people, too frequently special interests receive favorable treatment or regulatory exceptions. In many cases, the regulations are drafted by the special interests being regulated.

Judiciary and the Democracy of Dollars

The Supreme Court and the rest of the federal judiciary remain outside the triangle, but their responsibility is less independent, primarily because political party judicial appointments aim for political likeness, not political balance or pure judicial competence. The Court's deference, particularly to the executive branch, has the effect of denuding people's rights and denying them important constitutional remedies without judicial engagement in their claims.

The fundamental problem for the people in a Democracy of Dollars is the idea that the people don't have enforceable remedies for rights infringement when their natural and constitutional rights are not protected by the Court. When it comes to remedies, citizens are unlike shareholders of corporations. Corporate law provides shareholders with the right to bring "derivative actions," lawsuits brought by shareholders to benefit the corporation and shareholders when boards of directors and corporate executives breach their responsibilities. Breaches of responsibility by any of the three branches of government leave the people with no similar remedies.

Can Shareholders Influence Special Interests?

With shareholders having derivative rights remedies, what about the remedies available to corporate shareholders regarding public corporations? Can concerned shareholders assert control over the businesses in which their companies have invested? Today most of America's public businesses are not owned by individuals, but by three index funds: Blackrock, Vanguard, and State Street. The "Big Three" collectively own at least 40% of all S&P 500 listed American companies. In 2017 Cambridge University Press published an article with a long title, "Hidden Power of the Big Three? Passive index funds re-concentration of corporate ownership, and new financial risk." The authors found that the "Big Three" cooperate with each other on shareholder voting.

The Big Three also influence corporate direction through coordinated direct conferences with management. Thus, it should not be surprising that 90% of the time they vote with management. Cambridge also reports, "The Big Three did not follow Institutional Shareholder Services (ISS) recommendations and as such voted against most of the regular short- and medium-term oriented shareholders."

A January 2020 follow-up article, "Three Investment Banks Control More Wealth Than GDP of China – and Threaten Our Existence" reported: "The financial services sector owns the controlling interest in all of the media companies that own major news networks (except Bloomberg and the Washington Post which are privately owned)...." As to the fossil fuel industry and climate change, the report warns: "In 2018 Blackrock and Vanguard voted against 80% shareholder initiatives to make industries more accountable for their effect on the environment and climate change. The finance sector is laser-focused on a maximum return on investment."

Thus, organic shareholder resolutions advocating corporate social responsibility have a slim chance of influencing corporate direction. America's return to a Democracy of People will not be sourced in the Big Three money firms.

Who Speaks for the People in a Democracy of Dollars?

A question remains in today's Democracy of Dollars. *Who speaks for the people?* We return to the question in Chapter 10.

The constitution was made for times of commotion. In the calm of peace and justice there is seldom great injustice. Dangerous precedents occur in dangerous times. It then becomes the duty of the judiciary calmly to poise the scales of justice, unmoved by the arm of power, undisturbed by the clamor of the multitude."

William Cranch
D.C. Circuit Chief Judge
United States v. Bollman, et al, 1807

Chapter 2 - Our Constitution

Our Constitution is a statement of rights and responsibilities for each of us and the three branches of our federal government. The Constitution does not create rights, but its first eight amendments identify rights that are constitutionally protected.

The Ninth Amendment confirms the rights identified in the first eight amendments are not our only rights. The Ninth Amendment confirms there are more, called our unenumerated rights, which, by logic, include "life, liberty and the pursuit of happiness" expressed in the Declaration of Independence.

The Tenth Amendment confirms that powers delegated to the federal government are limited powers. Whatever powers are not delegated to the government in the Constitution belong to the people and the states. Thus, the Constitution is a limited grant of authority. If the federal government is not granted authority to take an action or limit a right under the Constitution, any such action or rights-limitation is unconstitutional.

The Constitution's Preamble states that the government created by the Constitution was created "for ourselves and our Posterity." Thus, responsible government considers the effect on future generations of today's actions and inactions.

Seven Key Passages

Seven key passages, one in our Declaration of Independence, and six in our Constitution and its Bill of Rights, when read together, state the purpose our government was formed and the limitations on the power the American people have delegated to the three branches of our federal government. These passages are cornerstones for the analysis and recommendations presented in this book:

1) ***Declaration of Independence*:** "We hold these truths to be self-evident, that all men are created equal, that they are endowed by their Creator with certain unalienable Rights, that among these are Life, Liberty and the pursuit of Happiness — That to secure these Rights, Governments are instituted among Men, deriving their just powers from the consent of the governed...." The Declaration, which is Lincoln's *Apple of Gold,* is first discussed in our framing chapter, *The Problem.*

2) ***Constitution Preamble*:** "We the People of the United States, in Order to form a more perfect Union, establish Justice, insure domestic Tranquility, provide for the common defense, promote the general Welfare, and secure the Blessings of Liberty to ourselves and our Posterity, do ordain and establish this Constitution for the United States of America." We discuss the Preamble in this chapter, as we consider the fiduciary responsibilities of the three branches of government.

3) *Article I, Section 8; Article II, Section 1; and Article III, Section 1*. These three articles specify the limited grants of authority to the three branches of government, legislative, executive, and judicial. These articles are the subject of Chapter 3.

4) *Amendment IX* - Construction of Constitution. "The enumeration in the Constitution, of certain rights, shall not be construed to deny or disparage others retained by the people." This amendment is a subject of Chapter 8.

5) *Amendment X* - Powers of the States and People. "The powers not delegated to the United States by the Constitution, nor prohibited by it to the States, are reserved to the States respectively, or to the people." This amendment is also a subject of Chapter 8.

Interpreting the Constitution

A challenge in constitutional interpretation is to decide whether the Constitution's meaning, including its Bill of Rights, is fixed and immovable. Is its meaning today to be understood with the meaning originally inscribed into our Constitution by the Framers? Or is the Constitution's meaning for us today finally revealed in the evolving growth of our culture and society and by events and discoveries that have occurred over the 230 plus years since the Constitution's adoption?

Some conservatives claim the Constitution as written is the end of it all. It is to be interpreted based on the Framers' "original meaning." Other conservatives argue that the meaning of the Constitution can be derived only from "textualism," the actual words used, regardless of the Framers' intentions explained in other documents, such as the Federalist Papers, or Madison's notes from the Constitutional Convention and his correspondence about constitutional issues.

A problem with both original meaning and textualism is that there is ambiguity. Historic documents are not always revealing, and meanings of words change over time.

Some liberals claim the Constitution is a "living document" providing a fundamental guidance and framework. They assert its meaning evolves to meet the values of the American people, which evolve over time.

As pointed out in the *Prologue,* the Constitution's fundamental meaning is found in the Declaration of Independence, Lincoln's *Apple of Gold,* rather than in the Constitution itself. Lincoln reasoned that the purpose our Constitution was adopted to fulfill is expressed in the Declaration of Independence, our Constitution's launchpad. That purpose, protecting our rights and liberty, "fixes" the Constitution's meaning. George Will explains in his 2019 *Conservative Sensibility*:

> "[T]he fixed meaning of the Constitution is to be found in its mission to protect natural rights and liberty in changing – unfixed – circumstances. Fidelity to the text requires fidelity to some things that were, in a sense, prior to the text - the political and social principles and goals for which the text was written."

I agree with Will.

The disagreement between liberals and conservatives is a debate about the constitutional interpretations of rights in a changing world.

However, there are some rights not detailed in the Constitution that have been approved by the Court that most of us agree on regardless of our political philosophy. For example, we can agree with the Court that expanding the right of free speech and free press over time to include radio, television, movies, and the internet is appropriate. Most of us also approve the Court's decision that certain rights are so fundamental (e.g., the right to marry, access to courts, and the right to privacy) that disputes over their meaning in the Constitution or Bill of Rights are unnecessary.

One of the most contentious debates between conservatives and liberals has been in defining what kinds of weapons are authorized by the Second Amendment's right to bear arms. A conservative Supreme Court, in *District of Columbia v. Heller*, had no difficulty deciding that the right to own guns includes today's AR-15 semi-automatic rifle. The Court determined the right to own weapons was not limited to front-loaded, single-shot muskets, prevalent in 1789 when the Constitution became the supreme law of the land. Another contentious debate has been about the Supreme Court's *Citizens United v. FEC* decision that the First Amendment right of free speech includes rights for "artificial persons" (corporations) who can spend unlimited money on political campaigns. These sorts of rights approved by the Court, ranging from agreeable to contentious, would have been impossible to foresee within the Framers' contemplations about the Constitution's Bills of Rights, no matter how farsighted they may have been.

Separation of Powers

The Constitution separates our government into the legislative, executive, and judicial branches, discussed in the next chapter. Each branch has unique responsibilities, although there is some overlap. For example, the legislative branch has the exclusive constitutional power to create laws, but the President, in the executive branch, has the right to veto any law presented to him for approval, unless the veto is overridden by a congressional two-thirds majority. Judges are members of the judicial branch, and administrative agency executives are members of the executive branch. The President appoints judges and executives, but both are subject to ratification by the Senate.

Why the separation of powers? The Framers were concerned about the influence of factions on our government. The powers of the three branches were divided to minimize their dominance and influence. Also, by separating the powers, each branch could provide checks and balances on the other two branches.

The role of the judiciary branch providing checks and balances over the executive and legislative branches was particularly important, as is pointed out over the following chapters. James Madison wrote in 1787 Federalist Papers #10 that "no man is allowed to judge his own cause." In 1788, Hamilton wrote in Federalist Papers #78, that "there is no liberty if the power of judging is not separated from the legislative and executive powers."

However, as pointed out in this book, the legislative branch has, with abandon, regularly delegated to the executive branch administrative agencies much of its legislative power and some judicial power reserved for the federal courts. Unfortunately, the Supreme Court has acquiesced, through its judge-made rules of deference. The Court's failure to provide judicial review over cases and controversies that provide constitutional issues related to legislative delegation or human rights is particularly disturbing. The Court's deference has been a major factor in our republic morphing from a Democracy of People into a Democracy of Dollars.

Fiduciary Responsibilities of the Branches of Government

The idea that our three branches of government have fiduciary responsibilities to the American people can be implied from the Declaration of Independence, where Jefferson writes: "That to secure these Rights [Life, Liberty, and the Pursuit of Happiness] Governments are instituted among Men, deriving their just Powers from the Consent of the Governed..."

The Preamble of our Constitution also confirms the idea our government and its three branches function as fiduciaries:

> "We the People of the United States, in Order
> to form a more perfect Union, establish Justice,
> insure domestic Tranquility, provide for the
> common defence, promote the general Welfare,

and secure the blessings of Liberty to ourselves
and our Posterity, do obtain and establish this
Constitution of the United States of America."

Fiduciary responsibilities are also captured in Lincoln's Gettysburg Address: "government of the people, by the people, for the people."

The three branches are constitutional creations of a government created by the people, for the people, seeking to "secure the blessings of Liberty to ourselves and our Posterity." Therefore, it should be clear that these three branches are fiduciaries for us, including our future generations. Does the Constitution use the word "fiduciary"? No, the Constitution doesn't use "fiduciary;" but the principle is systemic within the Preamble and in the Declaration, our *Golden Apple*. Fiduciary responsibility is also systemic within the responsibility of our government's three branches to exercise their delegated powers for the benefit of the people. The American people, as a people, are the sole beneficiaries of our Constitution.

Madison wrote in 1787 in Federalist Papers #10, that the legislature speaks for the people, a concept that is grounded in fiduciary responsibility. The title to Federalist Papers #51, written by Madison February 8, 1788, is "The Structure of Government Must Furnish the Proper Checks and Balances Between the Different Departments." The Paper begins:

> "TO WHAT expedient, then, shall we finally resort, for maintaining in practice the necessary partition of power among the several departments, as laid down in the Constitution? The only answer that can be given is, that as all these exterior provisions are found to be inadequate, the defect must be supplied, by so contriving the interior structure of the government as that its several constituent parts may, by their mutual relations, be the means of keeping each other in their proper places."

The legislative branch violates the principles Madison

expressed in Federalist Papers #51 by its over-delegation to executive branch agencies, and the judicial branch violates Federalist Papers #51 by its ubiquitous judicial deference.

Furthermore, the Court's failure to adequately take into effect the reality of today's Democracy of Dollars, which fails to "promote the General Welfare and secure the blessings of Liberty to ourselves and our Posterity" creates a serious problem. It too raises the question whether the Supreme Court is breaching its fiduciary responsibilities to the American people.

Presidential Elections: Electoral Collage

Bias

Electoral college votes (which elect our President) are allocated among our 50 states based on a state's total number of Senators and House Representatives members. We don't vote directly for our President. We vote for the portion of the college's 538 members allocated to the state in which we live. Each state has members in the college based on the number of senators (2 per state) and number of representatives (determined by population measured every 10 years by census). There is a slight bias in favor of small states (minimum of 3 electors). There is a significant bias from the "winner-take-all" allocation of electors.

Parliamentary governments, like England, give an active voice to minorities. Our constitutional system lacks a similar mandate. States decide how their electoral college votes are allocated. Forty-eight states award votes in the electoral college on a "winner take all" basis, which minimizes the voices of the minority factions within the states. Only Maine and Nebraska allocate electoral votes in the ratio of the popular votes cast. A winner-take-all allocation is neither mandated nor prohibited by the Constitution. States choose their own system. In February 2020, the Fifth Circuit Court of Appeals, in *League of United Latin America v. Greg A,* ruled that winner-take-all state laws electoral voting are constitutional.

Electoral College: Voter Dilution

The winner-take-all approach dilutes the votes of minorities and city concentrations of people. For example, in Wisconsin, the state where I was born and grew up, in 2016, the Republicans won Wisconsin's 8 presidential electoral votes with 47.22% of the votes, against the Democrats with 46.45% of the votes. That is less than a one percent difference between parties in the votes cast. If the allocation of electoral votes by Wisconsin was in the ratio of votes cast, the electoral votes most likely would have been assigned 4 and 4, or, possibly, the Republicans may have been assigned 5 and the Democrats 3. The allocation would have been aggregated with similar votes from the electoral colleges of other states. In the 2020 presidential election, Trump received four of the five Nebraska electoral college votes. In Maine, Biden received three out of its four electoral college votes.

In two recent elections (Bush and Trump), the President elected did not have the majority votes of Americans who voted, although they were awarded the majority electoral college votes. In the 2016 election, Hillary Clinton had the highest margin of popular votes (2.7 million more votes than Trump) of any candidate who ever lost the electoral college vote.

Some electors in the past took the position that the Constitution does not bind the vote of state electors to vote for the presidential candidate winning the state's popular vote. In 1948, a Democratic elector cast his vote for a segregation candidate instead of the winning Democratic candidate. In 2000, an elector from the District of Columbia refused to cast a vote for the District winner Al Gore. In the 2016 election, two electors for Trump and five electors for Clinton defected. In July 2020, the Supreme Court ruled unanimously in *Chiafalo et al. v. Washington* that states can compel electors to vote for the candidate with the popular vote within the state. The opinion written by Justice Elena Kagan holds, "electors are not free agents; they are to vote for the candidate whom the state's voters have chosen." This issue is discussed further in the *Epilogue.*

As of October 2020, fifteen states and the District of Colombia have entered an interstate compact mandating that the electoral votes of those states are voted for the presidential candidate winning the popular vote. The compact's electoral votes total 196 votes, which is 36% of the electoral college. It takes 270 votes to win the presidency, which leaves an additional 74 votes required for election. The compact goes into effect only when it has at least 270 votes. If more states join the compact, the President will be elected by the popular vote without amending the Constitution. However, to be effective, Article I, Section 10, of the Constitution requires congressional approval of state compacts.

To the Winner Belong the Spoils

Some Americans view an election like a football game, or perhaps a war, where to the victor belong the spoils. The winner-take-all approach may be appropriate for sports or wars, but despite the freedom of states to adopt such a system, I question whether it is appropriate for governing a nation composed of a large diversity of the people. A November 2020 Gallup poll found Americans identify as 31% Democrats, 30% Republicans, and 38% independent. A winner-take-all approach distorts the fundamental principle that the Constitution establishes a government of, by, and for the people.

A winner-take-all approach concerned James Madison, who wrote about it in a letter to George Hay in 1823. He wrote: "The part of the arrangement which casts the eventual appointment on H. of Rs., voting by states was, as you presume, an accommodation to the anxiety of the smaller States for their sovereign equality, and to the jealously of the larger States towards the cumulative functions of the Senate." Madison added that the electoral college system "is so pregnant also with a mischievous tendency in practice, that an amendment to the Constitution on that point is justly called for.... The States when voting for President by general tickets or by their Legislatures, are a string of beeds [sic]: When they make their elections by districts, some of these differing in sentiment from others, and sympathizing with that of districts in other States, they are so knit together as to break the force of those Geographical & other noxious parties which might render the repulsive too strong for the cohesive tendencies within the political System."

The Constitution's initial scheme did not contemplate political parties or the extremes in state populations, with large urban area population concentrations. Under the original Constitution, the President and ultimate Vice President were opponents in the presidential race. The President and Vice President were not from the same political party and were not elected directly by the people as they are today. Electoral votes would be cast by the states, as Madison pointed out. The winner became President and the second-place candidate became Vice President, providing at least some opportunity for a balanced voice.

But clearly, the Constitution does not contemplate that any person, or group of persons should remain unrepresented on the sidelines or be tread upon by winners until the next election – which, because of vote skewing may result in a perpetuation of the winner's power even without the popular vote. The Bill of Rights is intended to protect the minority from the tyranny of the majority. The judicial, legislative and the executive branches are responsible to all, not some, of the people.

A series of polls going back as far as 1944 indicate that Americans favor the President be elected by popular vote. However, resolving the problem of a candidate winning the electoral college votes while losing the popular vote is not as simple as stating the problem. For example, if the Constitution were to eliminate the electoral college, or if Congress approved the states' voting compact, the popular vote would be the presidential elector. That would skew elections in favor of states with the most populous cities, limiting the voice of the less populous states. That, too, would be contentious. The United States has been described by Colin Woodard in his 2012 *American Nations: A History of the Eleven Rival Regional Cultures in North America,* as a country that houses eleven different nations, each with different geography, different cultures, different priorities, and differing fundamental values. Our differing cultures, priorities and values require compromise within our system of government to assure the ultimate long-term success of what the late Supreme Court Justice Oliver Wendell Holmes called in his *Abrams v. United States* dissent as the American "experiment."

A direct popular presidential election vote could lead to a tyranny of the majority – a vote that favors cities and geographic areas that are most populous. The winner-take-all approach of assigning electoral college votes can also lead to the tyranny of the minority by the smaller states. Similarly, each state being represented in the Senate by two Senators can produce a similar tyranny, particularly when population concentrates in a few states, as we point out below in the Congressional Elections section.

In our country of 50 states with wide differences in territory and population, harmony in voting may not be possible. However, retaining the electoral college and eliminating the states' winner-take-all electoral votes, as Maine and Nebraska have, would, I believe, over time, produce a fairer, more realistic outcome, as Jesse Wegman suggests in his September 2020 New York Times article, "The Electoral College Will Destroy America — And no, New York and California would not dominate a popular vote." Following the 2020 election, despite heavy criticism, legislators in Nebraska introduced a bill to return Nebraska to a winner-take-all electoral college allocation.

Congressional Elections

Two Senators are elected "at large" from each state, and state Representatives for the House of Representatives are elected based on state population. Population is determined every ten years by the census. Each Representative is elected from within a voting district created by states, with each district providing one Representative. The congressional voting districts are of approximately equal population to facilitate one person, one vote (a district's size for federal elections is presently 710,000 people, which will be adjusted based on the 2020 census). A problem with state-designed voting districts is that they are easily gerrymandered. We discuss partisan gerrymandering in more depth in Chapter 6.

Senators, being allocated two for each state rather than allocated based on population, can also create a tyranny of the minority. The tyranny is evident when the Senate, dominated by one party, refuses to approve another party's presidential appointments.

In his 2020 *The Hidden History of the War on Voting,* Thom Hartmann writes: "Within the next two decades, half of the population of the United States will live in just eight states and be represented by only 16 (out of a hundred) senators." He also points out that today two-thirds of Americans live in fifteen states. Thus, they are represented by only 30% of the Senators. Hartmann recommends that our democracy would benefit by splitting up the most populous states, like California and New York, producing more equality in the Senate's representation. Doing so could go a long way in balancing the Court to be more representative of the American people. It should also result in a more balanced Supreme Court. We discuss the importance to each of us, conservative or liberal, of a more balanced Court in Chapter 9.

From Factions to Parties

In 1788 in Federalist Papers #10, Madison described "factions" as "a number of citizens, whether amounting to a majority or minority of the whole, who are united and actuated by some common impulse of passion, or of interest, adverse to the rights of other citizens, or to the permanent and aggregate interests of the community."

Madison continued: "A zeal for different opinions concerning religion, government, and many other points, as well of speculation as of practice; an attachment to different leaders ambitiously contending for pre-eminence and power; or to persons of other descriptions whose fortunes have been interesting to the human passions, have, in turn, divided mankind into parties, inflamed them with mutual animosity, and rendered them much more disposed to vex and oppress each other than to co-operate for their common good."

Unfortunately, our Constitution's Framers didn't plan for the emergence of political parties and their tribalism and winner-take-all philosophies that perpetuate the power of factions. As noted in the *Prologue*, factions developed early on between Washington's cabinet members. They disagreed about the meaning of the Constitution, and particularly, the scope of government.

Three years into Washington's first term as President, in January 1792, an article, "Parties," was published in the National Gazette. The publication was shortly after Jefferson formed the Republican Party. In the article, Madison championed the national need for political parties, writing, "In every political society, parties are unavoidable.... In all political societies, different interests and parties arise out of the nature of things, and the great art of politicians lies in making them checks and balances to each other."

Of course, as history tells us, when a political party becomes entrenched, supported by election processes that skew outcomes in its favor through partisan gerrymandering, corruption and self-interest replace checks and balances.

Political Party Democracy Distortions

In the Democracy of Dollars, winning and winner-take-all are prime. The fundamental principle that our Constitution is a document of accommodation, designed to protect the rights of a diversity of people with a diversity of beliefs, is nonexistent. Oligarchy, the government of the few for the benefit of a privileged few dominates, obliterating our constitutional Democracy of the People.

Voter Gerrymandering

We like to brag that fair representation is achieved by the "one person, one vote" rule. But, as we point out in Chapter 6, in today's Democracy of Dollars, votes are diluted by partisan gerrymandering so that, in many cases, a majority vote fails to determine election outcomes.

Congressional and state government voting districts have been skewed – the Supreme Court tells us, since the early days of our country – by gerrymandering, redistricting, or other political machinations that favor perpetual dominance by a party. One example of gerrymandering in state election districts is in my home state of Wisconsin. In their 2018 state election, the Republicans had 36% of the votes, but somehow won 53% of the state's legislative seats. Also, in the 2016 state election, Republicans won 65% of the seats with only 52% of the votes. (Wisconsin has 8 congressional voting districts and 99 State Assembly voting districts.)

Layering of Voting Requirements

Voting can be adversely affected by the political layering of voting requirements. An example of politicized election laws comes from Florida's Republican-dominated legislation that engaged in layering. In 2018 Florida voters approved a constitutional amendment restoring voting rights to ex-felons. The state legislature then passed a law adding a requirement that before ex-felons voted, they had to first repay any unpaid fees or court costs. This was not a stated requirement in the amendment. Florida's governor received an advisory opinion from Florida's Supreme Court that the voter-approved constitutional amendment granting felons the right to vote after serving their sentences was silent on the issue of fees. It ruled the amendment was therefore ambiguous, as to whether a felon was required to pay all fees and court costs before voting.

The Florida Supreme Court specifically did not address the issue as to whether a law requiring these payments violated constitutional requirements. The Florida law requiring fee payments was ultimately held by a federal district court to be unconstitutional. However, the state appealed, and a Court of Appeals reversed the decision on a 6 to 4 vote in September 2020. The Supreme Court refused to intervene.

Purging Voter Records

Efforts to maintain political party power also include eliminating the votes of voters who aren't members of the party in power. Returning to my home state of Wisconsin, in 2019, a state lower court with a conservative judge (judges in Wisconsin are elected), on the petition of a conservative advocacy group, ordered over 200,000 voters to be purged from Wisconsin's voting rolls. Most purged voters lived in Madison and Milwaukee, two cities with liberal and minority voting concentrations. In its December 2020 ruling, the Wisconsin Supreme Court rejected the purge, deciding that election laws must be challenged before, not after, the results are known.

Vote Blocks

Liberal voters are more likely to vote by mail than conservative voters. Efforts to minimize or eliminate the effectiveness of liberals voting by mail in the 2020 presidential election have included removing post office sorting machines and reducing postal services. In late summer 2020, the Post Office removed 711 sorting machines and reduced mail delivery services, which caused widespread mail delays. Removal and delays increased the risk of mail votes not being counted in time for the 2020 November election. A federal court order and public outrage forced the Post Office to reverse its decisions. The removal and reduced services had been ordered by Postmaster General Louis DeJoy, a Republican political appointee who made substantial political contributions.

On October 1, 2020, the Texas governor ordered each Texas county to close its satellite offices and reduce its mail ballot drop-offs to one per county. The governor's order also requires voting clerks to allow poll watchers (primarily Republicans) to "observe any activity conducted at the early voting clerk's office location related to the in-person delivery of a marked mail ballot." The governor used COVID-19 precautions as a rationale for his order. The Texas Governor was quoted in an October 9, 2020 story in The Hill as saying,

"As we work to preserve Texans' ability to vote during COVID-19 pandemic, we must take extra care to strengthen ballot security protocols throughout the state. These enhanced security protocols will ensure greater transparency and will help stop attempts at illegal voting." Texas, normally a Republican stronghold, exhibited a Democratic leaning in recent polls. We return to the use of emergency powers for political gain in Chapter 7.

Political party democracy distortions, like those illustrated in this chapter, may entrench political power, but they also increase factionalism. Democracy does not flourish in such an environment.

Madison and other Framers, who were philosophers from the Age of Enlightenment, appear to have overestimated the Constitution's ability to create an independent judiciary and an effective one person, one vote election process. Furthermore, these kinds of machinations have discouraged voting by too many Americans, particularly the young, who feel that their votes do not make a difference. For these disillusioned, the system is rigged.

Tampering with Judicial Independence

For the judicial branch, our Framers reasoned that lifetime appointments of federal judges would keep them independent. After all, if their appointment is for life, there is no worry about reelection or reappointment. They don't have to answer to any faction. The Framers would shutter at the prospect of the conversion of our Court into a political tool of the party in power. Politicizing of federal courts is a concern expressed in our *Prologue*.

Since 1953, federal judges nominated by the President and confirmed by the Senate were first vetted by the American Bar Association for judicial competency. George W. Bush and Donald Trump eschewed the ABA's review process. It is noteworthy that both campaigned on the importance of appointing "conservative" judges to the courts, apparently regardless of judicial competency or experience.

Barry Friedman tells us in his 2009 *The Will of the People* that federal court-packing – selecting judges for their political beliefs – has a long history, beginning in the late 1800s, when Republicans learned the value of the federal judiciary's support of their economic legislation favored by Republicans' corporate financial contributors. Their legislation promoted the rapidly growing economic power of the country. The Supreme Court learned the benefits of stability from being backed by a strong economic constituency. Several of the Court's decisions during the Reconstruction Period following the Civil War resulted in the Court suffering a loss of public and congressional support. This led to congressional court-packing and limitations on federal court jurisdiction.

Friedman adds, in our time, the idea of appointing judges with a compatible political philosophy began in the Reagan administration when he created the Office of Legal Policy (OLP) as part of the Justice Department. The OLP was heavily criticized for vetting candidates about their political views on "abortion and school prayer" and deprioritizing their legal qualifications. Although Reagan appointed roughly half of the federal bench during his two terms, the Court did not reverse prior opinions on school prayer, abortion, or other key conservative concerns.

During the Trump administration vetting Federal judges based on political views rather than legal competence continued at a fast pace. The Week Magazine reports in its November 6, 2020 issue article, "Barrett takes her Supreme Court seat," that since 2017, the Senate has confirmed 220 conservative federal judges, including three Supreme Court justices. Happy with the Senate's approvals, Republican Senate Majority Leader Mitch McConnell said that "Many GOP accomplishments 'will be undone sooner or later by the next election. They won't be able to do much about this for a long time.'"

Amend the Constitution?

Article V of the Constitution provides for amendments. Congress can propose an amendment by a vote supported by two-thirds of each house. Alternatively, at the request of the legislatures in two-thirds of the states, Congress is required to call a constitutional convention. Amendments become part of the Constitution upon ratification by the legislatures, or conventions, in three-quarters of the states. The last approved amendment was the 27th Amendment, approved in 1992, which dealt with congressional compensation. Six more amendments proposed by Congress are either pending among the states or their time for approval has expired. A child labor amendment has been pending since 1924.

The amendment process is not a "quick" process, nor is it a process immune from political influences. Any constitutional amendment is not likely to provide solutions that would reverse our transformation into a Democracy of Dollars. Not only is the process time-consuming, the American people can neither propose nor approve amendments directly. State legislatures, too frequently shaped by partisan gerrymandering, are not inclined to approve amendments that could cause them to share or lose power.

Solutions to the issues brought on by our slide into a Democracy of Dollars will be accomplished only by assertive public influence, the subject of Chapter 10. Solutions will make progress when, because of that public influence, the Supreme Court becomes hands-on sensitive to today's Democracy of Dollars and how its context has stripped the American people of key constitutional rights our Framers reserved to the people.

The Court must not continue as the handmaiden of the political branches of our government.

But what is government itself, but the greatest of all reflections on human nature? If men were angels, no government would be necessary.... the great difficulty lies in this: you must first enable the government to control the governed; and in the next place oblige it to control itself.

James Madison
#51 Federalist Papers, 1788

Chapter 3 - The Constitution's First Three Articles

All Articles of our Constitution and its 27 amendments are important. But the first three articles, defining the role of the three branches, legislative, executive, and judicial, are especially meaningful.

Constitution-Article I - Legislature

Article I begins "All legislative Powers herein granted shall be vested in a Congress of the United States..." Article I divides the Congress into the House and the Senate.

Members of the House, our elected Representatives, are "apportioned among the several States ... according to their respective Numbers...." Numbers were initially based on the number of "free people." In states that had "other people" (slaves), the Number of Representatives was based on the number of free people, plus 3/5's of "other people."

A hand-written note saved from 1785, the days of the Constitutional Convention, pegged the population of the 13 states at 3 million. Georgia was the smallest state with 32,060 people. Virginia was the largest with 512,974 people. Thus the constitutional idea developed that states should have a representative in the House based on the ratio of one person for every 30,000 people, with no state having less than one representative. The 14th Amendment changed that to apportion representatives based upon the numbers of people within a state without mention of the 30,000 population requirements. Congress ultimately limited the size of the House by legislation, a practical necessity with the growth of our country and the size of our governmental buildings.

The size of the House is limited to 435 Representatives, with reapportionment of the House every 10 years, based on census. For example, preliminary estimates of the 2020 census indicate that Florida's population growth compared to other states will result in Florida having an increase in the number of its Representatives. Because of the over-all 435-member limit, the Representatives in other states will be reduced in numbers to accommodate Florida's increase.

The census counts every person living in the United States, including citizens, non-citizen legal residents, non-citizen long-term visitors and undocumented immigrants. A person's residence is the place he or she lives and sleeps most of the time. Private citizens living abroad are not counted.

There has been growing political pressure to under-count minorities and exclude undocumented immigrants. For example, adding a citizenship question on the census was intended to discourage immigrants from participating in the census. In 2019, the Supreme Court ruled "no" to the Census Bureau proposal about adding a citizenship question to the census. President Trump's executive order directing the 2020 census exclusion of undocumented immigrants is a subject of Chapter 7.

As to the Senate, our Constitution's Framers decided that each state would have two senators, as noted in the preceding chapter. This decision was a result of the "Great Compromise" – the idea that small states should be able to stand up to the populous states so they wouldn't be overwhelmed. Hamilton hated the idea, as it risked creating a tyranny of the minority.

Madison wasn't supportive of the idea of two senators for each state either, but he saw it as a necessary compromise to keep the 13 states together, explaining in his notes from the Constitutional Convention: "A government founded on principles more consonant to the wishes of the larger States, is not likely to be obtained from the smaller States. The only option, then, for the former, lies between the proposed government and a government still more objectionable. Under this alternative, the advice of prudence must be to embrace the lesser evil; and, instead of indulging a fruitless anticipation of the possible mischiefs which may ensue, to contemplate rather the advantageous consequences which may qualify the sacrifice."

As important as this compromise was in the formation of our government, our Constitution's Framers could hardly have foreseen that America would have a state like California with 40 million people being represented by 2 senators, the same as North Dakota with 750,000 people. (Within the House, California has 53 Representatives and North Dakota has one.)

After our 230 plus years of operating under the Constitution, some of the mischiefs that troubled Madison have shifted us to a Democracy of Dollars from a Democracy of People. As pointed out in Chapter 1: special interests dominate and are not only the prime beneficiaries of the Democracy of Dollars, they are its architect. Special interests sit at the top of the upside-down Democracy of Dollars triangle; and their influence is enhanced by:

1) The power of lobbies over the executive branch and over Senators, particularly from smaller states.

2) Skewed electoral districts which shape the House membership.

3) Winner-take-all electoral college votes in presidential elections.

In Chapter 1's diagram, the legislature in the Democracy of

Dollars triangle is smaller than in the Democracy of People. The forfeited legislative space is taken up by the executive branch, as a result of the legislature's over-delegation of its legislative responsibilities to the executive branch. The over delegation is the subject of Chapter 4.

Constitution-Article II – Executive

Section 1 in Article II of our Constitution states, "The executive power shall be vested in the President of the United States of America." Under later sections of that Article, the President is granted other powers, such as the power to make treaties with the advice and consent of the Senate.

The Constitution is silent as to what the President's "executive power" includes. By logic, under the Constitution's grant of executive power, the President must operate our government within the framework of the Constitution and laws adopted by Congress. Thus, the President is to operate the government much as a corporate president operates a corporation under the authority of the corporate charter and the resolutions adopted by its board of directors. If a corporate president wants to do something that falls outside of what is considered the normal operations of his or her company, the president asks the board of directors to grant that authority. If the corporate president acts outside the board's grant of corporate authority, those acts are considered *ultra vir*es – illegal – done beyond the president's legal power and authority. If the corporate board of directors fails to bring the president into compliance, corporate shareholders have derivative rights granted by law to bring legal actions in the corporation's name to force the president and the board of directors to return to compliance. Such a right is not provided in our Constitution regarding government action or inaction.

Our country's President is far more independent from the legislative branch than a corporate president is from the corporation's board of directors. The corporate board not only elects its president to office but can also remove its president with a great deal more freedom than Congress has regarding its ability to remove our nation's President under the Constitution's impeachment provisions. Furthermore, citizens have no remedy equivalent to shareholders' derivative rights.

The executive branch is, constitutionally, a coequal branch with the legislative and judicial branches. However, we now live in the *Era of Presidential Administration* – a time when our government is dominated by a President more powerful and independent from oversight than our Framers imagined possible. Today, the executive branch dominates the judiciary and legislative branches. The Era of Presidential Administration is a subject of Chapter 7.

Constitution-Article III – Judiciary

Article III § 1 of our Constitution begins: "The judicial power of the United States shall be vested in one supreme Court and in such inferior Courts as the Congress may from time to time ordain and establish…" Article III § 2 describes the cases and controversies the judiciary is to decide.

As pointed out, executive branch administrative agencies have become our prime law givers, law interpreters, and law enforcers, despite Madison's comments in 1787 in Federalist Papers #10 that "No man is allowed to be judge of his own cause."

Congress has developed a pattern for liberal delegation to the executive branch of significant legislative authority. That over-delegation has been coupled with the Supreme Court's elevating a sweeping doctrine of deference regarding determinations by the executive branch's administrative agencies. The Court has also become reluctant to take on controversial issues that, in the minds of at least the majority of the judges in a particular case, are "political questions," or questions of "redressability." The Court equates political question and redressability issues as nonjusticiable and declines to hear those issues, preferring instead to defer to the political branches for resolution.

Contrary to the Constitution's First Amendment right to petition our government "for a redress of grievances," the

Court's deference denies people's access to the federal courts to resolve their grievances with the political branches of government. Deference is also contrary to what the Supreme Court has said in other cases. For example, in 1974, *United States v. Richardson*, where the Court denied a taxpayer standing to sue the government for its use of tax money, a claim the Court found amorphous, Justice Powell's concurring opinion explained:

> "The irreplaceable value of the [judicial] power articulated by Mr. Chief Justice Marshall [in Marbury v. Madison] lies in the protection it has afforded the constitutional rights and liberties of individual citizens and minority groups against oppressive or discriminatory government action. It is this role, not some amorphous general supervision of the operations of government, that has maintained public esteem for the federal courts and has permitted the peaceful coexistence of the countermajoritarian implications of judicial review and the democratic principles upon which our Federal Government in the final analysis rests."

Constitutional claims of rights violations by a political branch of government are anything but amorphous. Judge-made rules, like the Political Question Doctrine and redressability, which deny judicial review, should be inapplicable. These issues are addressed in Chapters 5 and 6.

The Long-term Influence of Judicial Dissent

However, life is not without hope when the Court denies persons the right to litigate grievances for rights violations against the political branches. Many of the ultimate decisions of the Supreme Court have come from the "Great Dissents" of earlier courts. There are many such Dissents. For example: In *Plessy v. Ferguson*, 1896, the Court ruled separate but equal educational facilities for black children satisfy the

Constitution's equal protection clause. However, Justice Harlan wrote a dissent, which ultimately was vindicated 58 years later in *Brown v. Board of Education.* Harlan wrote:

> "Our Constitution is color-blind and neither knows nor tolerates classes among citizens. In respect of civil rights, all citizens are equal before the law. The humblest is the peer of the most powerful. The law regards man as man and takes no account of his surroundings or of his color when his civil rights as guaranteed by the supreme law of the land are involved.... If evils will result from the commingling of the two races upon public highways established for the benefit of all, they will be infinitely less than those that will surely come from state legislation regulating the enjoyment of civil rights upon the basis of race."

In 1936, Chief Justice Charles Hughes stated that "A dissent in a Court of last resort is an appeal ... to the intelligence of a future day...." The intelligence may be that of a future court, or of a Congress that passes remedial legislation, or of a group of activists whose persistence results in a constitutional amendment. Although the eloquence of the dissent may motivate us, it is the dissent's effect on the evolution of history that will provide the defining events. There is a sense that the timing of controversial decisions of the Supreme Court that result in significant change must coincide with the willingness of the American people to accept the change. More than likely that is why it took 58 years for Harlan's dissent to become law.

Ultimate Limitations on Supreme Court's Authority

The Supreme Court has a limited ability to protect constitutional rights confirmed or granted by its decisions. Consider:

- The Court has no authority over the sword or

the purse, as Alexander Hamilton pointed out.

- The Court has no independent enforcement mechanism. Andrew Jackson reacted to an adverse Supreme Court decision, saying, "Well, John Marshall has made his decision, now let him enforce it." Lincoln ignored the Court without repercussions when his waiver of habeas corpus was declared unconstitutional.

- Barry Friedman points out in his 2009 *The Will of the People* that for the Court's decisions to be supported, the Court must enjoy high levels of legitimacy. If the Supreme Court or lower federal courts too frequently obstruct the other political branches, the Courts face political court-curbing measures, as it did during the Reconstruction Period following the Civil War. During that period Congress limited the Court's jurisdiction over specified cases, and passed other laws increasing, and later decreasing, the numbers of Supreme Court judges. As a result, the Supreme Court and the rest of the federal judiciary tended to avoid high profile clashes by using avoidance techniques – such as refusing to opine on what it viewed as being political questions or questions of redressability. However, these deference techniques, which we refer to as the Court's "Deference Doctrines," create their own set of problems. The 21st Century's contentious times are times demanding deeper Court involvement, not deference.

An Active People and a Supporting Court

In practice, in the 21st Century, with its mass

communications and constitutional complexity, the ultimate definers of constitutional rights are the people's protective constituencies, such as unions, trade groups, environmental groups, human rights groups, activist groups like the ACLU, Our Children's Trust, and religious groups that can make it politically difficult for either of our political branches of our government to ignore constitutional rights. To repeat: *Democracy is not a spectator sport.*

Certainly, an active and informed citizenry is important if the people are to be engaged with a strong voice – even though their voices may be filtered through the lens of a protective constituency. In the 2016 presidential election, 29% of people eligible to vote elected our President. Only 61.4% of citizens of the voting-age population voted. Low voter turnouts and uninformed citizenry were not within the expectation of our Framers. A 2018 Pew study done after the 2016 election indicates it was non-voters who determined the outcome. The 2018 Washington Post's article, "New data makes it clear: Nonvoters handed Trump the presidency," drew a shocking conclusion from the Pew study, "Demographic groups that preferred Trump were three times as likely to be a bigger part of the voter pool than nonvoters. Among groups that preferred [Hillary] Clinton, those were about 50% more likely to be a bigger part of the nonvoting community."

But, living in a Democracy of Dollars shaped by special interests and partisan gerrymandering, ballot-box preferences of the people are not enough. The rights of our people remain at risk. That risk is a point Chief Justice John Roberts did not speak about in his 2005 Senate nomination hearing. At that time, he assured the Senators that his Court would fairly, non-politically, and thoughtfully, call balls and strikes.

But that is a point Justice Neil Gorsuch is beginning to make in a loud and consistent way, at least in response to the legislative branch's expansive delegation of authority to the executive branch, and its deference paid to administrative agencies. However, Gorsuch's focus on deference and delegation has not yet reached the Supreme Court's Standing and Political Question Doctrines that we will discuss in

Chapters 5 and 6. These troubling Deference Doctrines, unlike the Chevron rules taken up in the next chapter, do not focus on excessive delegation by the legislative branch to the executive branch. These doctrines enable the Supreme Court and federal judiciary to evade judicial review, forcing individuals whose rights have been violated by a political branch agency to seek remedies from the same political branch which caused their initial harm. That is an impossible situation, and – the motivation for this book.

Playing by the Rules

In his nomination speech before the Senate in 2005, Chief Justice Roberts said: "Judges and justices are servants of the law and not the other way around. Judges are like umpires.... They make sure everybody plays by the rules."

We ask the question Justice Roberts didn't ask, "What happens when a political branch of government doesn't play by the rules and is flat out wrong?" We ask, "What happens when judges admit there is a wrong imposed by a political branch of government, yet refuse to act, as the 9th Circuit Court of Appeals has done in *Juliana v. The United States*?" The case is discussed in Chapter 5. We also ask, "What happens when the Supreme Court admits that state-imposed partisan gerrymandering dilutes votes of individuals who are not members of the political party in power, as it has in *Rucho v. Common Cause*, and yet refuses to act?" The case is discussed in Chapter 6.

These questions raise a further question: "Why isn't the Supreme Court insisting that our federal and state governments play by the rules?"

That question leads us to the ultimate question: "Was Supreme Court Chief Justice Marshall wrong?" He opined in 1803:

> "The very essence of civil liberty certainly consists in the right of every individual to claim the protection of the laws, whenever he

receives an injury. One of the first duties of government is to afford that protection…. The government of the United States has been emphatically termed a government of laws, and not of men. It will certainly cease to deserve this high application, if the laws furnish no remedy for the violation of a vested legal right."

Marshall was right. His conclusion that the Court's failure to provide remedies for violations of an individual's "vested legal right" makes us a government of men and not laws is why we argue that, in today's Democracy of Dollars, we must pay close attention to, and be activists for, the protection of our rights. By themselves, the written words of our Constitution are inadequate. There must be a strong voice of the people that demands the Supreme Court reassert its judicial review responsibilities in parallel to the problem-solving vision of the Marshall Court. In 34 years of decisions, the Marshall Court built the foundation on which today's Court stands. The Court must not turn away from its constitutional responsibility to secure "the very essence of civil liberty" for all of us.

Part II

Judicial Deference Doctrines and Their Effects

A constitution is not intended to embody a particular economic theory, whether of paternalism and the organic relation of the citizen to the State or of laissez faire. It is made for people of fundamentally differing views....

> Justice Oliver Wendell Holmes, dissent
> Lochner v. State of New York, 198
> U.S. 45, 1905

Chapter 4 – Judicial Deference: Congress's Over-Delegation

War Powers

Not only has Congress delegated much of its Constitutional legislative authority to the executive branch and its administrative agencies, it has also stripped itself of its fundamental war-making powers.

Article I, Section 8 of our Constitution, details the powers of Congress. One of its exclusive powers is the power to "declare War." Abraham Lincoln wrote in 1848:

> "The provision of the Constitution giving the war-making powers to Congress, was dictated, as I understand it, by the following reasons: Kings had always been involving and impoverishing their people in wars.... This, our [Constitutional] Convention understood to be the most oppressive of all Kingly oppressions and they resolved to so frame the Constitution that no one man should hold the

power of bringing this oppression upon us."

As one of the many necessary compromises during the Constitutional Convention, our Constitution's Framers used the word "declare," and not the word "make," in our constitutional grant of war power. The idea was to allow the President, as Commander in Chief of the military, to exercise Article II Section 2 powers to "make" defensive wars in emergencies to defend our country. Defensive wars, it was thought, require quick and decisive action. Assembling Congress for a formal declaration of war for defense would be unnecessarily time consuming.

In recent times, cold war threats, which developed in the aftermath of World War II, in the minds of many, necessitated expanding the President's authority to "make" undeclared wars, including when appropriate, a preemptive strike to deal with a complex, threatening world of competing philosophies and nuclear weapons.

The last time Congress declared war was in 1941 for World War II. Since then, our Presidents have led us to "military actions" in Korea, Cuba, Vietnam, Dominican Republic, Grenada, Panama, the Gulf War, Somalia, Haiti, Bosnia, Kosovo, Afghanistan, Iraq, Yemen, Syria, Pakistan, resulting – as one commentator totaled – 134 undeclared U.S. military operations around the globe.

In 1973, Congress had second thoughts about the numbers of undeclared military actions. Thus, in a War Powers Resolution, it reasserted that it retained its war powers. Congress passed the law over President Nixon's veto. But the Resolution has never been enforced or followed. Four times Congress has provided broad military authority to Presidents in "AUMF's" – *Authorizations for the Use of Military Force*. The most recent AUMF Resolution followed the 9/11 attacks in 2001. Presidents, Republican and Democrats alike, have viewed the 2001 AUMF as a continuing, open-ended grant of authority. Since then, the President's war powers have grown. In 2020, Congress voted to limit the President's power to wage war in the Middle East. In May 2020, the President vetoed the measure, as he did a similar Yemen resolution in April 2019. Congress has otherwise been reluctant to provide oversight to the executive branch's use of power.

Administrative Agencies

In the past, I've written about our government's heavy load of regulations emanating from executive branch administrative agencies. In a blog titled "Too Damn Many Regulations?" I pointed out that a 5-page tax statute I dealt with as a tax attorney was backed up by 200 pages of IRS regulations and 187 pages of IRS explanation. I added that in 1938, our Code of Federal Regulations consisted of 18,000 pages, and by 2014, the Code had grown to 175,000 pages. In 2016, Congress adopted 2,966 pages of laws only to see the executive branch add 97,110 pages of administrative law regulations. After a few more examples, I quoted conservative political commentator George Will, from his 2019 *Conservative Sensibility*: "Congress is no longer the primary institution of America's self-government."

When Congress delegates its critical legislative power to the executive branch administrative agencies, the consequences are troubling and significant – and far beyond the contemplation of the Framers:

1) Each newly elected President appoints political heads (frequently from regulated companies) to run executive branch agencies. An appointee typically has little or no expertise in the operation or mission of the agency he or she is appointed to lead. These appointments are subject to approval of the Senate – except when the President, as President Trump did with great frequency, appoints acting agency heads not approved by the Senate. (The 1998 Vacancies Reform Act limits the authority of acting agency heads after a specified time period, generally 210 days. It also specifies who can be an acting agency head without Senate approval. In a

September 2020 article, "At least 15 Trump Officials Do Not Hold Their Positions Lawfully," Becca Damante reports that Trump repeatedly ignored the time limit and requirements of the Act.)

2) Congress's delegation of rule-making authority to executive branch administrative agencies authorizes the agencies to adopt and enforce rules that have the force of law. Congress's delegation gives legislators the opportunity to pass vague laws – "politically correct" laws that provide both conservatives and liberals an opportunity to boast about what they have done, while doing little or nothing of substance. Thus, our laws are too frequently void of the details or instructive principles a conscientious executive – our President – and his administrative agencies need to guide their actions. This invites the President and his administrative agencies to fill in the vagaries and the details, providing the substance through regulations. Regulations are promulgated without ample consideration of the will or needs of the people. However, there is frequent and defining input from special interests who are the regulated.

3) Furthermore, the administrative rules adopted by administrative agencies under a President's leadership are frequently rolled back by the President's successor; particularly if the successor is from a different party.

4) What is missing throughout the entire administrative process is the give and take of legislative debate, effective public comment, and the finality of a well-drafted law passed by Congress. Although people elect congressional legislators, they have no direct role or voice in filling administrative agency vacancies. Filling

vacancies is the responsibility of the President.

5) With insufficient legislative guidance from Congress, the agency heads, frequently after presidential input, decide not only the breadth of the administrative regulations, but how they will be enforced. These decisions are too often guided by the industries being regulated. Regulated industries have been known to present their regulators with proposed rules, which are readily adopted. Regulated industries also champion self-regulation, with little governmental oversight. The ACLU and a few other legislative activists do their best to challenge agencies when they go too far astray. But courts are too often forgiving and tolerant of the agencies in measuring their responsibilities. These issues are discussed in additional depth in Chapter 7.

Chevron and Companion Deference Doctrines

Over the years, the Supreme Court has adopted the *Chevron Deference Doctrine*, under which the Court defers to an agency for its interpretation of the statutes regulating it. The Doctrine's standard is whenever a statute has ambiguity, and the Court concludes the agency's interpretation is "reasonable," the Court defers to the agency's interpretation. Similarly, under the *Auer Deference Doctrine*, the Court defers to agencies the right to interpret its own ambiguous rules.

Under the *Skidmore Deference Doctrine*, the Court defers to the presumptive expertise of the agency. In my mind, this deference is a most questionable practice. The original legislative objective of agencies was to provide expertise on complex matters. Today, agencies are too frequently run not by experts or scientists, but by political appointees from the industries they regulate.

A question arises when administrations change, appointing new leadership with allegiance to an incoming President. New administrations frequently seek different interpretations of ambiguous statutes defining agency responsibilities. Will their new interpretations prevail? If there are alternative, plausible statutory interpretations, an agency, supported by facts and policy reasons, most likely has the authority to pursue different policy objectives under its new administration.

These approaches are a far cry from the demands of "textualism" or "original meaning" of the Constitution. These Deferral Doctrines fail to meet the Constitution's checks and balances requirements. Rarely do agency interpretations of regulating statutes or its rules reflect the considerations a fiduciary for the people should have. Agency lawyers and other personnel come and go between the industries they are charged to regulate and the executive branch's regulatory agencies. Thus, agencies frequently fail to provide true oversight over the industries they are charged to regulate. Agency conflict of interest rules are of little help.

I remember a hearing for a client before the SEC in the 1980s. The SEC's hearing officer and the SEC counsel (the SEC's advocate) flew together to Tampa from and back to Washington for my client's hearing. Their conversations were those of obvious friends who have taken these trips together several times. There was no independence and little chance a court would overrule the administrative hearing officer's ruling. Special counsel for my client was also a former SEC counsel, having changed recently from representing the regulator to representing the regulated.

It took until 2018 for the Supreme Court to conclude that SEC appointment of administrative law judges by its staff members was unconstitutional. The SEC administrative law judges must now be appointed based on Article II, §2 of the Constitution. That article provides that "Congress may by Law vest the Appointment of such inferior Officers, as they think proper, in the President alone, in the Courts of Law, or the Heads of Departments."

The influence of lobbyists and their regulated industry clients are bolstered as agency staff members move back and forth between the regulating agencies and their regulated industries. The movement of staff personnel from the regulator to the regulated gives the lobbyists (who are frequently former regulators or former members of Congress) advocating for their industry clients special power to shape administrative law regulations in their favor.

Thus, industry lobbies have open access to achieve their sought-after results with little interference or effective oversight. Certainly, the back-and-forth discussions between congressional members of both parties participating in legislative hearings is missing. We return to this problem in Chapter 7.

George Will argues in his 2019 *The Conservative Sensibility*, that congressional legislative delegation to the executive branch is contrary to our Constitution's separation of powers requirements. As we point out in Chapter 3, Article 1, Section 1 of the Constitution articulates a legislative nondelegation doctrine.

Congress's legislative delegation to the executive branch also ignores Madison's caution in his 1788 Federalist Papers #47: "The accumulation of all powers, legislative, executive, and judiciary, in the same hands, whether of one, few or many, and whether hereditary, self-appointed, or elective, may justly be pronounced the very definition of tyranny." Yet, our Congress has fostered the accumulation powers in the executive branch with approval of the Supreme Court.

Will suggests what Congress should have done was to retain its legislative responsibility while strengthening its professional staffs to provide it with the necessary expertise to legislate with clarity. Such a process would minimize the current output of vague laws by Congress. It would also limit the output of substantive laws adopted in the form of regulations promulgated by administrative agencies run by unelected political appointees. Broad delegation enhances agency power to tilt the thrust of vague laws in favor of the special interests for whom the political appointees worked and will work again.

Will's suggestion has little chance of becoming law. Administrative agencies, our fourth branch of government, are too entrenched, too dominant, too powerful. However, Justice Neil Gorsuch, appointed to the Supreme Court in January 2017, has expressed skepticism of the statutory interpretive authority of the agencies. In his 2019 dissent in *Gundy v. United States,* Gorsuch said that the delegation appears to run counter to the Constitution's Separation of Powers Doctrine. Gorsuch argues that the Doctrine is a "vital guard against government encroachment on the people's liberties." Justices Roberts and Thomas joined in Gorsuch's dissent, stating that it was time to review the broad range of delegation by Congress of its legislative authority to the executive branch and its administrative agencies.

Justice Elena Kagan wrote the opinion for the Court, which held the law's delegation of decisional authority to the Attorney General was constitutional because it was based on an "intelligible principle." Writing as if in response to Gorsuch, Justice Kagan wrote that if the *Gundy* statute was unconstitutional, "then most of Government is unconstitutional — dependent as Congress is on the need to give discretion to executive officials to implement their programs."

The "intelligible principle" is sourced in the 1928 opinion of Chief Justice William Howard Taft. He opined in *J. W. Hampton, Jr. v. United States* that congressional delegation framed by an "intelligible principle," was constitutionally permitted. Taft wrote: "In determining what [Congress] may do in seeking assistance from another branch, the extent and character of that assistance must be fixed according to common sense and the inherent necessities of governmental coordination." So long as Congress "shall lay down by legislative act an intelligible principle to which the person or body authorized to [exercise the delegated authority] is directed to conform, such legislative action is not forbidden delegation of legislative power."

The intelligible principle has been used by the Court since 1928 as its measure of congressional delegation constitutionality. But what was an intelligible principle in 1928 no longer has traction. In the 21st Century, the intelligible principle that once enhanced the well-being of the people now results in special interests influencing government to the detriment of the people. Today, Congress has simply become too careless with our rights and its delegation. The idea of an intelligible principle must operate within a framework of enhanced standards and discernible checks and balances, both missing in today's environment.

A Supreme Court Rollback in the Making?

In 2017 Kevin Russell wrote an article, "Judge Gorsuch on separation of powers and federalism," on Neil Gorsuch's questioning the constitutionality of administrative law being delegated in its totality to the executive branch. Gorsuch's writings and speeches about administrative laws in various cases include:

- "To adapt the law to changing circumstances, the Framers thought, the collective wisdom of the people's representatives is needed. To faithfully execute the laws often demands the sort of vigor hard to find in management-by-committee. And to resolve cases and controversies over past events calls for neutral decisionmakers who will apply the law as it is, not as they wish it to be."

- "Might this arrangement [delegation of administrative law-making and enforcement authority to the executive branch], though arrived at with Congress's assent, still blur the line between the Legislative and Executive functions assigned to separate departments by our Constitution? Thanks to this and many other similar and similarly generous congressional delegations, the Code of Federal Regulations today finds itself crowded with so many "crimes" that scholars actually debate their number."

Gorsuch also makes the case in his 2019 book, *A Republic, If You Can Keep it*: "[T]he framers saw virtue in the separation of powers and a government that is deliberately deliberate…. By transferring more and more power from the legislature and judiciary to the executive, we alter piece by piece the framers' work and risk the underlying values it was designed to serve…. Madison and the framers held the view that '[n]o political truth is' more important to 'liberty' than the separation of powers because the 'accumulation of' power 'in the same hands' inevitably leads to 'tyranny.'"

University of Michigan law professors Julian D. Mortenson and Nicholas Bagley disagreed with Gorsuch's conclusions about delegation in their 2020 article, "There's No Historical Justification for One of the Most Dangerous Ideas in American Law." They argue, "The framers didn't believe that broad delegations of legislative power violated the Constitution, but conservative originalists keep insisting otherwise."

Mortenson and Bagley assert that congressional delegation to administrative agencies is "the indispensable foundation of modern American governance." They express concern that today's Supreme Court's conservative majority "is poised to breathe life into the 'nondelegation doctrine.'" The professors attribute the upheaval to Justice Neil Gorsuch's 2019 dissent in *Gundy v. United States*, where Gorsuch wrote, "that it would frustrate the system of government ordained by the Constitution if Congress could merely announce vague aspirations and then assign others the responsibility of adopting legislation to realize its goals." Their arguments include:

- The Constitution is silent on delegation.

- Locke's writings, important to Jefferson and the Framers, included "the legislature cannot transfer the power of making laws," relied on by the originalists, are misunderstood.

- In the Framers time, European parliaments delegated legislative authority "all the time."

- In their approval of the Constitution, States

delegated legislative authority to the federal government.

The professors conclude: "maybe the Constitution should be understood to prohibit Congress from closing up shop and making the President a permanent monarch. Indeed, a few contemporary theorists suggested as much. But that's worlds apart from saying that it's unconstitutional to delegate power when Congress remains on the scene to supervise, check, and withdraw that power."

Contrary to Mortenson's and Bagley's arguments, since the Constitution is a grant of power, its silence about delegation should mean the right of delegation has not been granted.

But what is our actual history? In July 2020, Professor Christine Chabot wrote "The Lost History of Delegation at the Founding." She observes, "Gorsuch's analysis relies on a deficient account of founding-era history." She views any restraint on congressional delegation by the Supreme Court as the imposition of "an unprecedented constitutional requirement."

Chabot argues that our Framers began our republic with a view that permitted congressional delegation: "Alexander Hamilton, James Madison, and the First Congress all approved of legislation that delegated highly consequential policy decisions to the executive branch." She points out that our first Congress approved Hamilton's recommendation that Congress's power to borrow money be delegated to the President to facilitate the federal government paying the Revolutionary War debts incurred by the states. Congress also passed a patent act under the Intellectual Property Clause of the Constitution, Article 1, Section 8. That clause gave Congress the power to protect intellectual property. Congress delegated the power to establish substantive and procedural patent rules to the executive branch. Chabot concludes: "The capacious language in founding-era statutes granted executive officers' powers that went far beyond finding facts and filling in the details."

Chabot adds, "Hamilton, Madison, and Jefferson fought

over many issues, but delegation of important policy questions was not one of them."

However, there is a pragmatic problem with delegation to the executive branch in the context of today's political environment. In America's Democracy of Dollars, delegation of power is frequently abused by the executive branch. Contrary to Professors Mortenson and Bagley's idea that "Congress remains on the scene to supervise, check, and withdraw that power," the President is in virtual control once a power has been delegated. Why? The President has the right to veto any corrective legislation not approved by two-thirds of both houses of Congress. A two-thirds vote is usually a political impossibility.

A veto of Congress's legislative attempt to take back a right granted is clearly illustrated by Trump's veto of the congressional attempts to rein in his war powers in the congressional Iran War Power and Yemen War Powers Resolutions. Trump also vetoed Congress's attempt to negate the controversial DeVos Rule about how student loans could be forgiven. These presidential vetoes confirm the error in Professors Mortenson's and Bagley's arguments.

In the past, Congress attempted to include in legislation the right of "legislative veto" to overturn agency abuse of delegated authority by reserving the right to withdraw legislated delegation. However, in 1983, the Supreme Court ruled in *INS v. Chadha* that reserved legislative vetoes in laws passed were not valid. Coupled with the judicial branch's deference, there are no effective remedies to protect us from the mire of over-delegation.

As a result of the Court's decision, Congress changed the National Emergencies Act. The Act initially empowered the President to activate special powers during a crisis, reserving to Congress the right to terminate any emergency declaration. When the Act was first adopted, the emergency could be terminated by resolutions of each house of Congress. It now requires a two-thirds majority in both houses when a termination is contested by the President.

Yes, Justice Gorsuch's concerns about Congress's

delegation have been challenged by Mortenson and Bagley as well as Chabot. Their challenges are supported by historical action of our first Congress, as well as an extensive legislative history. But the inability of Congress to supervise or withdraw its delegation when delegation is abused validates Gorsuch's concern.

Consider also Gorsuch's comments in *Damien Guedes et al; v. Bureau of Alcohol, et al.,* a March 2020 case the Supreme Court declined to hear. The Court did not write an opinion, but Justice Gorsuch added his statement to the Court's declination. He criticized the Bureau of Alcohol for changing its rules on gun bump stocks. The Bureau changed the category of gun bump stocks from not being categorized as machineguns to being in that category, even though the statute hasn't changed. Gorsuch wrote:

> "The agency used to tell everyone that bump stocks don't qualify as 'machineguns.' Now it says the opposite. The law hasn't changed, only an agency's interpretation of it. And these days it sometimes seems agencies change their statutory interpretations almost as often as elections change administrations. How, in all this, can ordinary citizens be expected to keep up — required not only to conform their conduct to the fairest reading of the law they might expect from a neutral judge, but forced to guess whether the statute will be declared ambiguous; to guess again whether the agency's initial interpretation of the law will be declared 'reasonable'; and to guess *again* whether a later and opposing agency interpretation will *also* be held 'reasonable'? And why should courts, charged with the independent and neutral interpretation of the laws Congress has enacted, defer to such bureaucratic pirouetting?"

The Bureau is a federal law enforcement organization

within the Department of Justice, under the authority of the President.

James Madison said during the first Congress's debate about its authority to delegate its constitutional borrowing power to the President — George Washington — was a decision involving "great trust." However, our times are dominated by America's Democracy of Dollars culture. The influence of special interests and their lobbies on an accommodating executive branch, which ignores its fiduciary responsibility of "great trust," raises Madison's concern, expressed in the 1788 Federalist Papers #47:

> "When the legislative and executive powers are united in the same person, or in the same body of magistrates, there can be no liberty; because apprehensions may arise, lest the same monarch or senate should enact tyrannical laws, to execute them in a tyrannical manner."

The critical point is that the Constitution must be applied in the context in which it operates. When the first Congress delegated authority to George Washington — elected as our President to two terms unanimously by the electoral college — the trust in the executive branch was well founded. It was a period of "great trust." Today, it is not and for good reason.

In this Era of Presidential Administration, a recapture of delegated lawmaking by a legislatively active and responsive Congress may be more of a dream than a reality. We now run our government through a bevy of executive branch agencies employing thousands of people. Shifting that responsibility back to the legislative branch would be an insurmountable task. But the Court's emerging conversations about congressional standards and Court oversight could bring reform within reach.

Hopefully, the Constitution's judicial responsibility that has been delegated to the executive branch can be reclaimed through enhanced judicial review, since the judicial branch is the most independent of our three branches. Perhaps we can even turn back today's politicization of the Court by reconsidering the judicial appointment process. Hamilton wrote in 1788, Federalist Papers #78 that "there is no liberty if the power of judging is not separated from the legislative and executive powers.... [T]he courts were designed to be an intermediate body between the people and the legislature, in order, among things, to keep the latter within the limits assigned to their authority." Hamilton concludes that the courts must be governed by the will of the people, not the will of the legislature. And certainly not by the will of the executive branch or special interests.

A 2020 5-4 decision of the Supreme Court, *Selina Law v. Consumer Financial Protection Bureau*, gives us an idea of the 21st Century Court's disposition. The Court held that, contrary to congressional prohibition, the President has the unrestricted right to fire heads of independent agencies without governing boards. An irony of the case is that the Constitution does not authorize the President to remove heads of any agencies. The Constitution's Article II removal remedy is impeachment by Congress. However, in 1926, the Supreme Court ruled that removal of appointed executive branch agency heads and executives was an incidental presidential power related to the President's power of appointment. The 2020 decision expands that authority to independent agencies that are not within the executive branch.

The 2019 5-to-4 Supreme Court decision, *Rucho v. Common Cause*, is discussed in Chapter 6. The Court opined that voting district gerrymandering is not a matter for courts to decide because the issue is a political question reserved to the states and Congress. This case may also indicate that today's conservative Supreme Court is less apt to resolve politically contentious issues involving an individual's rights tread upon by a state. However, the Supreme Court's 2020 6-to-3 decision, *Bostock v. Clayton County, Georgia,* protecting gay and transgender workers from sex discrimination indicates that the Court's ground rules regarding contentious issues can be complex and not always politically predictable.

There is an irony worth mentioning in how conservative and liberal judges apply the Deferential Doctrines, the judge-made rules, self-imposed by the Court. Conservative judges like Gorsuch oppose liberal delegation by Congress of legislative power to the executive branch and its administrative agencies. Liberal judges like Kagan have approved the Court's deference of legislative power delegation under the intelligible principle and similar Deference Doctrines that support congressional delegation. Conservative and liberal judges reverse their positions on deference when it is the Court's deference to the political branches through the Political Question and Standing Doctrines. Liberals object to the Court's deference under the Political Question and Standing Doctrines when individuals' rights are thwarted. In contrast, conservatives see that deference as presenting valid political questions not meant for the eyes of the Court. Chapter 5 considers the Standing Doctrine. Chapter 6, the Political Question Doctrine.

Whether we judges like to think so or not, courts are a part of the government against whom the constraints of the Bill of Rights operate.

Judge James L. Oakes
The Proper Role of the Federal Courts
in Enforcing the Bill of Rights, 1979

Chapter 5 – Judicial Deference: The Standing Doctrine

Definitions:

Redressability: The "standing" requirement that the plaintiff's claims or injuries must be redressable by a federal court under constitutional authority granted to them as Article III courts.

Standing: A plaintiff's right to make a legal claim and seek a judicial remedy, based on the plaintiff showing the court that (1) the plaintiff suffered an injury in fact, (2) the injury is fairly traceable to the defendant, and (3) the injury is likely redressable by a favorable judicial decision.

Marbury v. Madison and the Marshall Court

Debates as to what the Constitution means, and whether there are political questions, are not something new. These debates have been around since the days of the Framers. The most famous – and perhaps the most important – early controversy about the Court's constitutional role was between John Marshall, Chief Justice of the Supreme Court, and Thomas Jefferson, our third President (1801-1809). Marshall, who had been President John Adams' Secretary of State, was appointed Chief Justice in 1801 by Adams shortly before he left office.

During the Presidency of George Washington, two dynamically different views of government surfaced among members of Washington's Cabinet, one favoring a strong central government and the other a weaker central government.

Washington opposed the idea of political parties because, he reasoned, partisanship created factions and factions burdened the ability of an administration to function. In his 1796 Farewell Address, he said that one of the expedients of a political party is to "misrepresent the opinions and aims" of the other party. Washington concluded, "This spirit, unfortunately, is inseparable from our nature, having its roots in the strongest passions of the human mind.... The alternate domination of one faction over another, sharpened by the spirit of revenge, natural to party dissensions, which, in different ages and countries, has perpetrated the most horrid enormities, is itself a frightful despotism.... The disorders and miseries, which result, gradually incline the minds of men to seek security and repose in the absolute power of an individual... [who] turns this disposition to the purposes of his own elevation on the ruins of public liberty."

Despite Washington's advice, ultimately, the differences in views led to the formation of political parties. We noted in Chapter 1 that Madison moderated the concern about factions he expressed in 1787 in Federalist Papers #10. He later argued in a newspaper article that political parties were inevitable and would serve the Constitution's need for checks and balances, as each party would provide a check and balance on the other.

The rift between Adams and Jefferson, once revolutionary colleagues and the best of friends, resulted in a bitterly fought election in 1800 won by Jefferson. Adams and Jefferson didn't reestablish their friendship until 1812, when they began exchanging letters about their views on government. They exchanged 175 letters before their deaths, both dying on July 4, 1826, the fiftieth anniversary of the Declaration of Independence.

In 1801, as Adams was leaving office, he appointed Marbury and several others to government positions. President Jefferson directed his Secretary of State, James Madison, to refuse to accept the appointments. Marbury and the others sued Madison in the Supreme Court, asking the Court to issue a writ of mandamus ordering Madison to accept Adams' last-minute appointments.

Marshall ruled that Marbury had been properly appointed by Adams and was entitled to his governmental position. However, he opined that the Supreme Court only had appellate jurisdiction under the Constitution for these kinds of cases. Thus, the act of Congress passing a law that gave the Supreme Court jurisdiction as a trial court on a matter not specified in the Constitution was unconstitutional. Because the law was unconstitutional, the Supreme Court could not enforce the appointments.

Marshall concluded, "It is emphatically the province and duty of the judicial department to say what the law is." When the Constitution and a law both apply in a case, "the constitution, and not such ordinary act, must govern the case to which they both apply."

His opinion also commented on the powers of the President and his appointed executive officers. When powers are given by the Constitution to the President alone, presidential powers are political, entrusted to the President and his discretion. Discretionary powers are not subject to review by the Court. But "when the rights of individuals are dependent upon the performance of those acts; he is so far the officer of the law; is amenable to the laws for his conduct; and cannot at his discretion sport away the vested rights of others…." and is not immune from suit.

The *Marbury* opinion was a legal opinion artfully crafted within the context of politics. Madison and Jefferson were members of the new Republican party. Marbury had been appointed by Adams, a member of the opposing Federalist party. Marshall, also a Federalist, knew that if he ordered Madison to accept Adams' appointment, Jefferson would countermand the Court's order and the weakness of the Court – its inability to enforce its opinions – would be exposed. Marshall avoided a direct conflict with Jefferson by ruling that although the Court had the exclusive right to determine the enforceability of laws, the law before the Court was not constitutionally enforceable. While avoiding the conflict, Marshall was able to successfully affirm the Court's role as the ultimate determiner of the constitutionality of legislation.

Initially, Jefferson disagreed with Marshall on the role of the Court, arguing that the Court had less consequential responsibilities. Jefferson's idea was that the Court's authority to overturn laws conflicted with the peoples' right to rule through their elected representatives, Congress. (Jefferson did not take part in the Constitutional Convention or the writing of the Federalist Papers. He was on assignment by our young government in France. Thus, he missed the debates.)

Jefferson's position, however, was contrary to the intent of the Framers, expressed in 1788 in Federalist Papers #78 by Hamilton, who like Marshall was a Federalist. Writing as Publicus, Hamilton reasoned: "It is far more rational to suppose, that the courts were designed to be an intermediate body between the people and the legislature, in order, among other things, to keep the later within the limits assigned to their authority. The interpretation of the laws is the proper and peculiar province of the courts. A constitution is, in fact, and must be regarded by the judges, as a fundamental law.... Nor does this conclusion by any means suppose the superiority of the judicial to the legislative power. It only supposes that the power of the people is superior to both."

However, solidifying Hamilton's thoughts, and Marshall's *Marbury* decision into the minds and hearts of the American people was not an easy task. The idea of judicial review was an American creation, not part of our inherited English law. It took a lot of work by the Marshall Court, but, ultimately, the Court's responsibility for judicial review and saying what the law is became ingrained in our judicial and political systems.

The Supreme Court produced more than 1,000 opinions under its 34 years of John Marshall's leadership. Marshall personally wrote more than half of its opinions. *Marbury* and subsequent Marshall Court decisions firmly established the Supreme Court and the federal judicial system as independent and co-equal in responsibility to the executive and legislative branches.

History has proven the importance of the federal judiciary's role in providing checks and balances through judicial review, particularly in today's Democracy of Dollars, where the influence over the legislative and judicial branches by lobbyists and hefty political contributions, not the people, prevails.

Mariam Morshedi wrote in her 2019 article "Marbury v. Madison (February 24, 1803):"

> "*Marbury v. Madison* is one of the most important cases in Supreme Court history — perhaps the most important. The Constitution became the law of the land in 1789 with some very important principles that we take for granted today, like separation of powers and checks and balances. But there hadn't been enough time for the principles to be put into action.
>
> "*Marbury v. Madison* brought the first major checks and balances issue to the Supreme Court. The case solidified the Supreme Court's power to interpret the Constitution, and it also highlighted something else: The Court is not immune from politics."

Since 1803, when the Marshall Court delivered the *Marbury* opinion, there has evolved a fundamental understanding among legal scholars that the responsibility of the Constitution's Article III federal courts regarding the Constitution and the laws of our land include:

- Providing judicial remedies when there are legal wrongs. The Constitution's First

Amendment includes the provision that Congress shall make no law that abridges the rights of the people to "petition the Government for a redress of grievances." Marshall opined that providing people with the protection of the law is a principal responsibility of the Court.

- The Constitution is supreme over conflicting laws passed by Congress, conflicting rules and regulations crafted by executive branch administrative agencies, and executive orders of the President not supported by the Constitution or Congress's laws. The Constitution is also supreme over conflicting court-crafted rules used by the Court when rendering decisions.

- The Supreme Court has the ultimate duty to decide whether laws or executive actions violate the Constitution.

- The Supreme Court and the federal judiciary have a greater responsibility than to merely call non-controversial balls and strikes. The Supreme Court and the federal judiciary have an important role in calling balls and strikes that also provide constitutional checks and balances on the legislative and executive branches.

However, "what should be" is not necessarily what is. Over the years, as our Democracy of People morphed into a Democracy of Dollars, the debate about the role of the Supreme Court has continued. In 1967, Archibald Cox asked in his book, *The Warren Court* (the Court when I was in law school, 1964-67):

"What role should the judicial branch play in the government of American people? Should the court play an active, creative role in shaping our destiny, equal with the executive and legislative branches? Or should it be characterized by self-restraint, deferring to the legislative branch whenever there is room for policy judgment and leaving new departures to the initiative of others?"

During Marshall's 34 years the Supreme Court was energetic, architecting the Court's future. It crafted a balanced relationship not only with the two other branches of government, but with state governments as well. However, Cox points out, Marshall's judicial activism was ultimately met with opposition from those seeking a lesser role for the Court – one of judicial restraint rather than one of judicial problem-solving. The idea grew out of the Jeffersonian philosophy that government corrections must come through the political process, without judicial intervention or oversight.

Cox concludes that judicial restraint is too frequently the Court's loud, damaging, "no answer." When the legal process shuts down, he adds, "correction must come from outside and no violence is done to the principle of representative government if the court supplies the remedy." Cox closes:

"Ideally, the federal judicial branch ought not to enlarge its own jurisdiction simply because Congress and the state governments failed to solve the problem confided in them.... The ideal remedy is to reform the delinquents. But government is more pragmatic than ideal.... If one arm of government cannot or will not solve an insistent problem, the pressure falls on another."

Hence, the argument we set forth in this book: When the executive or legislative branches cannot or will not solve a problem involving governmental abuse or neglect of natural or constitutional rights, the pressure falls to the judicial branch, and when that occurs, the Court's judge-made rules that exclude judicial review, as presently applied by the Court, have no place within the Court's decisional process. This is particularly true when a political branch is the culprit, as it most frequently is in suppressing rights in today's Democracy of Dollars.

Stare Decisis

Change is never easy, and in law change is particularly difficult. Judicial decisions are based on *stare decisis*, on precedent. Absent a compelling need to change, Courts follow earlier judicial decisions when the same points arise in subsequent litigation. Stare decisis is intended to provide legal stability and continuity in the application of the law.

Over the years, the Supreme Court has acquired a portfolio of judge-made deference rules, which it also applies using stare decisis principles. The Court uses these rules to deny judicial review and defer resolution of selected cases or controversies before it to one or both political branches of government. The portfolio of deference rules comprises the Court's "Deference Doctrine." The Doctrine includes the Chevron Doctrine and companion doctrines discussed in Chapter 4. The Doctrine also includes the Standing Doctrine with its redressability requirement, discussed in this chapter. And it includes the Political Question Doctrine, the subject of Chapter 6.

Although the Court's consistent use of its deference rules should contribute to legal stability under stare decisis principles, in the context of today's Democracy of Dollars the Court's use can produce unintended harmful results. The Court's almost mechanical use of its deference rules has given too little consideration for the context of today's Democracy of Dollars. The Court's blindness to 21st Century reality also includes its failure to grasp that the Court itself has contributed to the growth of today's Democracy of Dollars, in part by its over-reliance on past decisions of deference, which were grounded in a different reality.

The Court's predilection for deference to the two political branches of government has become a systemic flaw in the judicial system.

The fundamental purpose of the law is to provide a remedy when there is a wrong. Judicial rigidity favors the status quo (stare decisis) and denies us the ability to right wrongs that accompany societal changes and changes in the way our government operates. Not all future changes can be expected to have been contemplated and thoroughly analyzed in earlier judicial decisions.

When human experience encounters a wrong not addressed by the law because of the Court's reliance on stare decisis, then the logic of the law must account for the realism of experience and reevaluate the precedents of the past. The judge-made rules of deference should not be applied without the Court's careful consideration of the context in which we are living.

Recrafting common law (judge-made law) is less difficult than recrafting statutory law. Statutory law, created by legislatures, places limitations on the authority of the judiciary. But we are talking about neither.

Judge-Made Rules

We are talking about judge-made rules, which judges can reevaluate and change. We are talking about the adverse effects these judge-made rules have on us.

When our natural and constitutional rights are abused or ignored by the legislative or executive branches, we look to the judiciary for remedies. Either we have these fundamental rights, or we don't. The legislative branch does not have the constitutional right to compromise, destroy or limit these rights. The executive branch does not have rule-making authority, or the right to issue executive orders, to deprive us of those rights.

It would be a rarity in today's contentious society, for any case involving human rights that comes before the Supreme Court not to have political implications. Human rights clearly have political implications. The Court errs by classifying such cases as political questions or non-redressable questions, which, with the Court's deference, deny aggrieved individuals remedies. The Court's disengagement from judicial oversight is an invitation to abuse of rights that are essential for life itself. The Court's responsibility, as John Marshall wrote so long ago, is to protect our rights.

Precedent for Change

Is there precedent for recrafting centuries-old judicial *stare-decisis* principles or holdings to deal with changing circumstances or evolving standards?

In the *Prologue*, we discuss how the definition of cruel and unusual punishment protected by the Eighth Amendment, changed as society evolved its standards of decency. In reflecting on earlier, acceptable but more severe forms of punishment, Chief Justice Earl Warren wrote that today's meaning of cruel and unusual punishment protected by the Eighth Amendment "must draw its meaning from the evolving standards of decency that mark the progress of a maturing society."

Although Warren was a Republican, the Warren Court is considered a liberal, progressive court. What about conservative Courts?

In Chapter 1, we discussed the Roberts Court opinion, *District of Columbia v. Heller* holding that the Second Amendment protection of an individual's right to bear arms wasn't limited to the front-loaded, single shot muskets common when the Constitution was adopted. Scalia opined that the kinds of weapons the Second Amendment protects include those weapons that are "common at the time" and are used for "self-defense." In 2008, the AR-15, a lightweight, semi-automatic rifle, was the most popular rifle in America and was, therefore, in "common use." Thus, today, AR-15 ownership by individuals is constitutionally protected.

Consider also the 2020 Supreme Court opinion, *Bostock v. Clayton County, Georgia*, written by Justice Gorsuch, joined by Chief Justice Roberts and four liberal members of the Court, relying on "textualism" and the meaning of the word "sex," holding that Title VII of the Civil Rights Act of 1964 protects

LGBTQ persons from being fired because of their sexual preferences. The three Judges dissenting argued that, when Congress passed Title VII, sex could not have included LGBTQ in its meaning, as then the word "transgender" did not exist.

With similar reasoning, today's Court should reevaluate the Constitution's application of its own deference rules against today's changed circumstances that comprise our Democracy of Dollars.

Our Children's Trust

In June 2015, at the age of 84, I shifted from a "mostly active" to "mostly retired" business/tax law practice. I called Julia Olson, chief counsel, and founder of Our Children's Trust ("OCT") and offered my help in their environmental litigation work, particularly should they decide to be involved in Florida, where I live. Florida is America's most vulnerable environment to the ravages of rising seas and global warming. Ultimately, OCT became active in Florida. The case is *Reynolds V. Florida*, brought by eight youth plaintiffs. The youths are represented by special counsel from OCT and seven Florida trial attorneys. The Florida trial court used the Political Question Doctrine as the basis for dismissing the kids' lawsuit. The case is on appeal.

Our Children's Trust, headquartered in Eugene, Oregon, "is a non-profit public interest law firm that provides strategic, campaign-based legal services to youth from diverse backgrounds to secure their legal rights to a safe climate."

OCT and their youth plaintiffs currently have active environmental lawsuits in Alaska, Colorado, Florida, Montana. North Carolina, Oregon, and Washington. Except for Colorado and North Carolina, trial courts have denied the youths' constitutional claims for a healthy environment by judicial deference to state political branches of government. In those states, their claims are on appeal. Colorado resulted in successful legislation requiring the state's Oil and Gas Conservation Commission to protect public health and the environment from oil and gas development. North Carolina has a rule-making procedure in progress.

Internationally, OCT and youth plaintiffs are active in 13 countries and before the United Nations. Many of the international actions are at early stages. Two are on appeal. However, there have been five significant international decisions:

- The Columbia Supreme Court of Justice ruled in favor of the youth plaintiffs' claims that deforestation in the Amazon and increasing temperatures threatened their constitutional rights to a healthy environment, life, health, food, and water.

- A Dutch Court of Appeal ruled that the Dutch government must do more to protect the environment. The court recognized the "grave danger" of climate change and called for the government to reduce greenhouse gas emissions.

- The Pakistan Supreme Court reversed a lower court rejection of the youth's petition and ruled that the constitutional climate lawsuit should proceed on its merits.

- The Ukraine court ordered the government's Cabinet of Ministers to prepare an assessment of the Country's progress in realizing the goals of the Kyoto Protocol on climate change.

- Fifteen young Mexicans living in the state of Baja in Mexico filed a climate lawsuit against the Mexican government. An early decision from the trial court authorized the suit to proceed on its merits.

OCT's federal case, *Juliana v. United States,* is OCT's most visible and its most important work in America. The 2020 dismissal by the 9th Circuit Court of Appeals of the 21 youths' claims illustrates the issues that concern us.

As we reflect on *Juliana* below and admire OCT's tenacity, we should remember the comments of Supreme Court Chief Justice Hughes in 1936, quoted in part in Chapter 3:

> "A dissent in a court of last resort is an appeal to the brooding spirit of law, to the intelligence of a future day when a later decision may possibly correct the error into which the dissenting justice believes the court to have been betrayed."

Juliana v. United States Chronology of Legal Actions

Definitions:

Answer is the response filed by the defendant to the complaint addressing the merits of a complaint, denying, or agreeing with the various allegations of the plaintiff.

Complaint is the initial pleading filed in a noncriminal court case stating the authority of the court to hear the claims and relief sought by the plaintiff, the complaining party, from the defendant.

Motion is a written or oral appeal by a defendant or plaintiff to a court requesting a specific ruling or order by the court.

Pleading is a formal document (e.g., complaint, answer, motion, writ) filed with the court by a party to litigation setting forth the claims, denials, defenses, requests, or allegations of the party.

Writ of mandamus is an order from a higher court (appeals court) to compel a lower court (trial court) to do its bidding.

A detailed *Chronology of Legal Actions*, briefly summarized below, is included in Appendix A.

The initial pleading, the *Juliana* complaint, was filed with the federal trial court in Oregon by 21 youths in September 2015. The complaint alleges that, through the federal government's affirmative actions that contribute to climate change, the federal government violated the youth's constitutional rights to life, liberty, and property. The pleading also claimed that the government failed to protect essential "public trust resources," which include the air we breathe and the water we drink.

As is typical in constitutional challenge litigation, the government filed a motion to dismiss the youth's complaint. When the motion was denied by the trial court, an appeal was filed by the government with the 9th Circuit Court of Appeals. When that motion was denied by the Court of Appeals, a further appeal was filed with the Supreme Court, which was also denied.

After more motions and appeals filed by the government, on November 21, 2018, following the recommendation of the 9th Circuit Court of Appeals, the trial court reluctantly referred the *Juliana* case to the Court of Appeals to determine if the case should go to trial. The Court of Appeals had requested the referral because of the concerns expressed by the Supreme Court that the breadth of the claims in *Juliana* youths presented "substantial grounds for difference of opinion."

On January 7, 2019, in response to the trial court's referral, the Court of Appeals granted the government's motion to file an interlocutory appeal.

Juliana v. United States: The Government's Interlocutory Appeal

Definition:

Interlocutory appeal: An appeal that occurs

before the trial court's final ruling on the entire case. Some interlocutory appeals involve legal points necessary to the determination of the case, while others involve collateral orders that are wholly separate from the merits of the action.

On January 17, 2020, in a 2 to 1 decision favoring the government's interlocutory appeal, the 9th Circuit Court of Appeals recognized the gravity and truthfulness of the evidence supporting the youths' claims. The decision also recognized the role of the government in causing harm. Despite it finding that the government violated the constitutional rights of the youths, the majority opinion ruled that under the constitutional Separation of Powers Doctrine the youths did not have standing and the case must be dismissed. Their claims were not redressable by the court. The third judge dissented and confirmed the children had standing, writing "our nation is crumbling – at our government's own hand – into a wasteland."

What is the essence of the 21 youth plaintiffs' claims that were before the court? Simply, that they have a constitutional right to a "climate system capable of sustaining human life." The trial court agreed and defined that right as climate system free from catastrophic climate change that "will cause human deaths, shorten human lifespans, result in widespread damage to property, threaten human food sources, and dramatically alter the planet's ecosystem."

The case summary of the Appeals Court's opinion includes the following conclusions: "[T]he record left little basis for denying that climate change was occurring at an increasingly rapid pace: copious expert evidence established that the unprecedented rise in atmospheric carbon dioxide levels stemmed from fossil fuel combustion and will wreak havoc on the Earth's climate if unchecked; the record conclusively established that the federal government has long understood the risks of fossil fuel use and increasing carbon dioxide emissions; and the record established that the government's contribution to climate change was not simply a result of inaction...

"The panel considered the three requirements for whether the plaintiffs had [Constitution] Article III [judicial branch] standing to pursue their constitutional claims. First, the panel held that the district court correctly found that the plaintiffs claimed concrete and particularized injuries. Second, the panel held that the district court properly found the Article III causation requirement satisfied for purposes of summary judgment because there was at least a genuine dispute as to whether a host of federal policies were a 'substantial factor' in causing plaintiff's injuries. Third, the panel held that the plaintiff's claimed injuries were not redressable by an Article III court. Specifically, the panel held that it was beyond the power of an Article III court to order, design, supervise, or implement the plaintiff's requested remedial plan where an effective plan would require a host of complex policy decisions entrusted to the wisdom and discretion of the executive and the political branches [legislative or executive] or to the electorate at large.

"District Judge Staton dissented and would affirm the district court. Judge Staton wrote that the plaintiffs brought suit to enforce the most basic structural principle embedded in our system of liberty: that the Constitution does not condone the Nation's willful destruction. She would hold that plaintiffs have standing to challenge the government's conduct, have articulated claims under the Constitution, and have presented sufficient evidence to press those claims at trial."

In his 91-page opinion, Judge Andrew D. Hurwitz defined the issue: "The central issue before us is whether, even assuming such a broad constitutional right exists, an Article III court can provide the plaintiffs the redress they seek.... Reluctantly, we conclude such relief is beyond our constitutional power."

The majority opinion denies that it bases its decision on the case presenting a political question; rather Hurwitz states that the youth plaintiffs lacked standing because standing's third factor, redressability, is lacking. However, the majority opinion admitted overlap between redressability and the political question. The dissent argues, and we agree, that "finding this case nonjusticiable blur[s] any meaningful distinction between the doctrine of standing [and its requirement for redressability] and political question."

The application of the Political Question Doctrine discussed in Chapter 6 requires a court to consider the *Baker Factors*. These are judge-made rules setting standards to determine whether an individual's claims have a judicial remedy when political questions may be present. Redressability is a judge-made rule that permits a court to conclude whether an individual's claims have a judicial remedy without considering the Baker Factors. For all practical purposes, there is no difference in effect. Finding the existence of a political question or an "inability" to provide redressability have the same results: total and absolute deference by the Court to the other two branches of government. In today's Democracy of Dollars, with our political branches answering to special interests and not to the people, that's a loud "no" to remedies.

In his consideration of the role of the Court and separation of powers, Judge Hurwitz wrote, "[S]eparation of powers depends largely upon common understanding of what activities are appropriate to legislatures, to executives, and to courts."

But what is the common understanding? Hurwitz never adequately explains. Certainly, the common understanding of the responsibilities of courts include their obligation to protect an individual's fundamental rights, particularly rights injured by one of the political branches of government.

Yet, ironically, Judge Hurwitz concludes: "The plaintiffs have made a compelling case that action is needed; it will be increasingly difficult in light of that record for the political branches to deny that climate change is occurring, that the government has had a role in causing it, and that our elected officials have a moral responsibility to seek solutions. We do not dispute that the broad judicial relief the plaintiffs seek could well goad the political branches into action..... We reluctantly conclude, however, that the plaintiffs' case must be made to the political branches or to the electorate at large, the latter of which can change the composition of the political branches through the ballot box. That the other branches may have abdicated their responsibility to remediate the problem does not confer on Article III courts, no matter how well-intentioned, the ability to step into their shoes."

Hurwitz doesn't address Chief Justice Marshall's 1803 *Marbury* conclusions, which are fundamental to the Court's role in reining in abuse by the legislative and executive branches:

> "The very essence of civil liberty certainly consists in the right of every individual to claim the protection of the laws, whenever he receives an injury. One of the first duties of government is to afford that protection."

Nor does he address the concerns of Archibald Cox in 1967, expressed in part earlier in this chapter:

> "When it comes to fundamental constitutional, human rights, judicial restraint is too frequently a 'no answer,'" for the restraint "closes the political process to particular ideas or particular groups, or otherwise distorts its operation. Then the correction must come from outside and no violence is done to the principle of representative government if the court supplies the remedy."

Nor does he address critical cases, addressed by Judge Josephine Staton in her dissent. She points out:

- In *Brown v. Plata*, the Supreme Court addressed cruel and unusual punishment in prisons, opining "Courts may not allow constitutional violations to continue simply because a remedy would involve intrusion into the realm of prison administration."

- In *Brown v. Board of Education*, the Supreme Court's "finest hour," the Court mandated racial integration, pointing out, "In the school desegregation cases, the Supreme Court was explicitly unconcerned with the fact that crafting relief would require individualized review of thousands of state and local policies that facilitated segregation. Rather, a unanimous Supreme Court held that the judiciary could work to dissemble segregation overtime while remaining cognizant of the many public interests at stake…. As we all know, it took decades to even partially realize *Brown's* dream."

In contrast, Judge Hurwitz concludes by relying in part on the 2019 *Rucho* case we discuss in the next chapter, "Not every problem posing a threat – even a clear and present danger threat – to the American Experiment can be solved by federal judges."

Judge Hurwitz punted. In my view, Judge Hurwitz is too timid, lacking the bravery and creativity John Marshall exhibited when he faced up to the challenge of Jefferson, and shaped the Court's responsibility for judicial oversight.

Yes, the government would have appealed to the Supreme Court had Hurwitz ruled in favor of the youths. The conservative justices, being the Supreme Court's majority, may have reversed. But Chief Justice Roberts has publicly said that the judges fill a role like that of an umpire. That means, he says, calling balls and strikes and seeing that everyone plays by the rules. Hurwitz called the balls and strikes in favor of the 21 gutsy kids. He admits the government was not playing by the rules. But, unlike an umpire, he gives the government a free pass. He tells the kids that if they want a solution, they must go to the bad guys who damaged them and plead with them to come up with a solution. That's the opposite of what umpires do. That's also the opposite of what fiduciaries do with the people they are charged with caring for.

In 1788, Federalist Papers #78, Alexander Hamilton wrote about the necessity for the judiciary branch to be separate from the two political branches, for "there is no liberty, if the power of judging be not separated from the legislative and the executive powers." He concludes, "liberty has nothing to fear from the judiciary alone but would have everything to fear from its union with either of the other two departments." Madison wrote in 1787, Federalist Papers #10, that "No man is allowed to be a judge of his own cause, because his interest would certainly bias his judgment, and, not improbably, corrupt his integrity."

Yes, there is a dangerous and unconstitutional effect in deference. When a political branch damages the fundamental rights of anyone, and the Court's deference gives that branch a pass, the political branch remains its own judge and jury without accountability. The constitutional protection the Court is mandated to provide us is totally lost.

In *Juliana,* the 21 gutsy kids brought to the Court their deep concerns that the Constitution does not condone willful destruction of our environment by the actions of the federal government. The Court's dismissal means that whatever chance the kids had to present their evidence and the science supporting their claims is gone forever, unless they can win on further appeal. The youths filed a motion for a rehearing before the 9th Circuit's full panel of judges. The motion was denied without opinion February 10, 2021. OCT announced that it plans an appeal to the Supreme Court, and with the change in administrations, is requesting a meeting with the Biden-Harris administration and the Department of Justice. In frustration, OCT's press release concludes that the court's decision "says that the courts are powerless to set constitutional parameters on what the political branches must and must not do to remedy the climate crisis. In the words of dissenting Judge Staton, it 'throws up (the court's) hands' in the face of humanity's greatest existential crisis ever and places the crisis solely in the hands of our ever-changing political branches. Until the courts mandate the government stop perpetuating the crisis, youth and humanity will face ever more threatening climate chaos. This is an enormous legal error not corrected today by the Ninth Circuit."

Is *Juliana* the kind of case that should linger without a judicial remedy?

Clearly not. These youth plaintiffs are not requesting that the Court direct the political branches of government to do their bidding. Such a request would be beyond the reach of the Court. They are asking the Court to direct the political branches of government to stop damaging their rights, which are constitutionally protected.

In Chapter 8, we discuss the Court's balancing rules, under which the Court considers the rights at issue and the needs of our government or communities. For example, during a pandemic, an individual's right to liberty may be restricted by the government to protect the community. Individuals may be required to wear masks to thwart the spread of disease like COVID-19. By denying judicial review, the Court has even failed to consider whether balancing of rights is appropriate.

The role of the Court in *Brown v. Board of Education* should be the Court's guide. After all, did not Chief Justice Roberts tell the Senate in his 2005 nomination interview, "The role of an umpire and judge is critical. They make sure everybody plays by the rules…"? The kids are simply asking the political branches to play by the rules.

As I reflect, I wonder how, as people, we would have fared over the past two centuries under our Constitution, which Justice Oliver Wendell Holmes called "an experiment, as all life is an experiment." What kind of country would we have if in 1803 Marshall had been as timid as Hurwitz is in 2020?

Do we want the Supreme Court to return to the nondescript role the Court had before Marshall breathed life into it and defined its important role? John Marshall confirmed the Court's role was not merely calling balls and strikes but calling balls and strikes in ways that provide necessary checks and balances envisioned by the Framers. In Federalist Papers #51, titled *"The Structure of Government Must Furnish the Proper Checks and Balances Between the Different Departments,"* Madison famously wrote in 1788:

> "Ambition must be made to counteract

ambition…. If men were angels, no government would be necessary…. In framing a government, which is to be administered men over men, the great difficulty lies in this: you must first enable the government to control the governed; and in the next place oblige it to control itself. *A dependence on the people is, no doubt, the primary control on the government; but experience has taught mankind the necessity of auxiliary precautions.*" [emphasis added]

The Court's use of deferential rules allowing it to avoid a threat to our fundamental rights by a political branch's unconstitutional behavior is like a World Series umpire letting a pitcher call his own balls and strikes. When that happens, the Court fails its fundamental obligation to assure us that the political branches are playing by the rules. That is a role only the Court can effectively provide.

The Court's deference to the political branches when rights are involved is potentially more damaging than its deference to Congress's over-delegation to the executive branch. We expressed Justice Gorsuch's concerns of congressional over-delegation in Chapter 4. Justice Thomas has expressed similar concerns, as has Chief Justice Roberts and Justice Alito. What is missing is the Court's failure to understand that its deference regarding rights has more dire consequences. When the Court won't right a constitutional wrong it clearly recognizes, while the executive branch abuses that wrong and Congress won't act, the affected American people are left without a remedy.

For our democracy to work, the Court must not fail us in providing what Madison calls our necessary "auxiliary precautions." The Court's failure to provide judicial review in cases like *Juliana* is the failure of the Court to provide those necessary precautions. The political branch favored by deference has no incentive to provide a solution, particularly one adverse to the special interests it favors.

The Court's use of the Political Question Doctrine and

Standing Doctrine (with its redressability) effectively license the executive branch to operate in near dictatorial form with special interests its paramount concern. Furthermore, Congress lacks motivation to provide legislative solutions. Or if it is motivated to rein in the executive branch, it faces a presidential veto.

Judge Staton points out in her *Juliana* dissent that the majority reaches its conclusion "not by marching purposefully through the [Political Question Doctrine's] *Baker* factors, which carve out a narrow set of nonjusticiable *political* cases, but instead by broadly invoking *Rucho* in a manner that would cull from our docket any case that presents administrative issues 'too difficult for the judiciary to manage.'... That simply is not the test." We examine *Rucho v. Common Cause* in the next chapter.

Deference Should Not Mean Denial

The time has come when a well-thought-out change is needed in the Court's reliance on its judge-made rules denying judicial review. Deference rules are championed because they create the illusion of smoothing out court processes with the added benefit of reducing judiciary branch conflict not only with the constitutional political branches of government, but also the fourth branch of government — the administrative agencies. The unfortunate consequence of reducing conflict is that the constitutional role of the Court being our umpire disappears.

The conservative Cato Institute had a challenging discussion about deference in a 1991 blog, "Restricting Judicial Restraint." The blog's point: "[C]onservatives and liberals alike – indeed, anyone who favors limited government and a wide range of personal and economic liberties – should be concerned when the third branch of government effectively withdraws from the scene." Cato then asked, how can a judiciary that is dedicated to restraint be "the bulwark of our liberties," our protector against the overreach of the political branches of government? "[I]t is no answer to the perennial problem of securing ordered liberty to ask the judiciary to serve as handmaiden to the other branches." Yet, that is the result of judicial deference.

Think again about the *Juliana* case. After the Court of Appeals' deference, were the gutsy kids left better off? Did the Court of Appeals provide them with a remedy? Did the Court of Appeals leave them in a position to obtain a meaningful remedy from a political branch of government?

No.

In *Juliana*, even though the Court admitted the kids had stated their case about environmental damage and destruction, which is exacerbated by government action, the damage to the youth plaintiffs – and to each of us – continues. The political branches have done, and will do, nothing to change their conduct. Nor are the branches motivated to do so. A change in conduct would lessen the political support of special interests, primarily the fossil fuel industry. In fact, as we point out in Chapter 7, during the Coronavirus pandemic, the government worsened the kids' plight.

Deference to the political branches who are the wrong-doers creates within the political branches a systemic cancer – an arrogance toward the will of the people with an accompanying political corruption funded by special interests. This incestuous cancer not only metastasizes throughout our government, but it causes people to lose faith and trust in the value of our Constitution and the fair workings of government, as polls constantly tell us.

When Judicial Concerns Rise From "Theoretical" to "Experiential"

On September 17, 2020, Our Children's Trust Senior Litigation Attorney, Andrea Rodgers, wore a COVID-19 face mask while appearing before the Washington State Court of Appeals. She was arguing against the trial court's dismissal of thirteen youth plaintiffs' climate change litigation. The court hearing was before a panel of three masked judges. Outside their courtroom the air was thick with the smoke that emanated from historic wildfires devastating Washington and neighboring states, Oregon and California. During arguments from the state's attorney who claimed the kids' case had no merit, Judge Mann asked:

> "For the past seven days, I can't go outside. If I go outside, I'm threatening my life. I have asthma so I have to stay inside with the windows shut. I don't have an air conditioner. *Why isn't that affecting my life and liberty?"*

We argue in this book that the judiciary's application of its judge-made deference rules involving rights is too often too theoretical, too impractical – too removed from the context of our 21st Century reality. Must judges personally experience deadly airborne viruses and pollution so they understand why youth plaintiffs concerns about climate change and health deserve a judicial review? Maybe such painful touches of reality are needed to move judges from their ivory towers onto the streets where people live. Maybe addressing context has a role in the arguments before the Court.

And, just maybe, we are near a congressional awakening. On September 23, 2020, a concurrent congressional resolution was introduced by members of Congress to support the principles underpinning *Juliana*. Our Children's Trust's release about the historic resolution is included as Appendix F.

Scarcely any political question arises in the United States that is not resolved, sooner or later, into a judicial question.

Alexis De Tocqueville
Democracy in America, 1835

If a litigant claims an individual right has been invaded, the lawsuit by definition does not involve a political question.

Howard Fink and Mark Tushnet
Federal Jurisdiction: Policy and
Practice, 1987

Chapter 6 – Judicial Deference: The Political Question Doctrine

Definitions:

Baker Factors: Court-designed tests to determine if an issue before the court is a political question: [1] a textually demonstrable constitutional commitment of the issue to a coordinate political department; or [2] a lack of judicially discoverable and manageable standards for resolving it; or [3] the impossibility of deciding without an initial policy determination of a kind clearly for nonjudicial discretion; or [4] the impossibility of a court's undertaking independent resolution without expressing lack of the respect due coordinate branches of government; or [5] an unusual need for unquestioning adherence to a political decision already made; or [6] the potentiality of embarrassment from multifarious pronouncements by various departments on one question.

Political question: A question that a court will not consider because it involves the exercise of discretionary power by the executive or legislative branch of government.

A Political Question: Rucho v. Common Cause

In 2019, the Roberts-led Supreme Court was presented with two gerrymandering cases, consolidated as *Rucho v. Common Cause*. One case involved a case that favored the Democrats, the other the Republicans. The Court held in a 5-4 decision that "partisan gerrymandering" was a political question, a question that lacked Baker Factor #2: "judicially discoverable and manageable standards, for resolving it." Thus, the case presented a controversy to be resolved by Congress or by state governments, not by the Court.

Chief Justice Roberts wrote the opinion, distinguishing partisan gerrymandering from racial gerrymandering and "one man, one vote" questions. The latter two issues — racial gerrymandering and one man, one vote — are addressable by the Court. Partisan gerrymandering, Roberts wrote, was well known in our Constitution's Framers' time, yet there is no mention of it in the Constitution; and our Constitution provides that voting is a matter for the states. However, Congress has the authority to alter state voting regulations applicable to congressional elections when it chooses to do so, which it has from time-to-time. But Congress has never addressed gerrymandering. In contrast, Roberts writes, the Constitution provides "no basis whatsoever to guide judicial discretion," concluding, "partisanship in districting leads to results that reasonably seem unjust. But the fact gerrymandering is incompatible with democratic principles does not mean the solution lies with the federal judiciary…. Federal judges have no license to reallocate political power between the two major political parties, with no plausible grant of authority in the Constitution, and no legal standards to limit and direct their decisions.... [W]e have no commission to allocate political power and influence in the absence of a constitutional directive or legal standards to guide us in the exercise of such authority." He closed with, "We conclude that partisan gerrymandering claims present political questions beyond the reach of the federal courts." Although the conservative majority could have established "legal standards" – since that is what courts do — they declined to do so. Thus, partisan gerrymandering must be resolved by the states or by Congress.

The four liberal judges dissented, Justice Elena Kagan writing for the dissent: "For the first time ever, this Court refuses to remedy a constitutional violation because it thinks the task beyond judicial capabilities.... The partisan gerrymanders in these cases deprived citizens of the most fundamental of their constitutional rights: the rights to participate equally in the political process, to join with others to advance political beliefs, and to choose their political representatives. In so doing, the partisan gerrymanders here debased and dishonored our democracy, turning upside-down the core American idea that all governmental power derives from the people. These gerrymanders enabled politicians to entrench themselves in office as against voters' preferences."

Justice Kagan continued, "Using sophisticated technological tools and precinct level election results selected to predict voting behavior, Hofeller [the map specialist, drawing the maps for the Republicans in the Republican-favored state], drew district lines to minimize Democrats' voting strength and ensure the election of 10 Republican Congressmen." She quoted Republican state representative Lewis, "I think electing Republicans is better than electing Democrats. So, I drew this map to help foster what I think is better for the country." She then provided a similar example from the state gerrymandering that favored the Democrats, followed by her frustration:

> "Is that how American democracy is supposed to work? I have yet to meet the person who thinks so."

Kagan continued, "Indeed, the majority concedes (really, how could it not?) that gerrymandering is 'incompatible with democratic principles.' ... And therefore what? That recognition would seem to demand a response.... (as the majority rightly notes), racial and residential gerrymanders were also once with us, but the Court has done something about that fact. The majority's idea instead seems to be that if we have lived with partisan gerrymanders so long, we will survive. That complacency has no cause. Yes, partisan gerrymandering goes back to the Republic's earliest days. (As does vociferous opposition to it.) *But big data and modern technology—of just the kind that the mapmakers in North Carolina and Maryland used—make today's gerrymandering altogether different from the crude line drawing of the past.* [emphasis added] ... And gerrymanders will only get worse (or depending on your perspective, better) as time goes on—as data becomes ever more fine-grained and data analysis techniques continue to improve. What was possible with paper and pen—or even with Windows 95—doesn't hold a candle (or a LED bulb?) to what will become possible with developments like machine learning. And someplace along this road, 'we the people' become sovereign no longer.... In short, the mapmaker has made some votes count for less, because they are likely to go for the other party."

After the *Rucho* opinion became final, other pending gerrymander cases, including a challenge to Wisconsin gerrymandering discussed in Chapter 1, were dismissed by lower courts. However, the Brennan Center for Justice's September 2020 article, "Gerrymandering and Racial Justice in Wisconsin," has a subtitle "Partisan maps have yielded a legislature that fails to respond to Black Voters." The report's author, Julia Kirschenbaum reported:

> "Indeed, the wave election of 2018 is a powerful lesson in just how rigged Wisconsin's

maps are in favor of the Republicans who drew them. Despite winning every statewide office and a majority of the statewide vote that year, Democrats managed to win only 36 of the 99 seats in the Assembly. Republicans won the remaining 63 seats with a minority of the statewide vote, losing only a single seat that they had previously held."

Kirschenbaum found that the maps were drawn with a total disregard of Wisconsin's constitutional requirements that voting districts respect county lines when possible. Despite 70% of Wisconsin's Black population living in the Milwaukee County area, the lines were meandered between the County and surrounding areas, which were predominantly white, in ways that allowed Republicans to carry "seven of these eight districts in 2018."

Despite the Supreme Court's refusal to deal with partisan gerrymandering, the Court has ruled on racial gerrymandering, which with Wisconsin's reality – and the reality of most states – is the same thing. Thus, Wisconsin will soon be back in the courts.

Noted in the preceding chapter, Judge Hurwitz relied on *Rucho* in deciding the *Juliana* plaintiffs did not have standing because of redressability (a political question without Baker Factors), opining, "*Rucho* found partisan gerrymandering claims presented political questions beyond the reach of Article III courts…. The [Rucho] Court did not deny extreme partisan gerrymandering can violate the Constitution."

In Chapter 4, in our discussions about the over-delegation of legislative power from Congress to the executive branch, I agreed with Justice Gorsuch, a conservative judge, that legislative delegation to the executive branch can be harmful to the people, and its constitutionality should be reconsidered by the Court during this period of our Democracy of Dollars. In this chapter, I agree with Justice Kagan, a liberal judge, that partisan gerrymandering can be harmful to the people and should be reconsidered by the Court.

In the *Prologue*, we observe that our Constitution did not contemplate political parties — political parties grew out of the contrasting views of the role of government that sprouted over the eight years of Washington's presidency, coming to fruition as separate parties when our second President, John Adams, was seeking reelection. In that election, Adams and his adversary Jefferson had differing views. It is not surprising that political parties and partisan gerrymandering may not have crossed the minds of our nation's Framers. But does that justify allowing the harm of partisan gerrymandering, particularly in these contentious times?

Beyond Kagan's comments above, I cannot forget the comments of Archibald Cox in *The Warren Court*, "Lobbyists for special interests prefer the status quo because they find it easier to influence the votes necessary to defeat regulatory measures in legislatures where rural counties are heavily overrepresented." Lobbyists, architects in today's Democracy of Dollars, and their special interest clients benefit from a system where dollars, not voters, are the ultimate ballots cast for the direction America takes.

As Paul Weyrich, co-founder of the conservative Heritage Foundation and the Moral Majority, put it in his 2007 speech, "Now many of our Christians have what I call the 'goo-goo syndrome' – good government. They want everybody to vote. I don't want everybody to vote. Elections are not won by a majority of people. They never have been from the beginning of our country and they are not now. As a matter of fact, our leverage in the elections quite candidly goes up when the voting populace goes down."

I live in Florida, which includes a state constitutional provision that provides no districting plan "shall be drawn with the intent to favor or disfavor a political party." Justice Roberts saw the Wisconsin requirement as a standard that other states could consider. Why didn't the Court adopt Florida's approach as a constitutional standard? Yes, the standard would be a judge-made rule, but so is the Baker Factor used by the Court in its determination that partisan gerrymandering is a political question. Let us look briefly at some history.

No Political Question: Baker v. Carr

The 1963 Supreme Court case, *Baker v. Carr*, is famous for more than one reason. First, the Supreme Court, under Chief Justice Earl Warren, developed its now famous Political Question Doctrine "Baker Factors," which the Court uses when determining whether a question before it is a political question that the Court will not decide under our Constitution's Separation of Powers Doctrine.

Second, the *Baker* case was also a case, overruling the lower court, deciding that apportionment of state-legislator districts was a justiciable question. Thus, the Court developed the six Baker Factors introducing this chapter to determine if voter-district reapportionment was justiciable. Since the case before the Court had been dismissed by the lower court, the Supreme Court sent the case back to the lower court for resolution. As to the Baker Factors, the Court held, "The question here is the consistency of state action with the Federal Constitution. We have no question decided, or to be decided, by a political branch of government coequal with this Court."

The Court's opinion, written by Justice William Brennan, was in part based on Marshall's *Marbury* opinion: "The very essence of civil liberty certainly consists in the right of every individual to claim the protection of the laws, whenever he receives an injury."

Judge Brennan wrote: "Of course the mere fact that the suit seeks protection of a political right does not mean it presents a political question. Such an objection 'is little more than a play upon words.'"

The *Baker* case arose in Tennessee, where state legislature districts had not been redistricted since 1901, rather than every 10 years as constitutionally required. With the concentration of population growth in cities, some rural districts had 20 times the representation of city districts. The result? Thirty-seven percent of the voters elected about 2/3 of the state senators. A similar disparity occurred in state house representation.

The Warren Court determined the district size inequity was a Constitution question of voter "equal protection" the Court could resolve. Later cases defined the measure of voter district apportionment, in absence of unusual circumstances, as "one man, one vote."

Justice William Douglas, in his concurring opinion, noted, "So far as voting rights are concerned, there are large gaps in the Constitution." Douglas also wrote that the equal protection clause prohibited "invidious discrimination," and with the fact voters in some counties had 20 times the voting power of those in other counties, invidious discrimination existed.

However, the Court's decision attracted a strong dissent from Justice Frankfurter, who felt the Court was deciding a political question meant for the legislative branch or the states. Frankfurter had written a decision for the Court in 1946, concluding that questions about congressional district apportionment were political questions, not to be answered by the Court. In *Baker*, Frankfurter objected to the Court's use of a "destructively novel political power."

Perhaps Frankfurter's most important arguments: "This [decision] of course implies that geography, economics, urban-rural conflict, and all the other non-legal factors which have throughout our history entered into political districting are to some extent not to be ruled out in the undefined vista now opened up by review in the federal courts of state reapportionments. To some extent — aye, there's the rub. In effect, today's decision empowers the courts of the country to devise what should constitute the proper composition of the legislatures of the fifty States. ... 'Federal courts consistently refuse to exercise their equity powers in cases posing political issues arising from a state's geographical distribution of electoral strength among its political subdivisions.'"

Stare Decisis

Although the *Baker* decision held that an apportionment case was justiciable, and not hampered by the Political Question Doctrine, the Roberts Court distinguished *Rucho* as being the first case before the Court specifically dealing with "partisan gerrymandering," words not coined as a form of gerrymandering in *Baker* or other prior cases. Thus, for Roberts, the Court was not bound by the *Baker* decision as stare decisis. Stare decisis had no application.

Mirror of Representation

In his 1997 *Original Meanings,* Jack N. Rakove has a chapter titled "The Mirror of Representation." He begins the chapter quoting John Adams' *Thoughts on Government in 1776.* John Adams wrote that a representative assembly "should be in miniature an exact portrait of the people at large." Of course, that never occurred, in part by the Constitution's original design, limiting voting to white males, and in part because of the Framers' compromise with the states, which granted the states the right to set voting rules.

The Framers assigned the right to states to set their own voting rules for selecting House of Representative members to defuse state concerns that they were surrendering too much power to the new federal government. However, as Rakove points out, "[B]y allowing the state legislations so much discretion in setting election rules, they left the national government susceptible to both the aspirations and the abuses of democratic policies." To which, as a result of the Supreme Court's approval of partisan gerrymandering, we now can add, "including designing voting districts to perpetuate control of a particular political party, while diminishing the effective votes of other voters within the gerrymandered district."

With the Supreme Court bowing out on partisan gerrymandering, how will the states respond? Abusively, it turns out. In the *Epilogue* we discuss the rush of voter restraints and gerrymandering imposed by Republican-run states after the 2020 election.

What is the Role of Political Parties?

On May 19, 2015, Brigham Young University political

science professor Dr. David Magleby gave a talk entitled "The Necessity of Political Parties and the Importance of Compromise." His remarks included: "Think of the Constitution as an engineering blueprint for the design of a functioning and enduring government." Magleby then discussed two contradictory elements of our democracy, the "necessity of political parties and the importance of compromise." Political parties are democracy's organizers, simplifying candidate selection and the process of voting. Parties "also in a broad sense stand for a particular view of government," and provide voters with insights into those seeking election. Strong party partisans, Magleby says, are the most knowledgeable and active citizens. In reality, most of us vote for a party and not a person. He also points out that our Constitution's Framers were mistaken in "assuming their system would work well without parties."

In Chapter 2, we referenced Madison's newspaper article about the important checks and balances role political parties play, written during Washington's presidency as differing views on the role of our federal government were developing. We could add Jefferson's comments written a few years later in a letter to John Taylor, "In every free and deliberating society, there must, from the nature of man, be opposite parties, and violent dissensions and discords; and one of these, for the most part, must prevail over the other for a longer or shorter time." Parties are necessary, Magleby concludes, because parties organize us into groups to pursue our common objectives.

Magleby also points out that "since the 1980s members of Congress have become more and more polarized in comparison to those serving in Congress from the 1930s through the 1970s." What is the result? Fewer Congressmen are willing to work with members of the other political party. He then addresses our need for political compromise, saying, "Government is necessary because people need it to resolve their conflicts," referring to James Madison's, "If men were angels, no government would be necessary."

Magleby confirms what I have learned over my more than 50 years of law practice: The best settlement of an honest dispute is when both sides are a little unhappy:

> "Compromise has been and will remain vital to sustaining our two-hundred-year-long experiment with self-government. Compromise is a process of give and take, of blending and adjusting, of accommodating competing interests and views in order to find a position most acceptable to the largest number or, at a minimum, the majority. It is not consensus, for rarely is consensus possible, and to make it the standard makes self-government possible.... Compromise is not wrong in public life, it is the way we reconcile our differences."

Magleby's advice, however, does not address the fact that opportunity for political compromise on the most troubling issues in today's Democracy of Dollars is rare. The contentions that trouble us most are not simply between political parties. The contentions that trouble us most are those of lobbyists who cast their votes of dollars among elected politicians of both parties who bow to their wishes. Will fossil fuel continue to suppress clean energy, despite its damaging effect on our earth, the only home we will ever have? Will gun lobbies continue to block regulation of gun sales desired by 64% of Americans? Will pharmaceutical companies continue to raise prices to irrational multiples of cost?

In 2009, in *The Will of the People*, Barry Friedman points out a flaw emanating from our reliance on political parties. Too few American people vote in the primaries. Thus, the primaries are dominated by extremes who select candidates representing political positions outside of the political mainstream. The result? Voters are left to choose between two candidates closer to party extremes. Furthermore, because of the low turnout for primary elections, parties can play to their extremist base without appealing to the moderates in the middle. Friedman concludes that while the people generally want their politics to be near the center, because of low-turnout primaries, today's political parties offer candidates from the extreme – not only in beliefs but in their unwillingness to listen to conflicting views and compromise. Taking into consideration varying views coupled with a willingness to compromise is at the heart of a successful democratic government of a diverse people.

The Bipartisan Policy Center's "2018 Primary Election Turnout and Reports," found: "[I]n 2018, 9.9 percent of eligible voters cast a vote for a Democratic candidate, 8.8 percent for a Republican candidate and 80 percent cast no vote at all." Five states had a total primary turnout of 12 percent or less. The five highest turnout states averaged about 33 percent. The Policy Center's recommendation: States should open primaries to independents partly to "increase primary turnout and partly because their presence can help moderate candidates and lead to nominees whose views are more closely aligned with the general public."

The 2020 primaries appear to be a repeat of 2018. The Hill reports in "Five things we learned from this year's primaries": "It is very hard to be a sitting incumbent in a party primary." Several Democrat Congressmen lost their seats to far-left activists. As to Republicans: "This year, a host of Republicans poised to win office in November will make the Tea Party look like genteel moderates." In August 2020, Statista published, "Voter turnout rate in presidential primary elections in the United States in 2020, by state," reporting Montana had the highest turnout with 45.6% and North Dakota had the lowest with 2.6%. My state, Florida, had a 19.4% turnout. Twenty-six states had less than a 25% turnout. Eight states had 12% or less turnout. The five highest states averaged 42.9%.

The difficulties in solving problems and in resolving conflicts presented in today's Democracy of Dollars are not easily resolved by traditional methods. Furthermore, the control our Democracy of Dollars has over our government has led to a great distrust among voters, too many of whom – particularly the young – have given up, as reflected by low voter turnout in the primaries. However, there may be hope. Setting aside the poor turnout in the primaries, the youth turnout (ages 18-29) in the 2018 mid-term election reached a

100-year high, jumping to 36% from 16% in 2014. For young adults, age 30-44, the jump was from 36% to 49%. On November 4, 2020, Rani Molla reported "Voter turnout is estimated to be the highest in 120 years," that the 2020 presidential election turnout is the highest percentage voter turnout since 1900. Whether the presidential election turnout was an aberration or lasting change is too early to tell.

What is the Gerrymandering Role for the Supreme Court?

Baker and *Rucho* cases raise the fundamental question we posed in Chapter 5, quoting from Archibald Cox's *The Warren Court* (Cox, as solicitor general filed an amicus [friend of the court] brief in *Baker*): "What role should the judicial branch play in the government of American people?"

Cox pointed out three problems with reapportionment established by Court rule instead of legislative action:

- There is no standard as to how strict per capita equality is determined. Can there be variations between rural and city districts? Can districts encompass more or less population than a county? How does a formula allow for new conditions?

- Does the "one man, one vote" rule apply to, say, county commissions, school boards, city councils, and similar bodies? Will malapportionment give "political dominance" to a class of voters in these elections?

- The Baker case, and the thrust of the cases before *Rucho*, primarily dealt with apportioning representatives among geographical districts. They did not require the Court to redraw maps to control gerrymandering.

Essentially, those three unsolved problems underpin the *Rucho* decision. Voters each had a vote, so the "one man, one vote" criteria were recognized. But partisan skewing made too many of the votes less effective, and more unequal, than others. The skewing wasn't made to solve race problems, at least superficially, or any of the problems that concerned Justice Frankfurter: "geography, economics, urban-rural conflict, and all the other non-legal factors which have throughout our history entered into political districting."

In contrast, partisan gerrymandering tolerated in *Rucho* is nothing but the seizure of power by a political party from the other political party. Essentially, partisan gerrymandering is a legal way to rig elections and perpetuate the dominance of a political party, even when the party no longer represents the majority of the people.

This issue was raised by The Week Magazine staff in its 2016 article, "How to rig elections, the legal way": "The word gerrymander comes from a salamander-shaped district in Massachusetts, redrawn that way by then-Gov. Elbridge Gerry ... in the 1812 election." The article points out that over-all, partisan gerrymandering favors the Republicans, because Democrats concentrate in cities, with most suburbs and rural areas leaning Republican. The article concludes, "As Karl Rove put it, 'he who controls redistricting can control Congress'.... The data and technology make tilting a district map almost as easy as one-click ordering on Amazon."

That point — about technology and data manipulating partisan gerrymandering to a fine point inconceivable by our Constitution's Framers — is the point Justice Kagan made in her *Rucho* dissent. The context of everyday living has changed dramatically since the Constitution was written, and the Court must adapt, as is repeatedly emphasize in this book. The Court recognized the change in context when it decided AR-15 rifles were constitutional. Why does the same rationale not apply to voting rights?

That sort of problem raises another issue: How does the Court break "new ground" where there are no standards? The strength of the common law is that the standards used to decide cases are judge-made "on the go," decided and modified, not by statutes or constitutions, but by experience as cases arise, and circumstances change. Relying on "original meaning" or "textualism" fixed in time in a written document, whether the Constitution or statutes or regulations, with circumstances far different today than when adopted, is the source of a problem for the Court.

The Constitution is not simply a collection of a list of "dos and don'ts." It is a statement of fundamental principles, intended by our Founders to have application in changing future circumstances. As pointed out in Chapter 2, quoting George Will's 2019 *The Conservative Sensibility*, "[T]he fixed meaning of the Constitution is to be found in its mission to protect natural rights and liberty in changing – unfixed – circumstances." In Chapter 9, we add Edmund Randolph's instructions to his committee at the Constitutional Convention: "In the draught of a fundamental constitution … insert essential principles only, lest the operations of government should be clogged by rendering those provisions permanent and unalterable."

The Court is constantly required to face monumental challenges — such as the challenges exhibited by both *Juliana* (destructive effect of climate change exacerbated by industrial growth) and *Rucho* (partisan redistricting honed with 21st Century tools of technology). However, "solving" the problem in each case by refusing to provide judicial review, based on judge-made rules, which have the force of law, is not a solution. Nor is it, in my view, constitutional.

Are we, as a society, better served by a Court that side-steps the challenge with such tools as the Baker Factors, or are we better served by a Court that is an intermediary between governmental action and the American people as Hamilton wrote in 1788 in Federalist Papers #78?

Our system of candidate election in voting districts is essentially a winner-take-all system. But is representing voters in each district— whether winners or losers in the candidate selected — a winner-take-all proposition? We've pointed out that nationwide about 30% of us are Republicans, 31% are

Democrats, and the rest of us are independents. For our democracy to work, winners must end up with not too unhappy losers. And the representatives selected, by oath of office, as fiduciaries, must represent everyone, both winners and losers.

Democracy doesn't win when winners suppress losers. Is not the "Great Compromise" of our Constitution's Framers, which resulted in each state having two senators, a decision that was unrelated to population, a worthy model? The interchange of contrarian thoughts, beliefs, and ideals, coupled with discussion, understanding, and compromise is what makes democracy better.

Without it, democracy is severely handicapped. Whether we have politically conservative or liberal leanings, our beliefs depend on how we value each of what psychologist Jonathan Haidt identified in 2013 as our six "moral foundations" in *The Righteous Mind.* The six foundations are care/harm, fairness/cheating, liberty/oppression, loyalty/betrayal, authority/subversion and sanctity/degradation. Democrats are more concerned about the moral foundation of care than are Republicans. Republicans prioritize the foundations of loyalty and authority more than Democrats. Conservatives and liberals are each partially right in what they emphasize. Being right comes from listening to and learning from the other.

A related issue is that each of us tend to believe first and then approve and accept facts that support our established beliefs. No better examples of this can be found than in majority and dissenting court opinions. Our Supreme Court justices went to the same two law schools. Most likely, they had many of the same professors and read the same casebooks. When cases are presented to them in court, they each are exposed to the same set of facts. They each have heard the same arguments from opposing counsel. They each have read the same cases used as precedent in shaping their legal opinions. And there has been a discussion and exchange of ideas among the justices before they vote.

Yet, on cases that deal with human rights or the meaning of our Constitution, they come to contrasting opinions representing either a conservative or a liberal interpretation of the law and facts. Their beliefs trump the facts, and they arrange the facts in different syllogisms to confirm their beliefs. The judges are not alone. We have the tendency to do the same thing. As imperfect as it may be, as a society we achieve our best decisions from the Court's judges when the Court is balanced with conservatives and liberals who listen to each other and influence each other's final decisions; and when there are dissents. Well-written dissents, along with the decisions, speak clearly to guide future generations.

Since federal judges are lifetime appointments, as we change over time from Democratic administrations to Republican administrations, and then back again, balance is achieved in judicial appointments among liberals and conservatives as long as each political party respects the process. Court-stuffing – or the refusal of, say, a Republican Senate, to consider the judicial appointments of a Democrat President – do not benefit the process. Court stuffing is contrary to democratic principles, which require an independent Court that is balanced, not a Court that is an unelected branch speaking only for the political party that happens to be in power when the justice was confirmed by the Senate. A single-minded, unbalanced Court is also subject to groupthink. Groupthink decisions may be harmonious, but they risk confirmation bias and lack of critical evaluation. Executive branch examples include John Kennedy's Bay of Pigs fiasco and George Bush's Middle East wars, discussed in Chapter 9.

In a complex, diverse society, we don't benefit from a group of judges representing a singular, unchallenged point of view, whether conservative or liberal. Our creator didn't make some of us liberals because being liberal is always right. Nor did our creator make some of us conservatives because conservatives are always right. Our creator relied on diversity, not only among all species, but of thought and human interaction, since diversity produces the best long-term results. With diversity of thought and interaction, listening and compromise are key ingredients.

The Voice of the People

The *Baker* decision was criticized by politicians, to the point a constitutional amendment was proposed to offset its effect. The House of Representatives, where redistricting was perceived as a threat to congressional jobs, adopted a jurisdiction-stripping bill, which failed to pass the Senate. However, the Senate expressed its displeasure by passing a bill limiting pay increases for Supreme Court justices.

But what about the people? In 2009 in *The Will of the People,* Barry Friedman wrote that the *Baker ruling* was extremely popular with the people. Adaptation of reapportionment statutes occurred at a rapid rate in several states, much faster than school integration. *Baker* may have shattered the Court's reputation with politicians, but it enhanced the reputation of the Court with the people.

What about *Rucho?* As one might suspect, *Rucho* has been popular with politicians whose political future is enhanced by gerrymandering. Thus, the howl that arose in Congress from *Baker* has produced not even a whimper about *Rucho*. However, the New York Times saw the decision as dragging the Supreme Court into the mud. While approving partisan gerrymandering, the Court confirmed that racial gerrymandering was still prohibited. Richard Hasen of the New York Times reported in a July 2019 article, "The Gerrymandering Decision Drags the Supreme Court Further into the Mud," that the decision "force courts to make logically impossible determinations about whether racial reasons or partisan motives predominate when a party gerrymanders for political advantage," a prime difficulty in states with large minority voting populations. In most situations it is impossible to separate racial from partisan gerrymandering. In North Carolina, one of the two states before the Court in *Rucho,* 90% of the black community voted Democrat. Republican "partisan" gerrymandering limited the effectiveness of minority votes.

In a 2019 article for the American Constitution Society titled "Dirty Thinking About Law and Democracy in Rucho v. Common Cause," Professors Charles and Fuentes-Rohwer wrote, "Rucho is not an easy case to take seriously as doctrine.

… Critically, the opinion is an amalgam of misdirections, distortions, and less-than-pellucid thinking about the constitutionalization of political-gerrymandering claims." The authors raise a question as to why the Court's conservative and liberal justices are so divided regarding its responsibility to "safeguard the fundamental rights of democracy?" They see the Court's primary responsibility as "defending the foundations of representative democracy." The authors list four standard objections the Court uses when it decides judicial supervision is inappropriate:

- The Court should not involve itself in what are "essentially political disputes."

- The Court should not decide cases about group rights, only individual rights.

- The Court's intervention to protect racial groups does not apply to other groups, such as political parties.

- The Court cannot manage without a justiciable manageable standard.

The authors describe Roberts' arguments in his majority opinion as "fairytales" that illustrate a deeper truth: despite the Constitution's objectives of protecting the rights of the people, the Court has decided that there is no objection to political parties seeking to advantage their voters at the expense of opposing voters. Quoting from Justice Kagan's dissent, they close with: "Is this how American democracy is supposed to work? I have yet met the person who thinks so."

The underlying idea, it seems to me, in partisan gerrymandering, is that it is another form of winner-take-all voting, with a similar result of losers not being represented after the election. It's winning party versus the rest of the people. Professors Charles and Fuentes-Rohwer conclude that *Rucho* is a defense for—not from—today's "dirty politics." It reflects the political polarization that has dominated our Democracy of Dollars, where racial and partisan polarization go hand in hand.

But do the American People want dirty politics? In "Americans Are United Against Partisan Gerrymandering," the Brennan Center for Justice reported in 2019, "opposition to gerrymandering spans the country and party lines." In its 2019 article, "Gerrymandering: Why only 2 percent of Americans feel elections work properly," The Hill's Lon Johnson reports, "fighting gerrymandering and corruption has bipartisan support, with 82 percent of Americans saying they are concerned about corruption of the system, and believe gerrymandering is undemocratic and should be illegal." Polls indicating the public's great dislike of gerrymandering predate the Court's *Rucho* decision, but apparently to no effect.

Why hasn't there been more of an outcry? Probably because it is the minorities whose rights have been most damaged. Instead of becoming a political force for change, minorities have avoided the voting booths in disgust, only minimally exercising their voting rights. There hasn't been a political outcry, because gerrymandering perpetuates political power for those who possess it. As The Hill report put it, gerrymandering allows parties to "pick their voters, instead of the other way around."

The Unsolved Problem

We leave the subject of the gerrymandered voter with an unsolved problem for voters whose voice is stifled by partisan gerrymandering. These voters are left with a denial of a legal remedy by the Supreme Court, and no political remedy from the legislative branch, or the states, in sight. Today's congressional members and their political parties see themselves prospering from the status quo of skewed partisan representation, serving only the party in power and not all the people. Over time, as population demographics continue to change, and white Americans are no longer politically the largest voting group, this decision may end up producing a power-change effect contrary to what today's political supporters see it as preserving.

A personal observation: Similar to my conclusions regarding the Standing Doctrine and its redressability, expressed in the preceding chapter, I think the Court too theoretical, too impractical, in its denial of voting rights by its unwillingness to decide partisan gerrymandering as it has in the past decided racial gerrymandering. Gerrymandering, whether racial or partisan, has but one objective: the perpetuation of political power. *Rucho* is based on the subordination of factual reality of no solutions for disenfranchised voters to the theoretical belief that voters, who no longer can cast a majority vote because of disenfranchisement, can somehow cast a majority vote to improve their plight. In the Democracy of Dollars world, a judicial "no" rendering from the Ivory Tower of the Supreme Court is a forever "no" for the disenfranchised people in the reality show of life in America. Why?

- Those in power are disinclined to relinquish power.

- Serious communication with politicians elected to represent the people too frequently requires a plush political contribution (beyond the capability of most of us) to gain a serious hearing — and even then —any contribution is too frequently overmatched by lobbyists and their special interest political contributors.

In a Democracy of People, dilution of the vote of the people – Democrat or Republican – resulting from partisan gerrymandering, not tied to a healthy reason resulting from a carefully negotiated political compromise, would be disconcerting; but in a Democracy of Dollars where special interests too frequently trump the vote of the people it is simply deplorable.

Marshall's 1803 conclusion in *Marbury,* that legal wrongs destroying legal rights have legal remedies, must control. This is the mission for the Court, the last bastion for the people. The votes of the people should not be diluted by gerrymandering.

Judge-Made Deference Rules: Unconstitutional?

Chapter 4 made note that the Roberts Court may be positioning itself for a retreat from the Court's long history of supporting Congress's legislative delegation to our fourth branch of government. The concerns have been expressed strongly by Justice Gorsuch in his writings and his dissents, most recently in the Court's 2019 *Gundy* decision. In contrast, liberal justices' views are more tolerant of the vast growth congressional delegation and the dependency of government on the executive branch's administrative agencies. Justice Kagan wrote the *Gundy* opinion that prompted Gorsuch's dissent. Kagan wrote that if the *Gundy* statute is unconstitutional, "then most of Government is unconstitutional — dependent as Congress is on the need to give discretion to executive officials to implement their programs."

In his 2019 New York Times article, "Most of Government is Unconstitutional," Nicholas Bagley writes, "To run a functional, modern government, Congress has no choice but to delegate authority and discretion to federal agencies. Doing so allows Congress to make use of agencies' resources and scientific expertise, to enable a nimble response to emerging problems and to insulate technocratic decisions from raw politics." Bagley concludes, "Congress does not *surrender* its legislative power by delegating. It *exercises* that power."

Earlier in this book, I wrote that I agree with Gorsuch on congressional delegation, not Kagan. I also disagree with the New York Times. Too much power has been delegated by Congress to the executive branch and its agencies. The executive branch's unfettered right to change agency leadership with new political appointees and gut or change existing agency's rules with every change of administration is neither practical, cost effective, nor healthy for our democracy. These issues are the subject of Chapter 7.

Ironically, as noted earlier, the positions of conservative

and liberal judges are reversed when it comes to the Court's own delegation through its judge-made rules that deny judicial review, the Political Question and the Standing Doctrines. In this chapter, in response to the conservative justices deciding that gerrymandering was a political question, beyond the reach of the Court, Kagan wrote in dissent: "For the first time ever, this Court refuses to remedy a constitutional violation because it thinks the task beyond judicial capabilities." Although the *Juliana* case, the subject of Chapter 5, has not yet been before the Supreme Court for its decision, the 2 to 1 decision of the Court of Appeals that the Standing Doctrine's redressability requirement received a similar dissenting opinion.

As I agreed with Gorsuch, I also agreed with Kagan. Both forms of deference violate the Constitution's purpose, the protection of our rights, and the Constitution's separation of powers requirements.

Thus, a strong case can be made that deference by the Court to a political branch of government through its Political Question and Standing Doctrines is unconstitutional. After all, judges too are constrained by the Constitution and its Bill of Rights.

In *Federal Jurisdiction: Policy and Practice,* 1987, Fink and Tushnet argue, and we agree: "If a litigant claims an individual right has been invaded, the lawsuit by definition does not involve a political question."

Consider:

- When the Court defers through its Political Question or Standing Doctrines to the political branches, and the political branches are the culprits suppressing rights, the injured have no solution. The practical result is that the collusion between the political party controlling the political branch and special interests supporting the party in power blocks meaningful solutions. This point is illustrated by *Juliana*, Chapter 5, and *Rucho* in this chapter.

- The Court errs when advising injured parties that solutions must come through the ballot box when voting districts are skewed to solidify the political party in power. Furthermore, there is no accountability to the people by the political branch, no judicial requirements for it to change its ways. The political branch remains its own judge and jury. Deference Doctrines clearly put individual rights and liberties at risk.

- Much of the harm to individuals from our government originates from administrative agencies. These harms are traceable back to the influence of special interests and their lobbies. This point becomes clear in Chapter 7, particularly during our discussion of the actions of the EPA under the direction of the President.

- Judicial review is a prime constitutional tool for the protection of rights. Jefferson reminds us in the Declaration of Independence that rights-protection is why governments are formed. The Court's denial of judicial review in today's Democracy of Dollars is a denial of protection of our constitutional rights. The Court enables the loss of rights by deference to a congressional delegation of authority to an executive branch agency. Similarly, Court deference to a political branch enables the loss of rights by denial of individuals' access to their courts. They are both equally wrong. Gorsuch gave voice to this concern in *Gundy*. The reason for his concern is also evident in *Juliana* and *Rucho*.

- Failure to provide judicial review violates the Separation of Powers Doctrine, which was established in the Constitution to control the influence of factions, explained by Madison in 1787, Federalist Papers #10, and Hamilton in 1788, Federalist Papers #78. The entire idea is based on the assumptions that factions will always be with us, and our political branches will never be disinterested umpires of their own actions and inactions. If the separation of powers is to be maintained, the judicial branch cannot consign itself to a spectator role observing the political branches judge themselves.

- The federal courts cannot be throttled by the legislative or executive branches if the courts are to perform their duties. The Florida Supreme Court has expressed the essence in 1953, when it ruled in *Boynton v. State*, "It matters not that whether the usurpation of power and the violation of rights guaranteed to the people by the organic law results from the activities of the executive or legislative branches of the government or from the officers selected to enforce the law, the rights of the people guaranteed by the Constitution must not be violated."

A Democracy of Dollars is not governed by the rule of law. Rather, a Democracy of Dollars is governed by bought and paid for political influence. A Democracy of Dollars is governed by the *Rule of Lobbies*. The result of the Court's rule-made, often-mechanical deference to the political branches of government has provided tacit approval of a legislative branch that no longer sees itself as the prime lawmaker, and an executive branch that sees itself as being above the law, with a fiduciary responsibility to no one. In *Madison's Nightmare: How Executive Power Threatens American Democracy*, Peter M. Shane wrote in 2016, "[T]he growing concentration of executive power and the campaign for party predominance have produced an era of aggressive presidentialism, a theory of government and a pattern of government practice that treat our Constitution as vesting in the President a fixed and expansive authority largely immune to legislative control or judicial review."

The far-reaching effect of deference of the Court, not only denies individuals an opportunity to have judicial review of the merits of their claims, it places the individuals with grievances into the hands of the political branch harming them for fair treatment.

The accumulation of all powers, legislative, executive, and judiciary, in the same hands, whether of one, few, or many, and whether hereditary, self-appointed or elective, may justly be pronounced the very definition of tyranny.

James Madison
#47 Federalist Papers, 1788

A feeble executive implies feeble execution by the government. A feeble executive is but another phrase for bad execution; and a government ill executed, whatever it may be in theory, must be, in practice a bad government.

Alexander Hamilton
#70 Federalist Papers, 1788

Chapter 7 - The Era of Presidential Administration

Definitions:

Administrative Law: The law governing the organization and operation of administrative agencies (including executive and independent agencies) and the relations of administrative agencies with the legislature, the executive, the judiciary, and the public.

Cabinet: The advisory council to an executive officer, especially the President.

> ***Executive Order:*** An order issued by or on behalf of the President, usually intended to direct or instruct the actions of executive agencies or government officials or to set policies for the executive branch to follow.

Introduction

At the beginning of this book, we pointed out in our statement of *The Problem* that the executive branch has replaced the legislative branch as our prime law giver. It generates pages of administrative rules and regulations, having the force of law, which dwarf the production of Congress. Furthermore, it is the prime interpreter and enforcer of its own laws.

Add to Congress's abrogation of its legislative responsibilities and unrestrained delegation to the executive branch, the numbers of executive orders issued by Presidents. Many executive orders are not supported by congressional action nor constitutional authority assigned to the President. Thus, we have a concentration of power in the executive branch and our President — the concentration the Framers thought our Constitution would protect us against. Of course, the Framers' assumption is that each of our government's three branches would perform their constitutional duties and, thus, balance each other. Such is not the case.

As, perhaps unusual, background for the comments that follow, we refer to our *Prologue.* In the *Prologue* we discussed the Warren Court's willingness to evolve from the Founders' historic understanding of cruel and unusual punishment to a modern understanding.

In an unsigned opinion issued at 2 A.M. regarding a federal execution planned for July 14, 2020, the Supreme Court decided that the request of Daniel Lee to have an opioid dose to mitigate any pain he might have from his death row lethal injection should be denied. The decision was 5 to 4, with all five conservative judges in agreement on the decision and with the Department of Justice that the dose should be denied. Thus, on the scheduled day, the federal government executed Daniel Lee. It was the first federal execution since 2003. Several more executions took place in the following weeks. As he was being executed, Lee professed, "I didn't do it. I've made a lot of mistakes in my life, but I am not a murderer." The trial evidence indicated that the actual killing was by Chevie Kehoe. Lee accompanied him and went along with the idea. Kehoe was sentenced to life in prison in a separate trial.

In her July 2020 article, "The Return of Federal Executions," Mary Harris interviewed Slate's Mark Stern, who said: "It is relatively rare, but it is increasingly common for these late-night [unsigned] decisions that the court hands down that could cause public backlash."

I personally oppose the death penalty. Many people do. However, it remains the law of thirty states, although 11 states have placed the death penalty on moratorium for more than a decade. The military has the right to enforce a military execution but hasn't done so since 1961.

Among the reasons I oppose the death penalty is that, beyond it being Old Testament "eye for an eye" and inhuman, there have been many on death row that DNA and other evidence later proved their innocence. The problem with the death sentence is that it is irreversible even when it's wrong.

But it remains the law of the land. However, beliefs against the death penalty are slowly building. The death penalty is on its way to being considered a cruel and unusual punishment, as the ACLU advocates it is. However, as a society we have not yet reached that conclusion. The Supreme Court has not yet been presented with idea that the death penalty as cruel and unusual punishment. However, as a nation, until Lee's execution, we had put off death row executions, as if moratoriums make the problem go away.

In 2009, the Death Penalty Information Center released a report, "Smart on Crime," stating, "The death penalty in the U.S. is an enormously expensive and wasteful program with no clear results." The Center's surveys with police chiefs conclude that police chiefs think politicians support the death penalty to show they are tough on crime, but the focus on the death penalty detracts from focusing on real solutions. The police chiefs see the death penalty as one of the most inefficient uses of tax dollars, and they do not believe it deters crime.

From time to time the death penalty claims the lives of innocent men and women. National Geographic reported in its March 2021 issue that "During the past five decades 182 former death-row prisoners, an average of four people a year, have been exonerated of all charges related to their death sentences."

In Justice Breyer's dissent to the unsigned Lee opinion, he wrote that he was deeply troubled that Lee had been on death row since 1999, "Such lengthy delays inflict severe psychological suffering on inmates and undermine the penological rationale for the death penalty." In her dissent, Justice Ginsburg wrote that the difficulties in administering death penalties have reached the point where "The solution may be for the Court to directly examine the question whether the death penalty violates the Constitution."

We include this discussion, not as advocacy as to whether the death penalty should evolve within our collective consciences into a cruel and unusual — and therefore, unconstitutional — punishment, but to point out a problem.

In the past 17 years, why have not prior Presidents proposed solutions to an obviously difficult problem about which they were willing to bury by deferring action? Why hasn't Congress?

Inaction, deferral, and unwillingness to provide solutions for difficult problems facing our people have become a too common modus operandi for our executive and legislative branches. Problem-ignoring instead of problem-solving has become too common an approach of government, not only regarding the death penalty, but regarding a galaxy of other issues. Issues like gun control, pharmaceutical prices, health care, public education, climate change, gerrymandering, and the dominance of lobbies. These are issues for which our people and our democracy desperately need solutions. Yet, these problems remain unresolved. The reason? Is it not because of what could most charitably be called the willful blindness of the political branches of our government?

In Chapter 3, we note that the Supreme Court is aware of its limitations. The Court is aware that for it to be effective, the mindset of the people must be ready for its decisions. Furthermore, the Court must enjoy a high level of legitimacy. Deference and inaction regarding tough human rights issues will not improve the Court's standing nor solve the problems these rights issues present. Nor will it serve as a check and balance over the willful blindness of the political branches of government.

Let us begin our discussion.

George Washington's Cabinet Beginnings

The executive branch didn't start out with a great deal of complexity. But after our first President, George Washington, took office in April 1789, he soon realized that Article II of the Constitution, providing a broad outline of the duties of the President, wasn't complete enough in its elaboration. Washington knew he needed advisors – a cabinet, as it was to be called by James Madison, our 4th President. The Constitution was silent on that point. However, he found a cabinet "implied" in Section 2 of Article II, which included a provision that the President "may require the Opinion in writing of the principal Officer in each of the executive Departments, upon any Subject relating to the Duties of their respective offices."

His first cabinet of advisors? Thomas Jefferson, Secretary of State, appointed March 22, 1790, Alexander Hamilton, Secretary of Treasury, appointed September 11, 1789. Henry Knox, Secretary of Defense, appointed September 12, 1789. And Edmund Randolph, Attorney General, appointed February 2, 1790.

Although, today, most Presidents select cabinet members to support their personal political philosophy, Washington intentionally chose men who represented a diversity of perspectives on the role of government. They also came from different geographic areas. (Abraham Lincoln took a similar approach. He appointed his political rivals to his cabinet.) The full cabinet met for the first time on November 26, 1791.

Today's Presidential Cabinet and Administrative Agencies

The President's Cabinet, in 2020, includes the Vice President and the heads of the 15 administrative agencies within the executive branch. The cabinet leaders are the Secretaries of Agriculture, Commerce, Defense, Education, Energy, Health and Human Services, Homeland Security, Housing and Urban Development, Interior, Labor, State, Transportation, Treasury, and Veterans Affairs, and the Attorney General. Additionally, the Cabinet includes the White House Chief of Staff and heads of a few of the independent and regulatory agencies, technically not in the executive branch. These include the Environmental Protection Agency, Office of Management and Budget, United States Trade Representative, Central Intelligence Agency, Office of the Director of National Intelligence, and Small Business Administration. Appendix B provides a list of the names of 2020 Cabinet Members.

The number of federal employees in the administrative agencies operated under the direction of presidential cabinet members is overwhelming. We include a detailed list in Appendix C of the executive branch administrative agencies, their employees, and budgets. Excluding the Department of Defense, which includes Army, Navy, and Air Force personnel, the numbers of employees run at the low end from 4,200 employees in the Department of Education, to, at the high end, 216,000 employees in the Department of Homeland Security and 235,000 employees in the Department of Veterans Affairs.

The enormity of the management problems for these agencies become apparent when we consider that every time there is an election that produces a political change in our nation's leadership, there are new presidential political appointees of agency chief executives. Furthermore, each agency adopts policies reflecting the views of our new President. Not only are there new policies, in many instances, there is a revamping of agency rules and regulations. Many of the existing rules and regulations are revoked and replaced, frequently with a different interpretation of existing laws and agency mission. The missions of the agencies to provide expertise is also politicized. It's politicized by agency policies that favor the industries meant to be regulated and by presidential appointment of non-expert political leaders, or lobbyists from regulated industries, that minimize or reject expert or scientific advice, which agencies were formed to obtain and provide. What business corporation could efficiently operate under such management chaos?

The agencies become political tools used to provide the short-term, constantly changing political objectives of whichever party is in power with little regard to the mission the agency was created to fulfill. Also ignored is our need as people for agency problem-solving. Agency rules and regulations, and enforcement, are driven by special interests and their lobbies and not the needs of the people.

Constitutional Background: Legislative Delegation

The White House's webpage introduces *The Cabinet* with: "Established in Article II, Section 2, of the Constitution, the Cabinet's role is to advise the President on any subject he may require relating to the duties of each member's respective office." As pointed out in the preceding section, the authority to establish a presidential cabinet is implied, and came from George Washington's initial interpretation of the Constitution, which is silent on the subject.

The Constitution provides absolutely no guidance as to what has become our fourth branch of government – the administrative agencies in the executive branch. Yet, today, it is in the executive branch and its administrative agencies where the real government action is.

Reuben Oppenheimer's 1937 Columbia Law Review article, "The Supreme Court and Administrative Law," begins, "The nine judges of the Supreme Court are in agreement on the importance and necessity of a form of a governmental institution to which no reference is made in the Constitution. The Court sharply divides upon questions as to what constitutes interstate commerce, due process of law, and the division of power between the Federal Government and the States, but it unites in its recognition of the administrative tribunal as a vital and permanent part of our system of government."

The rationale was expressed in 1935 by Chief Justice Hughes in *Schechter v. United States*, "the necessity of adapting legislation to complex conditions … which National Legislature cannot deal directly." Justice Sutherland followed up in 1936 in *Jones v. Securities and Exchange Commission*, adding, "necessarily called and being called into existence by the increasing complexities of our modern business and political affairs."

Oppenheimer writes that the "sweeping" authority granted by Congress to the executive branch and other administrative agencies is not supported by the Constitution and "there is no reason to suppose that the existence of our modern administrative bodies, with their diversified authority, is in line with the philosophy of the framers of our Constitution at the time of its writing. The conditions of modern life, with the close interrelation between all parts of the country and all elements of the economic structure are so different from those of Colonial America, where the emphasis of life was still upon the individual and local unit, that with all their perspicacity, the framers could hardly have imagined this aspect of the future."

It was Chief Justice John Marshall, who in 1825, in *Wayman v. Southard*, came up with the idea that the separation of powers did not prohibit the delegation by the legislative branch to another branch of authority to "fill up the details" in matters of "less interest," keeping to itself the decisions regarding "important subjects."

Marshall's dictum evolved into the idea expressed 1904 in *Buttfield v. Stranahan*, that it is okay for the legislative branch to proceed as far as practicable, leaving it to the executive branch "the duty of bringing about the result pointed out by the statute" – when, Oppenheimer cautions, the executive officials are *"guided by experts"* [emphasis added]. The initial idea that administrative agencies would be guided through our complex world by experts was an early theme of the Court's endorsement of administrative agencies and their functions. That theme has drifted far away from its foundation.

Oppenheimer also points out that, for Congress's delegation of its legislative authority to an administrative agency to be constitutionally valid, "There must be a declared legislative policy [based on a statement of facts supporting the legislation] and a reasonably clear standard whereby discretion must be governed." Noting there is no constitutional authority for Congress's delegation, Oppenheimer concludes the congressional power to delegate to the executive branch is an implied power, supplied by judicial interpretation.

Oppenheimer's article was written during the Great Depression, when the Supreme Court was initially hostile to unfettered delegation by Congress under Roosevelt's New Deal legislation. The Court held Congress's early attempts at delegating to the executive branch and its administrative agencies unconstitutional. The prime concern centered on delegation without adequate standards. But constitutional due process of law was also involved. Since Oppenheimer wrote in 1937, the idea that Congress must provide a clear standard has drifted away. Congress has come to paint agency authority with a broad brush.

In a 1920 case, *Ohio Valley Water Co V. Ben Avon Borough*, predating the Great Depression (and, perhaps, a precursor to Justice Gorsuch's recent concerns about excessive delegation expressed earlier in this book) after noting that administrative agencies are exposed to "political demands," the Court opined: "But to say that [administrative agencies] findings of fact may be conclusive where constitutional rights of liberty and property are involved, although the evidence clearly establishes that the findings are wrong and constitutional rights have been invaded, is to place these rights at the mercy of administrative officials and seriously to impair the security inherent in judicial safeguards. That prospect, with our multiplication of administrative agencies, is not one to be lightly regarded."

In his 2019 *The Conservative Sensibility,* George Will calls the Great Depression, a period of "Temporary Departure" – a period when the balance between the legislative branch and the executive branch shifted to favor the President, inviting him to experiment and act quickly to get us out of the Great Depression.

However, what was once a temporary departure has become a permanent way of life. The shift of legislative authority to the executive branch and the President continues to grow exponentially, in part driven by the complexities of contemporary life, the conflicts between nations and the globalization of national economics.

The Interstate Commerce Commission was created in 1887. From that beginning, George Will points out, the fourth branch of our government has grown and taken over the prime legislative and executive functions, and many of the judicial functions of government. In 2016, the fourth branch of government produced 97,110 pages of regulations, 32 times the number of pages of laws Congress passed in the same year. Will's conclusion? We are left with administrative agencies "untethered from responsibility." Will followed up in his September 2020 Washington Post article, "The fourth branch of government is on its way to replacing Congress." The article is a justified criticism of the Centers for Disease Control's seizure of unconstitutional power during the COVID-19 pandemic. Will objected to CDC's dictatorial hierarchy, using the pandemic as an emergency to assert the superiority of CDC rules over state laws and existing contracts and its right to impose fines. Will writes in disgust, "Congress is, as usual, a bystander."

Today, we have a Congress whose members spend half their time in political fund raising to assure their reelection. The result has been an increased delegation of legislative responsibilities to administrative agencies, freeing up fund-raising time. Congressional concentration on fund-raising has increased the influence of lobbyists, whose special interests have become the prime source of campaign funding.

It should not surprise us when Presidents say, as Obama said in frustration during his presidency, "If Congress won't act, I will."

The Era of Presidential Administration

In her 2000 Harvard Law Review article, "Presidential Administration," Supreme Court Justice Elena Kagan (then a law professor at Harvard), traced the evolution of the regulatory state from its beginnings. Initially, Kagan wrote, Congress's legislative efforts regarding administrative agencies was clear in its directions that the executive branch and its administrative agencies were merely "transmission belts for implementing legislative directives." However, with the emergence of the New Deal, Congress was less specific, and provided agencies with broad discretion. Kagan concluded that this approach was justified by the perceived need "for professional administrators, applying a neutral and impartial expertise." But, as pointed out earlier in this chapter, over time, faith in the objectivity of administrators eroded as special interest groups increased their ability to influence agency actions.

To counter special interest influence, Kagan said that Congress and the courts provided "enhanced participatory opportunities" for a variety of people and interested groups. Providing enhanced participatory opportunities was intended to provide more interaction between a broad range of constituents. That interaction was envisioned as providing political control over special interests and their influence. The idea was like Madison's idea, expressed when political parties were formed. He reasoned that each political party would provide a check and balance on the other. Madison was wrong. In their race for money, both parties are beholden to contributors, who are often from the same interest groups. Similarly, enhanced participation opportunities didn't provide an effective check and balance over favored special interest groups denigrating public preferences, a situation Kagan criticized as the "abdication of regulatory authority to the regulated."

Kagan wrote that, although over time each of the three branches of government have competed for control of the policies of our administrative state, today, we live in an "era of presidential administration." She sees the era as being more responsive to the public, while it also promoted "important kinds of regulatory competence and dynamism."

The Era of Presidential Administration began to take its present form, Kagan said, during the Reagan administration. Ronald Reagan used his presidential powers to appoint agency heads with individuals who would be personally loyal to him, to his agenda and to his political ideology.

Because of his staffing and commitment, Reagan was able to influence the scope of administrative regulations and actions. Reagan's oversight control was exercised through the OMB – the Office of Management and Budget. Kagan wrote that the OMB "used its powers under executive orders to change or (less often) block some proposed rules deemed not fully consistent with Reagan's regulatory policies, including rules relating to environmental quality and workplace safety."

Over time, as the complexity of government increased, and administrative agencies flourished, the role of Congress lessened. The executive branch's role in planning and setting priorities increased, as did the role of the President and his advisors in coordinating government action.

Criticism of Reagan's form of presidential oversight came because of his "anti-regulatory bias." Critics claimed his policies violated the Separation of Powers Doctrine, since Congress had delegated legislative authority, not to the President, but to administrative agencies. Furthermore, in many ways the operation of government became less transparent, frequently carried on by agencies and the administration in private discussions with regulated entities. These private discussions reinforced the executive branch's "antiregulatory inclinations."

Reagan's system picked up pace during the Clinton administration. Kagan concluded that under Clinton, presidential administration became the most important tool a

President could have "to achieve his domestic goals."

Certainly, the Presidents that followed Clinton – Bush, Obama, and, particularly, Trump – honed their skills and promoted their policies, standing on the shoulders of Reagan and Clinton. Reagan, operating more privately than Clinton, dealt primarily with suppression of prior administrative regulations and actions, as did Bush and as has Trump. Clinton, operating more in the open than Reagan in the administrative process, acted primarily through directives furthering administrative action to meet presidential objectives, including the shaping of regulations, as did Obama.

I don't doubt future Presidents will utilize similar strategies to fit their political agendas. The Era of Presidential Administration is now fully integrated into our government, not likely to be vanquished by voters, legislation, or judicial review. But it requires some carefully thought-out presidential blunting, particularly when it comes to protecting the rights of the people.

That's where, today in America's Democracy of Dollars, the role of the Supreme Court in judicial statesmanship, sampling from the lessons provided by the Marshall Court, becomes so important.

What has been the role of the Supreme Court and the federal judiciary during the evolving Era of Presidential Administration? Kagan writes, "Although substantial, this role is now mostly indirect: the courts today do not so much exercise an independent check on agency action as they protect or promote (in various ways and to varying degrees) the ability of the other entities … to perform their functions."

Despite that deference, Kagan adds that "President Clinton's assertion of directive authority … raises serious constitutional questions," under the Separation of Powers Doctrine and the responsibility of the legislative branch. However, she finds President's directions to agencies supportable by principles of statutory interpretation, including the fact that heads of executive branch agencies serve at the pleasure of the President.

Justice Kagan's theme is that, ultimately, the Court should

consider promoting "presidential control over administrative power." It is that theme, in today's Democracy of Dollars, that is in need of course correction. The president and executive branch agencies are too subject to the pressures of special interests, unbalanced by the influence of legislative debate. In America's Democracy of Dollars and the Era of Presidential Administration, a point we continually make is that the Supreme Court is the last bastion to the people to protect their rights. Its constitutional obligation is not the promotion of presidential power, but, through its umpire role, to assure us that presidential power is being exercised within the limits of our Constitution, for the benefit of us all, not just the political elite.

In 1967, in *United States v. Robel,* a case involving the Subversive Activities Control Act, in holding a provision of the Act unconstitutional, Chief Justice Earl Warren wrote for the Court, "When Congress's exercise of one of its enumerated powers clashes with those individual liberties protected by the Bill of Rights, it is our 'delicate and difficult task' to determine whether the resulting restriction on freedom can be tolerated."

Contrary to Kagan's idea of presidential promotion and agency control, should not Warren's reasoning be applicable to the excesses of the executive branch in the Era of Presidential Administration?

Should not that same rationale – instead of deference denying judicial review – be applicable, for example in *Juliana,* when actions of the government, the evidence, and the findings of the Court clearly indicate the rights of the 21 youth plaintiffs who brought the lawsuit have been damaged by both the legislative and executive branches? The task in a case may be "delicate and difficult," but the reality is that there is no other practical remedy available.

When the executive or legislative branch operates unlawfully, as the complaint in *Juliana* alleges (and the Court says it agrees), the Court's deference, coupled with its idea that the youths only solution is to get the political branches to change their unlawful ways, is a naïve, impossible burden. The youth plaintiffs can't vote; nor can they earn money to make serious enough political contributions to get anyone's attention. Even if they could, the burden is impossible. The 21 gutsy kids can't change Congress or the executive branch.

President Harry Truman once famously said of his office, "The buck stops here." The public holds the President responsible for the government's performance. Kagan adds, "Presidents have a large stake in ensuring an administration that works, at least in the eyes of the public."

In theory at least, with a President's national constituency, transparency in presidential communication about what the President and the President's administration is or is not doing should, as Kagan puts it, "improve the connection between governmental action and electoral wishes." With today's never-ending news blasts, the Era of Presidential Administration could be said to be "transparent." News blasts are likely to influence votes in presidential elections. And when the known actions of the President or the administrative agencies exceed constitutional or statutory authority, interest groups, such as the ACLU or the NRA, will act and make their positions known in the public dialogue and the courts.

However, today's transparency is clouded by conspiracy theories and fake news – with the definition of fake news varying with the mindset of its promulgators. The transparency also doesn't reach into the private conversations between regulators and the regulated where the deals are done.

Pontificating leads us to a question critical to our discussion: How unitary and unchaperoned should Presidents be?

Consider Kagan's points:

- Americans have come to harbor high expectations about what a "President should be able to accomplish," particularly with Congress's failures to provide political leadership. The possibility of significant legislative accomplishment has "grown dim in an era of divided government" and polarized congressional parties.

- The press puts impossible pressures and demands on the President. "For the President not to lose control of the debate about him, he must grab the public stage and make news himself."

- To maintain control, Presidents must demonstrate accomplishment and leadership.

- For the most part, Congress has "proved feckless in rebuffing" the President's assertions of authority.

Kagan reasons that political polarization is disrupting the abilities of the political parties to engage in "concerted action to meet national needs." Thus, the resultant gridlock creates the need for reforms that "strengthen the President's ability to provide energetic leadership in an inhospitable political environment."

Unfortunately, as the Era of Presidential Administration has solidified itself as our government's *modus operandi*, judicial deference has diminished the checks and balances contemplated by our Framers. An unchaperoned and powerful President operating in an environment when the executive and legislative branches have pledged less of their allegiance to our flag and our people and more of their allegiance to monied special interests is unhealthy for our democracy.

The Democracy of Dollars environment is where those special interests offer high-paying jobs to retired Congressmen before they have retired from public office. It is where lobbyists raise substantial sums to further reelections of Congressmen and Presidents who support their interests. It is where special interests use the fourth branch of our government as training ground for their lobbyists who join the administration to learn how to better get their way when they return to their lobbying lives, as we point out under the section of this chapter titled the *Executive Branch's Reality Show*.

Kagan closes her article, noting, "Future developments in the relationship between the President and the agencies may suggest different responses; the practice of presidential control over administration likely will continue to evolve in ways that raise new issues and cast doubt on old conclusions."

That time has come for different responses!

Executive Orders – A Prime Tool in the Era of Presidential Administration

Although a prime tool of Presidents is the use of executive orders, the Constitution doesn't define executive orders, nor does it specifically grant a President the right to issue executive orders. Executive orders, like congressional delegation to administrative agencies and the implementation of administrative law, are implied by the Constitution. Executive orders are tools that facilitate the use of executive powers in meeting the Constitution's Article II requirement that the President "take Care that the Laws be faithfully executed." Of course, the reality is that the presidential use of executive powers and the delivery of executive orders frequently extend far beyond that mandate.

In theory, executive orders are issued to direct the operational parts of the government a President administers. The orders aren't supposed to create new laws, nor to revoke or modify laws. That is Congress's job. Nor are the orders to be used to add or delete administrative rules and regulation. The promulgation and revocation of rules and regulations are required to comply with the Administrative Procedures Act.

Executive orders are intended to deal with the discretionary powers the Constitution grants a President, or powers Congress assigns to the President. Historically, executive orders were most frequently used when there was a change in administration and a new President wanted to direct executive branch agencies regarding his policies that fit within the scope of applicable laws. That is not always the case, as illustrated in the following sections.

Lincoln's Order About Habeas Corpus

Executive orders have always been subject to legal

challenge. For example, during the Civil War, President Lincoln suspended the constitutional right to a *writ habeas corpus*. The writ is a court order issued to protect the right of a person arrested or imprisoned by requiring a court hearing. Section 9 of Article I of the Constitution provides that the right of habeas corpus "shall not be suspended, unless when in Cases of Rebellion or Invasion the public Safety may require it." Despite the Civil War, the Supreme Court declared Lincoln's order banning the writ unconstitutional. But Lincoln ignored the Court, Congress did not override him, and apparently, he had no more legal challenges.

Youngstown Sheet and Tube Co.: A Landmark Case

In perhaps the most famous executive order case, during the Korean War, the Supreme Court ruled in 1952 in *Youngstown Sheet and Tube Co. v. Sawyer* that President Truman did not have the power by executive order to put steel mills under federal control during a serious labor dispute that the President thought threatened our war effort. The case is unusual, in that six judges affirmed the decision. Yet each justice who agreed with the decision felt compelled to write a separate concurring opinion.

We quote below from a few of those separate opinions to provide an idea about the Constitution's vagaries regarding the reach of executive branch responsibility. These vagaries, coupled over-the-years with Congress's extensive legislative authority delegation to the executive branch and the Court's deference, warped by the influence and power of lobbies and special interests, have created our Democracy of Dollars. We will follow this brief discussion with examples.

Justice Hugo Black wrote the 5-judge majority *Youngstown* opinion, which included: "The President's power to see that the laws are faithfully executed refutes the idea he is to be a lawmaker."

Justice Robert Jackson's concurring opinion is considered by many legal scholars as the most persuasive on the Court's later decisions. Jackson established three situations that can be used when determining the validity of the President's actions, including presidential executive orders:

1) A President's actions should be granted the greatest deference by the Court when Congress has granted power, explicitly or implicitly.

2) When Congress is silent, or has denied authority, a President has limited independent powers under the Constitution. However, there is a "twilight zone" where the President could have concurrent authority with Congress. Jackson wrote, "Therefore congressional inertia, indifference, or quiescence may sometimes, at least, as a practical matter, enable, if not invite, measures on presidential responsibility. *In this area, any actual test of power is likely to depend on the imperatives of events and contemporary imponderables, rather than on abstract theories of law.*" [emphasis added – think of Obama's "If Congress won't act, I will."]

3) When presidential action conflicts with the Constitution or with congressional legislation, as reflected by Truman's Youngstown seizure, the Court should have no deference.

Jackson's opinion includes this classic observation:

"Just what our forefathers did envision, or would have envisioned had they foreseen modern conditions, must be divined from materials almost as enigmatic as the dreams Joseph was called upon to interpret for Pharaoh. A century and a half of partisan debate and scholarly speculation yields no net result, but only supplies more or less apt quotations from respected sources on each side of any question. They largely cancel each other. And court decisions are indecisive because of the judicial practice of dealing with the largest questions in the narrowest way. The actual art of governing under our Constitution does not, and cannot, conform to judicial definitions of the power of any of its branches based on isolated clauses, or even single Articles torn from context. While the Constitution diffuses power the better to secure liberty, it also contemplates that practice will integrate the dispersed powers into a workable government. It enjoins upon its branches separateness but interdependence, autonomy but reciprocity."

In his concurring opinion, Justice Frankfurter quoted Justice Oliver Wendell Holmes, "The duty of the President to see that the laws are executed is a duty that does not go beyond the laws or require him to achieve more than Congress sees fit to leave within his power."

Justice Clark did not join the majority decision, but wrote a concurring opinion, tracing the vagaries of the Constitution's Article II regarding the powers of a President: "The limits of presidential powers are obscure.... Some of our Presidents, such as Lincoln, felt that measures otherwise unconstitutional might become lawful by becoming indispensable to the preservation of the Constitution through the preservation of the nation. Others, such as Theodore Roosevelt, thought the President to be capable, as a 'steward' of the people, of exerting all power save that which is specifically prohibited by the Constitution or the Congress."

Justice Clark concludes, "where Congress has laid down specific procedures to deal with the type of crisis confronting the President, he must follow those procedures in meeting the crisis; but that, in the absence of such action by Congress, the President's independent power to act depends upon the gravity of the situation confronting the nation."

As to Theodore Roosevelt, our "environmental president," one of my presidential heroes: Teddy was wrong. The President does not have the constitutional authority to do anything that is not specifically constitutionally prohibited. The Constitution is a "grant of power" from the states and the people. The terms of the Constitution's grant set the President's limits, despite its vagaries or the mindset of a President.*

Presidential Uses of Executive Orders

We include in Appendix D a list of the Presidents with the number of executive orders issued by each. The list is compiled by the University of California Santa Barbara in its "The American Presidency Project."

Executive orders weren't numbered until 1908. Since that date over 13,900 executive orders have been issued. Our first five Presidents – Washington, Adams, Jefferson, Madison and Monroe – issued a total of 15. Washington published 8 of the 15. He first directed his cabinet to issue reports about their operations. Another recognized Thanksgiving. The only President not to issue an order was Harrison, who died after one month in office.

Franklin Roosevelt tops the list with 3,721, including executive order 9066, which, on February 19, 1942, mandated the World War II internment of Japanese Americans, affecting the lives of 117,000 people. The internment camps ended when the Supreme Court ruled against it in *Endo v. the United States*. Avoiding the constitutional question, Justice William Douglas opined in December 1944, "In reaching that conclusion [that the defendant Mitsuye Endo should be freed] we do not come to the underlying constitutional issues which have been argued…. [W]e conclude that, whatever power the War Relocation Authority may have to detain other classes of citizens, it has no authority to subject citizens who are concededly loyal to its leave procedure." Alerted to the ruling, the Roosevelt administration immediately issued a public proclamation allowing the Japanese to return to their homes in January 1945.

I am writing this chapter in 2020, during the cresting of the Black Lives Matter movement and the peak of the COVID-19 crisis. Our nation is concerned about police brutality and the numbers of black people dying at the hands of law enforcement officers. On June 16, 2020 President Trump issued Executive Order # 13929, entitled *Safe Policing and Safe Communities*. Section 3 of that Order, "Information Sharing," provides that the Attorney General will create a database of information to share with federal, state, tribal, territorial, and local law enforcement agencies. If the executive order is challenged, this Order would most likely be upheld by the Court under Justice Jackson's first test – congressional authority – since it is supported by a 1998 law passed when Clinton was President.

Although each summer day in 2020 brought new highs in the numbers of Coronavirus cases, the Trump administration championed reopening schools in the fall. At the time, the COVID-19 threat to young children was viewed as slight. However, children were perceived to be disease carriers capable of infecting others, including teachers and parents. Concerned with the adverse health effect, schools and teachers struggled with the idea of a broad, uncontrolled opening. Local control of school openings that was responsive to circumstances was deemed important for everyone's health. Although no executive order was issued, Secretary of Education Betsy DeVos and the President put pressure on governors to open schools on a full-time basis. The pressure includes threats to cut federal funding for schools that don't open. If the threats were carried out, and challenged by affected parents, students, teachers, schools, or school districts, most likely withholding of funds would fail under Justice Jackson's third test – no congressional authority and no constitutional provision authorizing such presidential or agency action.

On July 21, 2020, President Trump issued a "Memorandum on Excluding Illegal Aliens from the Apportionment Base Following the 2020 Census." Although titled as a memorandum, its substance is an executive order directing that illegal aliens not be counted in the 2020 census. The executive order challenged the definition of "persons," which the Constitution requires to be counted in each census. The Constitution provides in Amendment XIV, Section 2: "Representatives shall be apportioned among the several states according to their respective numbers counting the whole numbers of persons in each state, excluding Indians not taxed."

The idea of not including illegal aliens in the census has been considered by Congress in the past, most recently following the 2010 census. On April 13, 2012, Congress's constitutional Research Service released its research paper, "Constitutionality of Excluding Aliens from the Census for Apportionment and Redistricting Services." (The names of the attorneys preparing the report are redacted.) The research paper concludes: The Constitution requires a decennial census to determine the "actual enumeration" of the "whole number of persons" in the United States. The data must be used to apportion the House seats among the states. The paper concludes that the constitutional term "whole number of persons" is broad enough to include all individuals, regardless of citizenship status, and thus "would appear to require the entire population be included in the apportionment calculation." As such, "it appears a constitutional amendment would be necessary to exclude any individuals from the census count for the purpose of apportioning House seats."

Thus, the research paper concludes, neither legislative action nor an executive order could change the requirement to count all persons, including illegal aliens within a state. Trump's order challenges those conclusions because Congress has provided in legislation that it is "the President's personal transmittal of the [census] report to Congress" that "settles the apportionment." Trump's order further provides "Excluding these illegal aliens from the apportionment base is more consonant with the principles of representative democracy underpinning our system of Government. Affording congressional representation, and therefore formal political influence, to States on account of the presence within their borders of aliens who have not followed the steps to secure a lawful immigration status under our laws undermines those principles." There has never been a census when aliens were excluded. Two censuses in the 1800s specifically asked the question about alien status, and then counted the aliens. The Supreme Court has not specifically ruled on the issue.

Congress has passed census laws and has not addressed the issue.

Does Trump's order violate the Constitution's plain words? Is Trump usurping exclusive legislative authority of Congress, which has been silent on the point and has not delegated the specific authority to the President?

On September 10, 2020, a three-judge panel for the U.S. District Court for the Southern District of New York blocked President Trump's executive order directing the census bureau to exclude undocumented immigrants from the census count. On September 30, 2020, the Supreme Court granted the administration's motion for an expedited review, holding, however, that the issue wasn't ready for determination.

Challenges of executive orders take both time and money, whether they are expedited or not. Roosevelt's Japanese internment order was issued in February 1942. Only after the December 1944 Supreme Court decision voided it were the Japanese Americans able to return home in January 1945. In the meantime, for almost three years, they were herded into camps. They lost their jobs and their businesses and their mortgaged homes. They lost their children's rights to attend public or private schools or colleges of their choice. They didn't receive medical care from doctors and medical facilities of their choice, or insurance protection through their desired insurance companies. They couldn't invest or save their money as they would choose. They lost their rights to attend churches or places of worship of their choice. Essentially, they lost their rights.

The Executive Branch's Reality Show

As I wrote in the *Preface*, I do not intend this book or this discussion to be political, favoring either conservative or liberal politics. A changing of the guard is not likely to change the problems, only the level and the purveyors of the problems. However, this book was written in 2020. Thus, our discussion, for the most part, includes events occurring during the Trump administration under a Republican-led and operated executive branch. The issues that require our attention, I believe, are amply illustrated by current events.

Ethics Statutes

There are several federal statutes, including criminal statutes, dealing with government employee ethics. In 2018, the Office of Government Ethics reported that the most common basis for disciplinary action taken against federal employees was the misuse of position. The Federal Manager's Daily Report noted that, in 2018, a total of 1,077 disciplinary actions were taken by 40 agencies. 23 of the agencies made 56 referrals to the Justice Department of possible criminal violations.

Executive orders do not have superiority over statutes. For example, the Ethics Reform Act of 1989 addresses the revolving door issue between regulators and regulated in several provisions, including:

- Lifetime bans on "switching sides" on matters an executive branch employee worked on "personally and substantially" while with the government. However, this law does not apply to broad policy matters including agency rulemaking.

- A two-year "cooling off" period for certain senior officers, including the Vice President and cabinet members, that bars representational communications before agencies or departments where the officers worked.

The predecessor to the Act is the Ethics in Government Act of 1978, which had as its source President John F. Kennedy's Executive Order 10939.

Generally, ethics executive orders expand statutory requirements. To the extent an executive order conflicts with the Act, or any other law, the executive order would be inoperative. To the extent the executive order provides restrictions in addition to those imposed by law in the form of a pledge signed by the employee or officer, the additional restrictions should be enforceable as a contract.

There are also *Standards of Ethical Conduct for Employees of the Executive Branch* that have been codified into regulations by the Office of Government Ethics. These too have the force of law.

Executive Branch Ethics Commitment

Definition:

Lobbying activities: Lobbying contacts and efforts in support of such contacts, including preparation and planning activities, research and other background work that is intended, at the time it is performed, for use in contacts, and coordination with the lobbying activities of others. (Lobbying Disclosure Act definition)

Shortly after Donald Trump was sworn into office as President in January 2017, he issued Executive Order 13770, "Ethics Commitments by Executive Branch Appointees." A copy of the Executive Order is included as Appendix E. The Ethics Commitments are based on similar Commitments issued by President Obama, but Trump's order revoked Obama's Commitments. Only two other Presidents, Clinton and Obama, have required executive branch personnel sign an ethics commitment.

Executive Order 13770 was issued as part of President Trump's plan to "drain the swamp," an important campaign promise. For the most part, the executive order received rave reviews. For example, CNBC touted it with a headline, "Trump imposes lifetime ban on some lobbying, five years on others."

CNBC's report included, "Trump has said individuals who want to aid him in his quest to 'Make America Great Again' should focus on the jobs they will be doing to help the American people, not thinking ahead to the future income they could rake in by peddling their influence after serving in government.... Trump said he talked about the ban a lot during the campaign and 'we're now putting it into effect.'" He also criticized Obama's prior 2-year ban as being "full of loopholes."

Section 1 of Trump's *Ethics Pledge*, starts off "I will not, within 5 years after the termination of my employment as an appointee of any executive in which I am appointed to serve, engage in lobbying activities with respect to that agency." That's the point that the favorable publicity picked up.

Another favorable point is that the *Ethics Pledge* also restricted "shadow lobbying." A shadow lobbyist is a person who engages in some lobbying activities but does not engage in all the activities that require the person to register as a lobbyist. Shadow lobbyists do not make lobbying contacts, but frequently "consult" with lobbying firms, influencing lobbying results.

The Swamp

But then, many lobbyists began to be employed by Trump's executive branch, including several Cabinet members with backgrounds lobbying for coal, energy, steel, banking, defense, automotive, and pharmaceutical companies – frequently, companies their agencies now regulate. In a June 2020 United Press International article, "D.C. Swamp has gotten swampier under Trump, report finds," Sarah Swann wrote: "Four years after Donald Trump campaigned on 'draining the swamp,' wealthy special interests wielding power in Washington have only become more pervasive.... Trump has named more lobbyists [in less than four years] to Cabinet-level positions than former Presidents Barack Obama [four lobbyists] and George W. Bush [two lobbyists] did in their eight-year terms."

The Report Swann referred to, "Spotlight on the Swamp," is the product of Issue One Action, released in June 2020. Issue One Action's Report describes Washington, D.C. as a stronghold for wealthy special interests. "In 2020, Washington, D.C., remains a place where wealthy special interests buy access and influence. While they have an outsized impact on policymaking, those who can't afford to pay to play are often shut out."

The Issue One Action Report states that lobbying spending reached $3.47 billion in 2019. The report also notes that almost 300 lobbyists have joined the Trump administration's executive branch. And almost 400 former congressional legislators registered as lobbyists. The Issue One Action Report also ferrets out that one of the sources of excessive lobbyist influence that keeps the doors between government regulators and their regulated industries swinging is in the "Definitions" section of Trump's executive branch Ethics Commitment, which contains an exception that negates critical components of the ethics pledge. (Neither the Clinton nor Obama pledges include such an exception.) The exception allows rulemaking, adjudication, licensing, and law enforcement lobbying without restriction, four of the most important aspects of agency work. The exception is highlighted below.

Section 2, Definitions, subsection (n), of Trump's pledge in Executive Order 13770, defines the prohibited "lobbying activities" by adopting the definition contained in the Lobbying Disclosure Act (the definition introduces this section). But the Commitment makes an exception to the definition allowing post-termination agency lobbying activity not contained the Lobbying Disclosure Act or prior ethics pledges. *The exception provides that "the term [Lobbying Activities] does not include communicating or appearing with regard to a judicial proceeding; a criminal or civil law enforcement inquiry, investigation, or proceeding; or any agency process for rulemaking, adjudication, or licensing, as defined in and governed by the Administrative Procedure Act...."* [emphasis added]

An irony of Trump' ethics pledge is that after he lost the 2020 election, and before leaving office, he revoked the pledge, releasing his executives from its requirements. The Associated Press reported January 20, 2021 in an article titled "Trump frees former aides from ethics pledge, lobbying ban:" "By rescinding his ethics executive order before leaving office, Trump freed former officials from lingering concern that they could face consequences for running afoul of the ethics policy as they return to the private sector."

The Center for Responsive Politics publishes a list of lobbyists in and out of the Administration. Their list is impressive and is noted in our References and Resources.

ProPublica also publishes a "Lobbying Registrations Report," which is updated daily. As of November 9, 2020, there were 17,218 active lobbying registrations. Fifty-four percent of the registrations involve a revolving-door lobbyist. A link is provided in References and Resources. Putting this in context, there are 100 Senators and 435 Representatives. Thus, there are 34 lobbyists for each Congressman.

Two Views of Lobbying by Former or Future Governmental Employees

A September 2017 report by Jacob Straus, "Ethics Pledges and Other Executive Branch Appointee Restrictions Since 1993: Historical Perspective, Current Practices, and Options for Change," published by Congressional Research Service, a public policy research institute of Congress, includes this perspective: "Some have argued that the revolving door can lead to undue influence by the private sector over the government or vice-versa.... Proponents of the revolving door, however, observe that the promise of future private-sector employment could potentially improve the quality of candidates applying for government jobs.... Another factor observers raise is that the flow of personnel between the public and private sectors may increase the knowledge base of both sectors." Nothing in the report addresses the critical issues of independence versus bias or integrity versus opportunity.

The Lobbying Reality

In July 2020, Politico reports in an article by Meyer and Kahn, "Dozens of Trump veterans cash out on K St. despite 'drain the swamp' vow," that 82 former administration officials have registered as lobbyists and several more now work for lobbying firms but have not registered with the government.

In 2019 David Mora of ProPublica reported in "Update: We Found a 'Staggering' 281 Lobbyists Who've Worked in the Trump Administration" that, in the Trump administration, there has been one lobbyist political appointee for every 14 appointees. "It suggests that lobbyists see themselves as more effective in furthering their client's special interests from inside the government rather than from outside."

Mora points out that it is difficult to determine the extent of the influence of the lobbying industries because of the lack of government cooperation. Mora writes, "federal agencies decline to share details of recusals granted to officials who disclose potential conflicts with their new government roles."

Mora then provides several examples, including one regarding a healthcare lobbyist who joined the Department of Health and Human Services as deputy secretary in January. He remained in Health and Human Services from January to early October when he returned to his former lobbying firm, where he began to lobby the legislative branch, not prohibited by current ethics rules, although it would have been under Obama's revoked rules. On his return, his firm announced, "Spending time at HHS will make [him] even more valuable to our team." The lobbyist is quoted by Mora as saying, "While working with the government I gained knowledge and background, intellectually and professionally, and I intend to unapologetically utilize those skills for my employer and clients."

Mora quotes Jeff Hauser at the nonpartisan Center for Economic and Policy Research, saying that the present administration "has organized the executive branch as a mechanism to reward allies and their political power. Lobbyists are hired not because they're great at the specific matter that they lobby for but because their specialty is delivering political results."

Of course, the swinging door didn't start in the Trump administration; it's just ran at a faster pace. In the Obama administration ProPublica reported a smaller version of the same problem.

How strong, overall, are the voices of lobbyists? Consider *5 crazy facts about lobbyists*, included in a 2020 report entitled "Is Lobbying Good or Bad?" from RepresentUs, which includes:

- Lobbyists raise gobs of money for elected officials. It takes about $14,000 a day to win a Senate seat and about $1.6 million for a House seat. A study found that "on average, for every dollar spent influencing politics, the nation's most politically active corporations received $760 from the government."

- Lobbyists frequently write our laws. For example, in 2013, the New York Times reported that, over the objections of Treasury, Citigroup's recommendations were reflected in more than 70 lines of an 85-line financial bill. Two critical paragraphs prepared by Citigroup were copied word for word.

- Lobbyists effectively influence members of Congress with lucrative job offers … to become lobbyists. Former lobbyist Jack Abramoff is quoted, "I would say to [the congressional member], 'When you're done working on the Hill, we'd very much like you to consider coming to work for us.' The moment I said that, we owned them." About half of retiring senators and about 42% of House members register as lobbyists. In the 1970s, less than 5% did.

The Report concludes that lobbying is constitutionally protected and needed; that overturning *Citizens United,* the 2010 Supreme Court ruling allowing certain political organizations to raise unlimited funds, won't help, because it doesn't deal with lobbying; and Congress won't fix the problem without pressure, because the problem keeps them in power.

What RepresentUs advocates is strong bipartisan action of the people to champion its proposed *American Anti-Corruption Act,* which limits lobbying donations, closes the "revolving door," and prohibits politicians from taking money from special interests, and in many ways, is an expanded version of the recommendations of Issue One Action in its report discussed earlier in this section, "Spotlight on the Swamp Report, Has lobbyist influence been reduced and the revolving door slowed?"

Cuts in IRS Budget, Minimizing Tax Collections from the Wealthy

In 1789, Benjamin Franklin wrote a letter to his friend, French physicist and clockmaker, Jean-Baptiste Le Roy, pontificating, "Our new Constitution is now established and has an appearance that promises permanency; but nothing can be said to be certain, except death and taxes."

Well, that's almost always true. But when our two political branches of government, the executive and legislative branches, underfund and understaff the Internal Revenue Service not only do our nation's deficits rise but we get another result: no certainty in collecting necessary revenues from taxes.

In 2010, the IRS employed 13,879 agents and received 230.4 million tax returns. In 2019, after budget cuts, the IRS employed 8,526 agents but received 253 million tax returns. The result? Davison and Versprille write in their 2020 article, "For now, millionaires face less chance of IRS audit," that if you earned $1 million or more, there's less than a 1% chance you will be audited.

But, there's more.

The Treasury Inspector General for Tax Administration reported on May 29, 2020: "The IRS did not work 369,180 high-income nonfilers, with estimated tax due of $20.8 billion. Of the 369,180 high-income nonfilers, 326,579 were not placed in inventory to be selected for work and 42,601 were closed out of the inventory without ever being worked. In addition, the remaining 510,235 high-income nonfilers, totaling estimated tax due of $24.9 billion, are sitting in one of the Collection function's inventory streams and will likely not be pursued as resources decline. The IRS removed high-income nonfiler cases from inventory, resulting in 37,217 cases totaling $3.2 billion in estimated taxes that will not likely be worked by the

IRS."

I was unable to locate any reaction from either Congress or the executive branch, although the President's proposed fiscal 2021 budget includes an increase for the IRS to add 1,700 personnel, along with a cut in Medicare and Social Security – thus, it's future is uncertain.

Agency Rollbacks

Another 2016 presidential campaign pledge was to reduce the administrative burden of the thousands of administrative rules and regulations imposed by our fourth branch of government, the Administrative State. An admirable objective, with which in principle I agree.

But, if you were a former industry lobbyist or executive now in charge of an administrative agency, planning to return to your lobbying business when your service to your government is up, what regulations would you revoke?

A prime example: The Trump administration appointed Andrew Wheeler as administrator of The Environmental Protection Agency. The Washington Post's Steven Mufson reported in a 2018 article, "Scott Pruitt's likely successor has long lobbying history on issues before the EPA," "Wheeler spent a decade lobbying for just the sort of companies the agency regulates."

On July 15, 2020, the New York Times published an article by Kendra Louis, "The Trump Administration is Reversing 100 Environmental Rules. Here's the Full List." The very detailed list comprises 68 completed and 32 pending reversals. Do these actions comport with concerns that we have too many rules, and that the plethora of rules generated by our fourth branch of government overburden our businesses and people?

In numbers the answer is "yes," but in substance the answer is "no." For the most part, the rules reversed are environmental rules authorized by Congress that assure us that we will have clean and healthy air and water, while minimizing pollution. The EPA reversals favor the fossil fuel industry to the detriment of our health and well-being. Nineteen of the rules address air pollution and emissions, four to water pollution, six to toxic substances. The rollbacks also eliminated the rights of affected communities to have a say on environmental projects that impact them, clearly a violation of the First Amendment right of free speech and totally contrary to the idea of a government "for the people."

Kendra Louis reports in her July 15, 2020 New York Times article that most of the rules repealed were rules adopted during the Obama administration. The rules withdrawn and replaced weakened wetlands protection, motor vehicle requirements and "withdrew the legal justification for restricting mercury emissions from power plants." The rollbacks most likely "significantly increase greenhouse gas emissions and lead to thousands of extra deaths from poor air quality each year, according to energy and legal analysts."

Brett Hartl, governmental affairs director of the Center for Biodiversity wrote EcoWatch an email in July 2020, that the present administration "is turning back the clock to when rivers caught fire, our air was unbreathable, and our most beloved wildlife was spiraling to extinction. The foundational law of the modern environmental movement has been turned into a rubber stamp to enrich for-profit corporations, and I doubt the courts will stand for that."

Most of the rollbacks do not appear to be within the discretion delegated to the EPA by Congress, and rollbacks are being legally challenged. As a result of legal challenges, at least ten of the rollback changes, the New York Times reports, were quickly reversed or suspended.

The Noll and Revesz Regulatory Review March 2020 article, "Regulatory Rollbacks Have Changed the Nature of Presidential Power," points out that the present administration is using three primary rollback tools:

- The Congressional Review Act, which allowed the 2017 Congress to disapprove regulations issued after June 13, 2017 (during the Obama era).

- Obama rules that were being challenged in courts were stayed by the administration during their time in court, which makes them ineffective.

- Suspensions deferring compliance with in-force rules, sometimes indefinitely.

The author's conclusions? "Because of these three aggressive rollback strategies, future one-term Presidents are unlikely to see a significant portion of their regulatory output on important matters survive."

We can now add a fourth technique: waiver of environmental protection provisions of laws and regulations to accelerate economic recovery during emergencies. Like during the COVID-19 pandemic.

On June 4, 2020, President Trump issued Executive Order (EO) 13927, "Accelerating the Nation's Economic Recovery From the COVID-19 Emergency by Expediting Infrastructure Investments and Other Activities." Among the EO's lengthy pronouncements, the EO provides in Section 6: "These regulations [Council on Environmental Policy (CEP) regulations issued under the National Environmental Policy Act] provide that when emergency circumstances make it necessary to take actions with significant environmental impacts without observing the regulations, agencies may consult with the CEP to make alternative arrangements to take such actions." The EO continues: "These emergencies have included not only natural disasters and threats to national defense, but also threats to human and animal health, energy security, agriculture and farmers, and employment and economic prosperity.... [T]he heads of all agencies (i) shall identify planned or potential actions to facilitate the Nation's economic recovery that (A) may be subject to emergency treatment..."

Similar provisions in the Executive Order are in sections addressing the Clean Air Act and the Endangered Species Act. Not surprising, legal challenges to the EO were quickly filed with the courts. A May 2020 Reuters report by Valerie Volcovici, "Nine U.S. states sue EPA for easing environmental enforcement amid pandemic," stated that, in addition to the nine states suing the EPA, a dozen environmental groups have done likewise, alleging that Trump's directions to the EPA in his Executive Order are unlawful, and the suspension exceeded EPA authority. Fifteen state attorney generals formed a coalition, sending a letter to the President, urging him to maintain environmental protections during COVID-19 pandemic.

Inside Climate News' March 2020 criticism of Trump's waiver, "Trump's Move to Suspend Enforcement of Environmental Laws is a Lifeline to the Oil Industry," has a sub-headline, "The American Petroleum Institute sought the EPA's help for companies hurt by COVID-19." One former EPA official called the suspension "an open license to pollute."

Inside Climate News continued: The EPA suspension occurred after Congress refused to include fossil fuel industry relief in its Coronavirus stimulus bill. A former head of the EPA office of enforcement commented, "I am not aware of any instance when EPA ever relinquished this fundamental authority." Speaking about the communities that surround refineries and other fossil fuel facilities, another commenter added, "We know that these are the communities where we have elevated levels of cancers and liver, kidney, heart and lung diseases. You're going to put more pollution into these communities, then you're also going to create more chronic health conditions which make you more susceptible to COVID-19." These communities are also poor and medically underserved.

The President's Executive Order also waived environmental reviews under the National Environmental Policy Act and the Endangered Species Act. His claim is that the waiver of these reviews will speed up projects and environmental recovery following the Coronavirus pandemic: "Unnecessary regulatory delays will deny our citizens opportunities for jobs and economic security, keeping millions of Americans out of work and hindering our economic recovery from the national emergency."

But are these rules unnecessary? These waivers are the type of government action that produces long term, permanent damaging results to the environment and human health. The waivers also defeat the purpose of the National Environmental Policy Act, adopted 50 years ago. Would not championing the development of clean technologies, where today's job growth is accelerating, and the results are not environmentally destructive, be more productive?

In his June 2020 Washington Post article, "Citing an economic emergency, Trump directs agencies across government to waive federal regulations," Jeff Stein writes, "The Trump administration is doing by fiat what it has struggled to accomplish through lengthy rulemaking – dismantling federal regulations designed to protect workers, consumers, investors and the environment.... This move comes on top of waivers that the federal agencies had granted businesses and industries earlier in the health crisis." Stein was referring to Executive Order 13924 issued in May which provided a generalized right to agencies to waive rules that could slow recovery.

Administration Rollback Legal Challenges

Executive Orders 13924 and 13927 illustrate a flaw in a government dominated by a President and the administrative state. Policies reflect the politics of the moment, changing from administration to administration, frequently with more damage and cost than positive effect. Policies should be carefully thought out, researched, and long-term oriented.

The actions of the President are being challenged legally, at a great cost of money and time. In an August 2020 article by Sheeler and Irby of The Sacramento Bee, California's attorney general reports that California has spent $43 million suing the Trump administration, an amount that's untouchable by most states and certainly by individuals. The attorney general says that the litigation has saved billions in funding the state would have lost had Trump been able to carry out his policies. The amount of our tax dollars spent by the federal government are not disclosed, but when all the litigation is considered, the costs must be astronomical.

The question before the federal courts, and ultimately the

Supreme Court, regarding Executive Order 13927 is whether the National Emergency Act's delegation of power permits the President to waive enforcement of environmental laws during a pandemic which will be with us not for days, weeks or a few months, as most emergencies are, but most likely for years. The letter 15 attorney generals sent the President argues that the National Emergencies Act doesn't permit the waivers. The attorney generals urge that the President revoke Executive Order 13927.

The President has not been successful in his efforts to unwind environmental regulation. In July 2020, EarthJustice reported in "Overruled: The Untold Story of the Trump Administration," that it has participated in 49 environmental lawsuits against the Trump organization, and to date Trump has lost 40 of them. The Institute for Policy Integrity at New York University School of Law reports in "Roundup: Trump-Era Agency Policy in the Courts," updated October 27, 2020, that out of 153 legal actions regarding the administration's deregulatory efforts, the administration has lost 127 of them. In a similar study dated August 2020 by Brookings Institute, monitoring 74 administration deregulatory actions, reports in "What is the Trump administration's track record on the environment?" that "Regulatory rollbacks are intended to boost fossil fuel production and use." Brookings reports the President's loss ratio is 87%.

Although the outcome over the pending litigation regarding the Executive Orders 13924 and 13927 has not been decided, in the context of his prior actions, it seems clear that the intended beneficiaries of presidential actions are special interests and not the people.

The cost to us as taxpayers? We will probably never know. Most likely it's several times the $43 million California has spent.

During the long periods of challenge, even if the challenges are successful, the failure of the agencies to enforce regulations Congress has charged them with enforcing is damaging to the environment and to the health of the country.

Pandemics Aren't the Only Excuse to Trample on Rights

Trump's delving into the reaches of the National Security Act during the COVID-19 pandemic is not the first time the Act has been used to expand presidential authority at the expense of individual rights. David Rudenstine's 2016 book, *The Age of Deference,* provides startling, in-depth detail, beyond the scope of this book – from secret Army experiments that have unknowingly harmed military personnel to kidnapping and torture policies that are disgusting.

Rudenstine concludes: "[T]he very governing institution most responsible for protecting individual liberty, upholding the rule of law, and preserving the constitutional order – the Supreme Court – has generally betrayed for over seven decades its responsibilities to hold the executive meaningfully accountable in cases the executive claims implicates national security."

Initially, Rudenstine writes, judicial deference reflected the security concerns that followed wars. But over time, the deference with minimal or no judicial review became settled procedure when claims of national security implications were made, providing "constitutional legitimacy in the Imperial Presidency and the rise of the National Security State."

The harmful results parallel those that concern us in this book:

- Individuals are denied judicial relief when their rights are violated by a political branch of government.

- Deference amounts to the Court abandoning its role, providing judicial review under our constitutional system of checks and balances, leaving individuals with no realistic remedy.

The Court's deference to the political branches, which minimizes the utility of judicial review also has another adverse effect. In *The Will of the People*, Barry Friedman wrote in 2009:

"The value of judicial review in the modern era is that ... [i]t serves as a catalyst for the American people to debate the polity of some of the most difficult and fundamental issues confronting them. It forces Americans to work to reach answers to these questions, to find solutions – often compromises – that obtain broad and lasting support."

Would not we, the American people, have a better chance to solve our accelerating climate change problems – problems that have more potential for long-term damage to our environment and our health than the COVID-19 pandemic – if in *Juliana* the appellate court had given credence to the harm being done to the youth plaintiffs by providing judicial review, and that credence could be a focus of our political debates?

Would not we, the American people, have more comfort with our electoral system if each of our votes counted with equal weight? Would it not encourage voters, particularly our young voters, to have less despair and more enthusiasm for participating in our democracy if *Rucho* had not been dismissed by the Court as a decision to be left to a political branch or state legislature that has absolutely no interest in rectifying the damage caused by partisan gerrymandering?

Rights to the Highest Bidder

In our Democracy of Dollars, in this Era of Presidential Administration – or as Rudenstine calls it, in the *Age of the Imperial President* – driven by the reality of the over-sized influence of special interests and their lobbies, we cannot afford a passive judicial system deferring to a political branch that is the culprit. Fortunately, on rollbacks, the judicial system has not been laid back. The Supreme Court and the rest of the federal judicial system must also step up on its protection of rights, as is argued in this book.

Without the Supreme Court and the federal courts stepping up to protect the rights of the people in face of the Democracy of Dollars real world, the people effectively have no rights. In a bygone era when special interest influence supported by lobbyists and their dollars were less dominant, the deference rules might have worked. But not today, at least when the deference is to the political branch culprit causing the harm.

In the Spring of 2015, Phi Beta Kappa's magazine, *The American Scholar*, shocked the academic world with its cover, a picture of the five conservative judges on the Roberts Supreme Court, overlaid with this title: *Company Men: Free Speech Goes to the Highest Bidder*.

If the article were written today, would it say *Company Men: Rights of the People Go to the Highest Bidder*?

If anyone cares to argue that the rights enumerated in the Declaration are not in the Constitution, they should re-read the [9th] Amendment until they get it.

Bradford Hatcher
"Notes for the Next Constitution,"
2016

The message of the Ninth Amendment is all the more important today, when the Supreme Court's protection of human rights is under such violent attack.

Daniel Farber, Professor, University of
California
Retained by the People, 2007

Chapter 8 – Natural Rights and the Ninth Amendment

"The enumeration in the Constitution, of certain rights, shall not be construed to deny or disparage others retained by the people."

Constitution, Ninth Amendment

In 2010, during Elena Kagan's Supreme Court Senate confirmation hearings, she was asked a question by Senator Tom Coburn from Oklahoma about her belief in "natural rights." The discussion was about guns and the second amendment, but Coburn framed the questions in the context of one's "natural rights of resistance and self-preservation."

Kagan: "Senator Coburn, to be honest with you, I don't have a view of what are natural rights, independent of the Constitution. And my job as a justice will be to enforce and defend the Constitution and the other laws of the United States."

Coburn: "So you wouldn't embrace what the Declaration of Independence says, that we have 'certain God-given inalienable rights' that aren't in the Constitution, that are ours and ours alone, and that government doesn't give those to us?"

Kagan: "Senator Coburn, I believe that the Constitution is an extraordinary document. And I'm not saying I do not believe that there are rights preexisting the Constitution and the laws, but my job as a justice is to enforce the Constitution and the laws.... I think that the question of what I believe as to what people's rights are outside the Constitution and the laws, that you should not want me to act in any way on the basis of such a belief."

Coburn: "I would want you to always act on the basis of the belief of what our Declaration of Independence says."

Kagan: "Senator Coburn, I think you should want me to act on the basis of the law, ... the Constitution and the statutes of the United States."

Before we comment on the exchange between Justice Kagan and Senator Coburn, and before we delve further into this chapter's discussion of natural rights and the Constitution's Ninth Amendment, let us first return to two questions we raised at the beginning of this book.

Two Questions About Democracy and Why Governments are Formed

Early on in this book, in our framing chapter, *The Problem*, we raised two questions about democracy and why governments are formed:

- Was Justice Scalia correct when he said, "The whole theory of democracy ... is that the majority rules; that is the whole theory of it. You protect minorities only because the majority determines that there are certain minority positions that deserve protection?"

- Or was Jefferson correct that fundamental human rights are not grants from a generous governing majority, but that governments are formed to secure our preexisting, unalienable rights? Jefferson wrote in the Declaration of Independence: "We hold these truths to be self-evident, that all Men are created equal, that they are endowed by their Creator with certain unalienable rights, that among those are Life, Liberty, and the Pursuit of Happiness. That to secure those rights, Governments are instituted among Men, deriving their just Powers from the Consent of the Governed."

Scalia's Democracy

The late Justice Scalia presents us with a *dictionary definition of democracy*: government by the majority – or, as Lincoln said, "government of the people, by the people."

Scalia's comments about democracy, reported by Frost and Sikkenga in their 2019 treatise, in *History of American Political Thought,* were made in a talk he gave in May 1996 at the Gregorian University in Rome, where his son was then a student. In his 1998 book, *A Matter of Interpretation*, also reported in the same treatise, Scalia said, "If you want aspiration, you read the Declaration of Independence, with its pronouncements that 'all men are created equal' with 'unalienable Rights' that include 'Life, Liberty, and the Pursuit of Happiness'.... There is no such philosophizing in our Constitution, which, unlike the Declaration of Independence and the Declaration of the Rights of Man, is a practical and pragmatic charter of government."

Unlike Scalia, Lincoln didn't stop with "government of the people, by the people," the dictionary definition of democracy. He added "for the people," the essential ingredient of constitutional democracy.

That fundamental addition – *for the people* – missing from Scalia's analysis reflects the difference between a mechanical *dictionary democracy* and a meaningful *constitutional democracy.*

Ralph A. Rossum, the author of the treatise's chapter on Scalia closes his discussion of Scalia on democracy with, "Scalia's critics also wonder how someone who argues, as he does, that 'In textual interpretation, context is everything,' could fail to consider the Declaration of Independence and its theory of democracy in constitutional context."

Jefferson's Democracy

In the Declaration of Independence, Jefferson makes two critical points:

- We "are endowed by their Creator with certain unalienable rights, that among those are Life, Liberty, and the Pursuit of Happiness."

- "That to secure those rights, Governments are instituted among Men, deriving their just Powers from the Consent of the Governed."

Unalienable rights include, "life, liberty and the pursuit of happiness," but, as Jefferson points out, the Declaration's reference to unalienable rights is not complete.

The fundamental reason for forming government — the protection of rights, not to perfect the will of the majority — is poo-poo'd as mere philosophizing by Justice Scalia, and surprisingly, is ignored by Justice Kagan in her exchange with Senator Coburn. Its significance is also too often ignored today by our Supreme Court.

First Amendment Right to Petition Our Government for Grievances

The First Amendment in our Bill of Rights provides constitutional protection not only for our right to free speech, press, assembly, and religion, but for our right to petition our government for grievances. The Constitution is silent on how grievances are to be brought before our government, but there are many forms, including litigation. The Constitution's plain words about our right to bring grievances without limitations or restrictions, indicate the importance of this constitutional right as a tool for us to keep our government in line, a necessity if we are to have a thriving democracy. The right to bring grievances has another aspect besides "bringing." To be effective, the response of the Court to the "bringing" must include "listening," "considering," and "deciding." A constitutional process is not intended to be perfunctory.

The right to litigate grievances with our government has a long history that predates the Constitution, going back to at least the seventeenth century under English common law, which became our American common law. But, as is pointed out, judge-made deference rules denying judicial review of grievances have shattered its effectiveness in protecting our rights, even when a federal court acknowledges a damaging wrong has been intentionally inflicted on us by our political branches of government, as it did in the *Juliana v. United States* case, the subject of Chapter 5. The deference rules have the potential for being particularly damaging with our "unalienable rights," which are not itemized in the Bill of Rights.

It is these unalienable rights that James Madison and the Framers recognized in the Ninth Amendment as belonging to the people and the states. The lack of success petitioning grievances about these rights places the political branches of our government in a position to abuse these rights. A flaw in the Constitution is that it does not specifically state that the government or its branches must respond to a person's petition. If the Constitution were more specific, the Court's ability to deny judicial review would be less troublesome.

Natural Rights: Our Unenumerated, Inalienable Rights

Definition:

Natural law: A philosophical system of legal and moral principles purportedly deriving from a universalized conception of human nature or divine justice rather than from legislative or judicial action; moral law embodied in principles of right and wrong.

In *The Problem* chapter we wrote that our Declaration of Independence was *Lincoln's Apple of Gold*, giving us the context in which our Constitution should be construed. The theme of our Declaration's 1,337 words is grounded in the rights that come to us, not from governments but from our Creator. These rights are ours forever. These rights are unenumerated, unalienable.

Protection of these rights is why our constitutional government was formed. It was not formed to preserve the control of the majority who might, if they feel generous, provide the minority with a few rights as their left-over crumbs of generosity. The Constitution is not a "top-down" document granting rights from kings or from the majority. It is a "bottom-up" document, a compact between all the people for all the people, granting their government certain powers to be used to protect their rights. In Jefferson's 1801 first inaugural address he spoke as if contradicting Scalia:

> "All, too, will bear in mind this sacred principle, that though the will of the majority is

> in all cases to prevail, that will to be rightful
> must be reasonable, that the minority possess
> their equal rights, which equal laws must
> protect, and to violate would be repression."

Yet, despite the Declaration's theme, no place within our Constitution do the Framers address the Declaration's unenumerated, unalienable rights, except in the Ninth Amendment. A few rights are scattered throughout the Constitution and, ultimately, when the first ten amendments were adopted as the Bill of Rights in 1791, the first eight defined specific rights as constitutional rights.

The Bill of Rights, of course, is a short 475 words. The Constitution, about 4,400 words without the amendments and about 7,500 words with them, is the shortest Constitution of any major government. Neither the Bill of Rights nor the Constitution is long enough to list all the unalienable rights Thomas Jefferson and the signers of the Declaration of Independence had in mind. Jefferson and the rest of our Founders were grounded in the Age of Enlightenment, and the philosophy of that age was based on the idea that each of us has natural rights – unalienable rights from our Creator, which include, but aren't limited to, "Life, Liberty and the pursuit of Happiness." Natural rights are fundamental. They're everyone's rights, not limited to rights granted by a constitution or a government. These stated and unenumerated rights are ours unless we voluntarily give them up.

Professor Randy Barnett points out in his 1991 "A Ninth Amendment for Today's Constitution," "Despite their many differences, the Framers of the Constitution shared a common belief that although the people may delegate certain powers to their agents in government, they still retain their natural rights."

Thus, the Framers' first thoughts were that the Constitution didn't have to say anything about natural rights. The Framers thought any discussion in the Constitution about natural rights irrelevant. After all, the Constitution was a delegation of power to the federal government. Whatever wasn't delegated was retained by the states or by the people. So, there was no necessity to write into the Constitution what was being retained, only what was being given up to the new national government. The Framers were also concerned about the difficulty in producing an appropriate list of rights. Barnett explained, "The Framers believed it was dangerous to enumerate any rights because the rights of the people are boundless and important rights might be lost by being left off the list."

But, despite the Framers' concerns and desire not to have a list of rights in the Constitution, there was a debate about whether something should be included about rights when the Constitution was sent to the states for ratification – a debate so intense that it almost sent the Constitution down in defeat. The debate centered around whether the broad swatches of powers granted to the new government in the Constitution could be corrupted, used by conniving political leaders to usurp the natural rights from the people.

Ultimately, there was agreement among the Framers and the states to include a Bill of Rights. Thus, the states began to approve the Constitution with the understanding a Bill of Rights would soon be added. During the approval process, five states assembled long lists of rights that could be included in the new Bill of Rights.

The idea of what to include in a Bill of Rights then created its own conundrum. In one of the debates, reported in *The Debates in the Several State Conventions on the Adoption of the Federal Constitution,* a debater, James Wilson, frustratedly challenged the participants to name all the rights, "Enumerate all the rights of men! I am sure, sirs, that no gentlemen in the late Convention would have attempted such a thing."

Ultimately, James Madison prepared two provisions the Framers and the states agreed upon to include in the Bill of Rights: Amendments 9 and 10. The first dealt with unenumerated rights; the second with undelegated powers.

- The Ninth Amendment: "The enumeration in the Constitution, of certain rights, shall not be construed to deny or disparage others retained by the people." This amendment provides that our Constitution and its Bill of Rights don't include the only rights we have; we have unenumerated rights. These rights are not listed constitutional rights, as are rights included in the first eight amendments. They are natural rights, ours as additional unalienable rights.

- The Tenth Amendment: "The powers not delegated to the United States by the Constitution, nor prohibited by it to the States, are reserved to the States respectively, or to the people." This amendment provides that if the Constitution doesn't state a power delegated to the national government, the national government doesn't have the power. The federal government wasn't delegated any powers that would take away our natural rights. Thus, the government is prohibited from adversely affecting unenumerated rights. They belong exclusively to the people.

We pointed out in prior chapters, that it didn't take long for our first President, George Washington, to figure out that the delegation of powers to the executive branch includes implied, but unstated, powers he needed to be an effective President. Over time, the breadth of implied powers grew exponentially. That growth is one of the concerns that led to this book; but that concern doesn't change the Constitution's framework or the conclusion: The Constitution is a delegation of specified limited powers. By interpretation approved by the Supreme Court, the Constitution also includes powers provided by implication from the powers stated.

Despite its straight-forward language, over the past 230 years, there has been a debate about what the Ninth Amendment means. Rather than take its words at face value, dozens of law review articles have been written about what scholars think the Framers really meant. We will return to this discussion shortly. But, first, another deference rule of the Court: judicial rights balancing.

Judge-Made Balancing Rules

Beyond the judge-made rules of Chevron and its companion rules of deference to administrative agencies and the Political Question and the Standing Doctrines, there are judge-made rules of balancing. The balancing rules are used when legislation or an executive act is challenged as conflicting with constitutional rights. For example, when rights are suspended by government action during an emergency, discussed later in this chapter. In describing its balancing responsibilities of the Supreme Court, its government web page titled "The Court and Constitutional Interpretation" assures us:

> "The Constitution of the United States is a carefully balanced document. It is designed to provide for a national government sufficiently strong and flexible to meet the needs of the republic, yet sufficiently limited and just to protect the guaranteed rights of citizens; it permits a balance between society's need for order and the individual's right to freedom."

Balancing complex issues between the guaranteed rights of citizens and the needs of the republic requires careful consideration and understanding of a wide variety of factors. Retired Supreme Court Justice David Souter made that point in his talk to the May 2010 Harvard graduation class: "The Constitution contains values that may well exist in tension with each other, not in harmony.... Constitutional facts may require judges to understand the meaning that the facts may bear before the judges can figure out what to make of them. And this can be tricky.... because [the Constitution's] language grants and guarantees many good things, and good things that compete with each other and can never all be realized, all together, all at once."

Balancing Rules in Emergencies

Is an unalienable right, enumerated or unenumerated, absolute? During pandemics or national emergencies? The Supreme Court webpage noted above points out that individual rights and the needs of the country frequently may have to be balanced, neither being absolute. But when emergencies arise, real or imagined, suspending rights can replace balancing rights.

However, in a Democracy of Dollars, emergencies are frequently a pretext to undermine constitutional rights and solidify authoritarian power and political views that would never be supported by democratic process, or judicial balancing. The difference between an emergency that justifies the exercise of constitutional power that results in the temporary suspension of rights, and the use of an emergency to create unlawful power that squelches rights and promotes a special interest is not always transparent, particularly when the Court relaxes its judicial review.

Suspending Rights

In 1905, in *Jacobson v. Massachusetts*, the Supreme Court was called upon to decide whether Massachusetts could mandate smallpox vaccinations. The Court opined that it could. The Court held that individual liberties are not absolute and are subject to the "police power" of the state. A state's police power is the inherent power of a state government to make laws necessary to preserve public security, order, health, morality, and justice. Justice Harlan wrote, "in every well-ordered society charged with the duty of conserving the safety of its members the rights of the individual in respect of his liberty may at times, under the pressure of great dangers, be subjected to such restraint, to be enforced by reasonable regulations, as the safety of the general public may demand…. Real liberty for all could not exist under the operation of a principle which recognizes the right of each individual person to use his own, whether in respect of his person or his property, regardless of the injury that may be done to others."

Thus, today's libertarian idea that it's an unconstitutional interference with individual freedom for governments to require persons to wear masks during the COVID-19 pandemic that began in 2020 is incorrect.

But Harlan closed his opinion with an important observation: "[T]he police power of a State, whether exercised by the legislature or by a local body acting under its authority, may be exerted in such circumstances or by regulations so arbitrary and oppressive in particular cases as to justify the interference of the courts to prevent wrong and oppression."

Consider: In response to the COVID-19 pandemic, many state governors issued orders that elective medical procedures would be barred during the emergency. The ban has been intended to assure hospitals and medical personnel have enough available facilities and protective equipment to treat COVID-19 patients. The governor of Texas issued such an order on March 22, 2020.

The Texas attorney general, a conservative Republican, promptly issued an opinion that the order prohibited abortions, because, he ruled, abortions are elective surgeries. Abortions are rarely performed in hospitals, and when they are, they are usually emergencies. COVID-19 abortion bans under the guise of being elective surgeries by Texas and eleven other states were heavily criticized and resulted in several patient-rights lawsuits. The American College of Obstetricians and Gynecologists, joined by other groups, issued a 2020 "Joint Statement on Abortion Access During the COVID-19 Outbreak," defining abortion as a time sensitive and "essential component of comprehensive health care," pointing out that even short delays "may increase the risks or potentially make it completely inaccessible." Before a final court decision was rendered in Texas, on April 17 – most likely because of public pressure – the Texas governor modified his order to allow elective surgeries that did not deplete hospital capacity, or the use of protective equipment needed to treat COVID-19. This led to the attorney general notifying the Texas court that abortion services were again available in Texas.

Was the Texas attorney general's ruling that abortions be suspended an appropriate, health-protecting response to the

COVID-19 pandemic or something else? The ruling appears to have been promulgated as a way around the Supreme Court's *Roe v. Wade* decision that abortions are lawful, a holding that many conservatives in Texas oppose. A June 2019 NPR/CBS poll places those conservatives in a small minority: "[T]hree-quarters of Americans say they want to keep in place the landmark Supreme Court ruling, *Roe v. Wade,* that make abortion legal in the United States…"

It is cases like the abortion cases that motivated professors Wiley and Valdeck to write in an April 2020 article, "COVID-19 Reinforces the Argument for 'Regular' Judicial Review – Not Suspension of Civil Liberties – In Times of Crisis," that rights in a crisis should never be suspended without a full judicial review based on non-crisis standards. The professors' reason that the courts are the only institution in a position to push back against the overreaching of the political branches. They add that judicial reviews of "government incursions on civil liberties" also force governments to communicate the reasons for their actions and how any imposed restrictions further legitimate purposes. They reason, "In the process, a robust judicial role may be indispensable not only in minimizing the loss of our liberties, but also in facilitating the development of a sustainable long-term response to this crisis."

In their follow-up article from July 2020, "Coronavirus, Civil Liberties, and the Courts: The Case Against 'Suspending' Judicial Review," Wiley and Valdeck warn: "More fundamentally, though, the more that courts coalesce around a standard in which governments are held to exceedingly modest burdens of justification for incursions into our civil liberties during emergencies, the more those same governments might be incentivized not only to use emergencies as pretexts for scaling back our rights, but also to find pretexts for triggering such emergencies in the first place."

Balancing Rules, the Presumption of Constitutionality and Footnote Four

In 1938, in *United States v. Carolene Products*, the

Supreme Court developed another judge-made deference rule, a "presumption of constitutionality." Under the presumption of constitutionality if there is any "rationale basis" that can be imagined for Congress's legislation being challenged in the federal courts, the legislation will be upheld.

The *presumption of constitutionality* has deep roots in America's jurisprudence, traced back to a Harvard Law Review article, "The Origin and Scope of the American Doctrine of Constitutional Law," written by James B Thayer in 1893. Thayer was an early champion of judicial restraint. Thayer's judicial restraint and the Carolene Products' *rational basis* test are subjects for another day. The critical point for our discussion is a footnote.

Footnote Four of *United States v. Carolene Products* – considered by many constitutional scholars as the most important Supreme Court footnote in history – provided dictum (dictum are nonbinding observations of a judge stated in an opinion) setting up a stricter standard of review when rights specified in the Constitution are involved:

> "There may be a narrower scope of operation of the presumption of constitutionality when the legislation appears on its face to within a specific prohibition of the Constitution, such as those of the first ten amendments…. In other words, the enumerated rights may narrow the presumption of constitutionality, *but one of the unenumerated rights retained by the people will have no such power-limiting effect.*" [emphasis added]

Is Footnote Four correct when it says unenumerated rights have less protection than the Constitution's stated rights? St. George Tucker, author of the first constitutional treatise, *View of the Constitution of the United States* (published in 1803, during Jefferson's Presidency), wrote that the Ninth and Tenth Amendments provide an interpretive requirement of strict construction, assuring that "the powers delegated to the federal government, are, in all cases, to receive the most strict construction that the instrument will bear, where the rights of a state or of the people, either collectively, or individually, may be drawn into question."

Ultimately, Footnote Four became a working tool of the federal judiciary, paving the way for many of the Court's Civil Rights decisions. But even though the Footnote includes all Ten Amendments within its umbrella, it left our unenumerated rights, the subject of the Ninth Amendment, dangling.

Thus, the validity of legislation not adversely affecting the Bill of Rights is presumed to be constitutional if a rational basis for the law can be imagined. If the law is shown to interfere with the unenumerated rights of the people, the law will also be constitutional if it meets the rational basis test. However, if the law interferes with rights specified in the Constitution or the Bill of Rights, the law will only pass muster if it passes a stricter review standard, placing "imagination" on a lower rung.

Professor Randy E. Barnett wrote in his 2006 *The Ninth Amendment: It Means What It Says,* that by leaving out the unenumerated rights, the judicial philosophy behind the Footnote Four limitation is contrary to the clear words of the Ninth Amendment. Barnett concludes, "Indeed, Footnote Four would seem to be the epitome of a constitutional construction that is expressly barred by the original meaning of the Ninth Amendment."

Over the years, the Court has tied a few unenumerated rights to the Bill of Rights' First Amendment, or to the Bill of Rights' "due process" clauses in the Fifth Amendment (federal rights) and Fourteenth Amendment (state rights). The due process clauses prohibit the federal and state governments from unfairly or arbitrarily depriving a person of life, liberty, or property.

But the Court's actions regarding the rest of the unalienable, unenumerated rights retained by the people have been sparse. The Court's "presumption of constitutionality" deference, coupled with its sparse attention to the Ninth Amendment's preservation of unstated rights, gives the political branches of our government the ability to deal with our unenumerated rights at will. This is particularly damaging when it comes to our fundamental rights to clean air, unpolluted water, and a healthy environment, essential to life itself.

There has been but one Supreme Court case in which the Ninth Amendment played a role, the 1965 case, *Griswold v. Connecticut*.

Griswold v. Connecticut – Marital Right to Privacy

In the 19th century, several states had laws that made it illegal to use drugs, medicinal articles, or instruments to prevent conception. Connecticut had such a law, the Comstock Act of 1873. Most states rid themselves of these acts; but in 1965, the law remained in force in Connecticut, though it had been enforced but once, to block a clinic from providing services and advice about contraception.

Griswold was arrested for operating a birth control clinic, charged with a crime under the Comstock Act of 1873. Griswold challenged the constitutionality of the Act. Ultimately, the case made its way to the Supreme Court. Justice William Douglas delivered the Court's opinion, holding Connecticut's anti-contraception law unconstitutional since it violated the marital right to "privacy."

Douglas wrote, "We do not sit as a super-legislature to determine the wisdom, need, and propriety of laws that touch economic problems, business affairs, or social conditions. This law, however, operates directly on an intimate relation of husband and wife and their physician's role in one aspect of that relation. The association of people is not mentioned in the Constitution nor in the Bill of Rights. The right to educate a child in a school of the parents' choice — whether public or private or parochial — is also not mentioned. Nor is the right to study any particular subject or any foreign language. Yet the First Amendment has been construed to include certain of those rights." As to the marital right to "privacy," Douglas concludes,

"The foregoing cases suggest that specific guarantees in the Bill of Rights have penumbras, formed by emanations from those guarantees that help give them life and substance."

He asks, "Would we allow the police to search the sacred precincts of marital bedrooms for telltale signs of the use of contraceptives? The very idea is repulsive to the notions of privacy surrounding the marriage relationship. We deal with a right of privacy older than the Bill of Rights – older than political parties, older than our school system."

Justices Black and Stewart dissented since privacy is not specifically stated as a constitutional right, with Black writing, "I like my privacy as well as the next one, but I am nevertheless compelled to admit the government has a right to invade it unless prohibited by some specific constitutional provision." (In more recent times, the late Justice Scalia expressed a similar opinion about privacy.)

Douglas found the right of privacy not in the text of the Constitution, but in the penumbra, "within the zone of privacy created by several fundamental constitutional guarantees."

Justice Arthur Goldberg wrote in his concurring opinion, joined by Justice Brennan and Chief Justice Warren: "I do agree that the concept of liberty [liberty is a Declaration of Independence stated unalienable right] protects those personal rights that are fundamental, and is not confined to the specific terms of the Bill of Rights.... The language and history of the Ninth Amendment reveal that the Framers of the Constitution believed that there are additional fundamental rights, protected from governmental infringement, which exist alongside those fundamental rights specifically mentioned in the first eight constitutional amendments.... The Amendment is almost entirely the work of James Madison. It was introduced in Congress by him and passed the House and Senate with little or no debate and virtually no change in language. It was proffered to quiet expressed fears that a bill of specifically enumerated rights could not be sufficiently broad to cover all essential rights, and that the specific mention of certain rights would be interpreted as a denial that others were protected.... Madison and [Justice Joseph] Story make clear that the Framers did not intend that the first eight amendments be construed to exhaust the basic and fundamental rights which the Constitution guaranteed to the people."

Disagreeing with Justice Black's dissent, Goldberg concludes, "The Ninth Amendment to the Constitution may be regarded by some as a recent discovery, and may be forgotten by others, but since 1791, it has been a basic part of the Constitution which we are sworn to uphold. To hold that a right so basic and fundamental and so deep-rooted in our society as the right of privacy in marriage may be infringed because the right is not guaranteed in so many words by the first eight amendments to the Constitution is to ignore the Ninth Amendment and give it no effect whatsoever.... [T]he Ninth Amendment shows a belief of the Constitution's authors that fundamental rights exist that are not expressly enumerated in the first eight amendments, and an intent that the list of rights included there not be deemed exhaustive.... In determining which rights are fundamental, judges are not left at large to decide cases in light of their personal and private notions. Rather they must look at the 'traditions and [collective] conscience of our people' to determine whether a principle is 'so rooted [there] ... as to be ranked as fundamental.'"

Ninth Amendment: Does it Mean What it Says?

Griswold was decided when I was in law school, and I can remember the excitement of our discussions about Justice Douglas' opinion, locating our right to privacy in the "penumbra" surrounding expressed constitutional rights, and Justice Goldberg's concurring opinion breathing life into the long-overlooked Ninth Amendment.

But the Reality? *Griswold* was the first and the last Supreme Court opinion stating our rights under the Ninth Amendment.

Professor Kurt Lash wrote in his 2013 "Inkblot: The Ninth Amendment as Textual Justification for Judicial Enforcement of the Right to Privacy" that Justice Douglas was criticized by legal scholars, some calling his penumbra metaphor a flight into "metaphysical poetry:" Lash's critique: "Douglas lost touch with the text of the Constitution altogether."

And the Ninth Amendment? Some scholars have taken the position that the Ninth Amendment with its unenumerated rights created a second, unwritten Constitution for Americans. Professor Suzanna Sherry wrote in her 1987 "The Founders' Unwritten Constitution," "the founding generation did not intend their new Constitution to be the sole source of paramount or higher law, but instead envisioned multiple sources of fundamental law. The framers thus intended courts to look outside the Constitution in determining the validity of certain governmental actions, specifically those affecting the fundamental rights of individuals."

However, for many judges and legal scholars, stepping outside the written Constitution to find rights that in some way have constitutional protection from interference by our two political branches was, and is, scary. Judicial excursions into the broad expanse of unenumerated rights could allow judges to become unelected legislators, despite Justice Goldberg's admonition that "In determining which rights are fundamental, judges are not left at large to decide cases in light of their personal and private notions. Rather they must look at the 'traditions and [collective] conscience of our people' to determine whether a principle is 'so rooted [there] … as to be ranked as fundamental.'"

In his 1991 article, "Judging the Ninth Amendment," Sol Wachtler, then Chief Judge of the State of New York, commented on the continuing debate regarding the meaning of the Ninth Amendment: "The act of assigning meaning to the open-ended language of this amendment requires judges to make political decisions about the provision's scope and effect. To give effect to the provision's obvious meaning is to sanction what many perceive to be untrammeled judicial activism. Yet to deprive it of any meaningful role in the protection of fundamental rights appears to violate the Founders' intent."

Wachtler concludes that the Ninth Amendment "requires judges to confront deeply held misgivings about the indeterminacy and the essentially undemocratic nature of the judicial process." The troubling thought process necessary to wrestle with the issues Wachtler projected for judges was resisted by Judge Robert Bork, once a candidate for the Supreme Court, known for his ultraconservatism. Bork wrote in his 1990 *The Tempting of America* that nothing in the Ninth Amendment "suggests that it is a warrant for judges to create constitutional rights that are not in the Constitution.... Nothing could be clearer, however, than that, whatever purpose the ninth amendment was intended to serve, the creation of a mandate to invent constitutional rights was not one of them.... What then can the ninth amendment be taken to mean?"

Bork surmises that the statement "retained by the people" refers to unenumerated rights existing when the Bill of Rights became effective, not later judge-invented rights. For Bork, that means the rights are limited to those "guaranteed by state constitutions, statutes and common law" in 1791.

The error in Judge Bork's analysis is that the object of the Ninth Amendment is not to "create constitutional rights." Its object is to identify a category of rights, unenumerated natural rights, that the Tenth Amendment prohibits the political branches of the government from usurping from us. He also misses the point that natural rights exist even when they have not become the subject of a grievance brought before a court for adjudication. We return to this point later in this chapter when we discuss the ancient Justinian Code.

In his 2017 Senate confirmation hearings, Justice Neil Gorsuch was asked about his understanding of the Ninth Amendment by Senator Ben Sasse. Their conversation:

> Senator Sasse: "[The Ninth Amendment] reads, 'The enumeration in the Constitution of certain rights shall not be construed to deny or disparage others retained by the people.' What does that mean?"
>
> Judge Gorsuch: "Well, Senator, I think it means what it says. There are different views about its effect and its meaning, and I do not

doubt there will be cases and controversies in which I would, if confirmed, and maybe if I am not, be asked to construe the meaning of that. It is one of those amendments that has not had a lot of judicial attention...."

The discussion between Senator Sasse and Judge Gorsuch never dug into the responsibilities of the Court or the political branches of our government to not interfere with our unenumerated rights. However, in his 2019 *A Republic, If You Can Keep it*, Justice Gorsuch expressed a concern similar to that expressed by Bork about justices creating rights by judicial activism: "Life tenure makes little sense if judges are supposed to be nothing more than politicians wearing robes.... Why would the Constitution bother to distinguish so carefully between the legislative and judicial powers if judges were really just supposed to be superlegislators free to alter not just statutes but the Constitution according to their own evolving sensibilities?"

Three decades earlier, Judge Wachtler expressed a similar concern that the Ninth Amendment, "however clear its language, cannot be given an expansive reading that would essentially sanction judicial authority to resolve disputes that are probably better left for the political process." He added that a broad interpretation of the Ninth Amendment may well be unnecessary today with the Supreme Court's "generous reading of the first eight and the fourteenth [due process] amendments," which have been used to protect individuals' rights not itemized in the Constitution.

But, as pointed out, the Ninth Amendment does not create rights, nor does it give unenumerated rights constitutional stature, as the Court has from time to time found other Bill of Rights provisions might do, such as the First Amendment or the due process clauses. It categorizes rights that are exclusively ours. In 2007's *Retained by the People,* an excellent analysis of the Ninth Amendment, Professor Daniel Farber writes that the Founders didn't think they were creating rights for us in the Constitution or its Bill of Rights. "Instead, they were *acknowledging* some of the rights no government could properly deny."

Although Goldberg's concurring *Griswold* opinion could have been clearer on this point, his opinion tells us that the right of marital privacy predated the Constitution. Thus, the right to privacy was not created by the Court or the Constitution. Both Douglas and Goldberg found that Connecticut statute interfered with that fundamental, unalienable marital right to privacy. It was interference with the marital privacy right, an unenumerated right, by the statute that was unconstitutional.

That is the critical point worth repeating: The Ninth Amendment does not create constitutional rights, nor does it give natural rights constitutional status. The Ninth Amendment (which confirms we have unenumerated rights), in conjunction with the Tenth Amendment (which confirms our federal government is a government of limited powers, delegated in the Constitution) run interference for us, protecting our natural rights from interference by our government.

Although the Supreme Court has had nothing further to say about the Ninth Amendment since the Griswold decision, several lower court cases have dismissed Ninth Amendment claims. Dismissals have been based on a court's conclusion that the Amendment provides no substantive rights, or is a rule of construction, or the rights sought to be protected were not fundamental. For example, *Concerned Citizens of Nebraska v. United States Nuclear Regulatory Commission*, held in 1992 that there is no constitutional right provided by the Ninth Amendment to be protected from non-natural radiation, because the right was not fundamental. The court opined:

> "To be considered fundamental, an unenumerated right must be 'deeply rooted in the Nation's history and tradition.'"

Nuclear power, the court reasoned, was relatively new, and not imbedded in tradition. In 1979, *Gasper v. Louisiana Stadium and Expo. Dist.*, the court held there is no fundamental right to a smoke-free environment, ruling "While a growing number of commentators argue in support of a constitutional protection for the environment, this newly-advanced constitutional doctrine has not yet been afforded judicial sanction..." When courts rely on earlier decisions by *stare decisis,* the availability of those earlier decisions means that some court at some time in the past did afford judicial sanction on a point of law which had not yet been decided. Thus, the lack of an existing judicial sanction is not evidence that a fundamental right does or does not exist.

The court could have afforded a judicial sanction. Fundamental rights include life and liberty. What causes an individual to lose life or liberty at any point in history may differ from what causes a person to lose life or liberty at another point in history. There is no reason to believe that, historically, humans would knowingly consent to losing their life by getting cancer from a polluted environment or from radiation. The court missed the fundamental principle that a person has a right to life and liberty. It is the life and liberty that are subject to constitutional protection, regardless of whether the cause of the loss by another has been before an earlier court.

In 2007 in *Retained by the People,* Professor Farber lists factors he believes could guide Courts in determining whether a right is fundamental, worth of protection under the Ninth Amendment:

> • "Supreme Court precedent establishing the right or analogous rights;"
>
> • "Connections with specific constitutional guarantees;"
>
> • "Long-standing, specific traditions upholding the right;"
>
> • "Contemporary societal consensus about the validity of the right;"
>
> • "Decisions by American lawmakers and judges recognizing the right;"

- "Broader or more recent American traditions consistent with the right;"

- "Decisions by international lawmakers and judges recognizing the right."

The Justinian Code

The Justinian Code is ancient. In 2015, Professors Blumm and Wood report in *The Public Trust Doctrine in Environmental and Natural Resources Law,* that it was codified "under the reign of the Roman Emperor Justinian between 529 and 534 A.D." The Institutes of Justinian, as the Code is formally called, was based upon an earlier, second century work that codified the natural law of Greek philosophers. "Ancient in their own right, as well as a recodification of even more ancient law, the Institutes of Justinian remain the touchstone of today's public trust doctrine." From the Justinian Institute Book II:

> "By the law of nature these things are common to all mankind – the air, running water, the sea, and consequently the shores of the sea."

Blumm and Wood continue, "Roman civil law eventually influenced the jurisprudence of all Western European nations. Most important to American jurisprudence, Roman civil law was adopted in substance (with modifications) by English common law after the Magna Carta.... From England to the American colonies, through the American Revolution to the 13 original states, tempered by the United States Constitution and the evolution of modern society, the public trust doctrine survives in the United States as 'one of the most important and far reaching doctrines of American property law.'"

What right could be more basic, more fundamental to each of us than the right we share with all of life to the air we breathe and to the water we drink? Air and water are basic to all of life. Certainly, these rights are more fundamental than marital privacy.

But our common rights to clean air and unpolluted water are being damaged, being trespassed on to our detriment by our political branches of government, particularly the executive branch. Special interests, led by the fossil fuel industry, have *colonized the atmosphere with pollution*. The colonizing has been not only with the blessings of our government, but by its promotion and financial incentives. Many of the executive branch's administrative environmental law rules and regulations are written and enforced to enhance the fossil fuel businesses to the detriment of the health and welfare of each of us. The pollution of our air also heats the atmosphere, creating health problems for all of life. In addition, the heated atmosphere acidifies and heats the oceans and the other waters of the earth, polluting them and endangering life dependent upon the waters, including the life of every human.

Professor Susana Borràs writes in her 2019 "Colonizing the atmosphere: a common concern without climate justice law?" "In the new 'Age of the Anthropocene', the Earth's atmosphere, like other elements of Nature, is rapidly being colonized by a minority of the world's population, at no cost, threatening the security of all humanity and the stability of the planet." Greenhouse gas emitters, she continues, have transferred humanity's costs, environmental and social, of their polluting atmospheric emissions, to "all the world population, especially the most impoverished ones." She warns that the failure of governments to meet their responsibilities to face up to climate change risks to protect their people is a threat to humanity's rights, including their present and future rights to a "healthy environment, the right of self-determination and even the right to life itself."

Our Constitution assigns no specific responsibility to our government regarding the environmental duties Borràs writes about. However, our Declaration includes our right to "life" as fundamental; and many of our laws, like the Clean Air Act, provide a framework for positive government action.

Our rights to the air we breathe and the water we drink, articulated and settled centuries ago in the Justinian Code, are fundamental. These rights are rooted in the history of humankind on all continents, shaping English and American common law as well as the laws of other nations. These rights clearly predate the Constitution. These rights are the most basic and important of all our unenumerated rights; and no one can deny the absolute necessity of healthy air and water.

Our right to air and water expressed in the ancient Justinian Code, and carried to our time in the common law, satisfies Farber's "long standing tradition" standard for Ninth Amendment protection. The right to air and water also meet his "contemporary societal consensus" standard, reflected in several United Nations reports, including its *Report of the Secretary-General on the 2019 Climate Action Summit*, America's periodic climate assessments, including our federal government's 2018 *Fourth Climate Assessment*, and in contemporary Gallup and Pew polls, in which two-thirds of Americans express concern about our environment and the lack of government protective action. Furthermore, as we observed in Chapter 5, there has been a small but growing body of international laws and judicial decisions meeting Farber's international standard, supporting the proposition that governments have a responsibility to protect the environment.

Thus, I am convinced that federal courts should be willing to opine that our right to clean air and unpolluted water is fundamental, unalienable, unenumerated, natural rights, within the meaning of the Declaration of Independence and the Ninth Amendment. Under our limited form of government, our federal courts should also be willing to confirm that our Tenth Amendment requires that our political branches of government face up to their support of the fossil fuel industry's colonizing our atmosphere and our waters with greenhouse gas emissions. We have a fundamental right to livable air and water that we share with all of life.

As if in confirmation of my conclusions, in his 2016 "Notes for the Next Constitution," Bradford Hatcher wrote about the Ninth Amendment's inclusion of unenumerated rights: "Will a federal court allow this? *A federal court does not even have a right to question this.* [emphasis added] A court has no rights – it only has a limited set of delegated powers.

Neither can a court look to its government's constitution as the source of the rights of the people. It is simply the instrument by which the rights of the people are secured. It is only the source of the government's delegated powers, granted for the purpose of protecting the rights of the people."

For those among us of the Justice Bork or Justice Scalia mindset, that no right exists worthy of constitutional protection if it is not stated in specific words and phrases in the Constitution, the following instructions given at the Constitutional Convention on July 26, 1787 by Edmund Randolph are illuminating:

> "In the draught of a fundamental constitution, two things deserve attention: 1. To insert essential principles only, lest the operations of government should be clogged by rendering those provisions permanent and unalterable, which ought to be accommodated to times and events; and 2. To use simple and precise language, and general propositions...."

With an understanding of the principles envisioned by our Founding Fathers, Abraham Lincoln envisioned the Declaration of Independence as our *Golden Apple*, framed by the silver of the Constitution. The Golden Apple's message, and the purpose of our Constitution envisioned by the Framers, is that our national government was formed to protect our Declaration's unalienable rights, stated and unstated. Unalienable rights are not those granted by the generosity of the majority, the whims of politicians or approval of the lobbyist with the highest bid. Nor are they limited to the written words of the free world's shortest Constitution. Unalienable means unalienable, worthy of defense by our judiciary system.

> *Will the Supreme Court's holdings confirm that it is the guardian of our unalienable rights, or will the Court continue to defer to the political branches on rights cases, regardless of the adverse effect deference has on our rights?*

A positive answer most likely will take the continued tenacity of gutsy kids and organizations like Our Children's Trust, followed by a series of dissenting opinions that ultimately become the law of the land, as dissenting opinions for other rights have in the past.

But, most of all, for the Supreme Court to reach its rights-protecting destiny envisioned by our Founders, it will require public influence, a strong, continuing message from the people: the subject of Chapter 10.

Part III

The Engaged Court & The Voice of the People

> *We must never forget that it is a constitution we are expounding . . . intended to endure for ages to come, and consequently, to be adapted to the various crises of human affairs.*
>
> John Marshall, Chief Justice
> McCulloch v. Maryland, 1819

Chapter 9 – The Engaged Court

We closed our discussion of natural rights with how things are, not how they ought to be. Our goal in this chapter and Chapter 10 is more ambitious. In our framing chapter, *The Problem*, we concluded that a substantial change in the way we are operating our government [through executive branch administrative agencies] is highly unlikely in today's political complexity. We also faced up to the unlikelihood of an operational change that veers away from our dependency on the fourth branch of government, the administrative state. These continuing factors place an extremely high responsibility on the Supreme Court to assert itself and fulfill its political branch checks and balances responsibilities, particularly in protecting the natural and constitutional rights of people. Furthermore, the increased political complexity of government and its vastness prevents even the most knowledgeable people from grasping the full understanding of the workings of our government. In his 2019 *The Conservative Sensibility,* George Will points out that this political opaqueness is another reason for a strong judiciary.

Chapter 2, *Our Constitution,* closed with:

Solutions to the issues brought on by our societal morphing into a Democracy of Dollars will have to be accomplished by assertive public influence, the subject of Chapter 10. Solutions will make progress when, because of that influence, the third branch of government – the "politically independent" Supreme Court and the federal judiciary – becomes hands-on sensitive to today's Democracy of Dollars, and how its context has stripped the American people of key constitutional rights that our Framers confirmed are reserved to us, the people.

The Court must not continue as the handmaiden of the political branches of government. The Court must affirm the rights of the people. That is its prime constitutional responsibility.

The 21st Century Court: Standing on the Shoulders of the Marshall Court

What is the ideal constitutional role for the Supreme Court and the rest of the judicial branch? Consider Archibald Cox's questions raised in Chapter 7:

"What role should the judicial branch play in the government of American people?

"Should the court play an active, creative role in shaping our destiny, equal with the executive and legislative branches?

"Or should it be characterized by self-restraint, deferring to the legislative branch whenever there is room for policy judgment and leaving new departures to the initiative of others?"

Cox points out, and this book confirms, that the Court's deference and restraint produce failure for the people and our democracy. Judicial deference is a loud "no" answer to aggrieved individuals entitled to a judicial remedy. However, the Court does not have to assume the activist role suggested by Cox's questions as the alternate. The activist role occupied the Warren Court when I was in law school. It is the Court Cox wrote about in *The Warren Court.*

Although the Court may not have to assume an activist rule akin to the role of the Warren Court, the Court must assume an *engaged role* sensitive to our times. In the *Preface*, I advocated that the Supreme Court must become sensitive to context, to today's Democracy of Dollars and the rapid political, cultural, and societal changes occurring in the 21st Century. If the Court's role is to be successfully changed from producing a "no" when it should produce a "yes," enhanced sensitivity requires the Court be less bogged down by what Friedman calls in his 2009 *The Will of the People,* the "phonograph theory of judicial function." The phonograph theory criticizes judges for basing their decisions on nothing more than replaying existing legal precedents as if they were infallible. Similarly, the Court's deference to the political branches is replayed time after time as if the Court had no responsibility to look deeply into Friedman's "hard facts on the ground," or consider the results of the Court's deferral on our constitutional democracy or the people.

The time has come for the Court to abandon its phonograph approach when it comes to the application of its judge-made rules of deference. The Court must assert the defining problem-solver role the Court occupied in the past, as it did for 34 years, beginning in 1803 – during the era of the Marshall Court. As the Marshall Court accomplished during the early beginnings of our republic, today's Court must accomplish in the 21st Century.

Our Founders had no intention to freeze us in the past. Our Founders created a Constitution of principles to last through the ages. The idea of replaying legal precedents as if they were the only phonograph recordings worth playing was far from their minds. John Marshall was clear about that. In 1819, he opined in *McCulloch v. Maryland,* that the Constitution is: "intended to endure for the ages to come, and consequently, to be adapted to the various crises of human affairs. To have prescribed the means by which Government should, in all future time, execute its powers would have been to change entirely the character of the instrument and give it the properties of a legal code."

The Constitution our Framers created was for them and their "Posterity." We are the Framers' posterity. We have the same responsibility to care not only for ourselves but for our posterity.

The Marshall Court was a problem-solver of first impression problems – defining the judicial branch's requirements within our new constitutional government, clouded by conflicting political considerations and factions. The Marshall Court created new precedents. Precedents necessary to strengthen our infant, unseasoned Constitution. Precedents that confirmed the Court's authority to provide judicial reviews and to decide whether the actions of the two political branches were constitutional. Precedents that were perceptive enough to survive the political tensions of Marshall's time and were so well-reasoned that many remain the *stare decisis* of today.

The problem-solver defining role of the Marshall Court created the tools the Court needed to fulfill its checks and balances responsibilities in the context of its day. The Supreme Court of the 21st Century can also be a Marshall-type problem-solver. We live in an era of problems clouded by political considerations and factions, not only as they existed during the early days of the Marshall Court, but as they exist today in our Democracy of Dollars.

Today's problems – the marginalization of our rights while favoring the wishes of special interests – have incubated over several decades. They have become insufferable. They have not been adequately addressed by the Court. The Court's mechanical deference has left these problems in the hands of the two political branches of our government. These problems remain unsolved and will never be solved while we are a Democracy of Dollars operating without the Court's insistence that the political branches respect the rights of individuals.

Thus, these unsolved 21st Century-problems are essentially judicial problems of first impression, problems that require a problem-solving approach that stands on the shoulders of the Marshall Court.

An engaged role requires the Court to reconsider the utility of many of its judge-made rules; in particular, the rules we discuss in this book. The role will require the Court to revise, or create new, check and balance rules for this era, solid enough to minimize the damaging impact on our rights by today's Democracy of Dollars. We have pointed out that judge-made rules of deference are neither fixed by written laws nor mandated by our Constitution. These rules are like the common law, shaped by judges out of necessity by experience. Thus, like the common law, these rules can change interstitially, as experience dictates. Stare decisis is a consideration, but the cold, hard facts of today must prevail when rights are trampled on by a political branch of government.

As pointed out, there is early movement in the direction of change, reflected in Justice Gorsuch's comments on a few of the judge-made rules: the "intelligible principle" and the Chevron Doctrine and its related rules. These rules relate to the Court's deference to Congress's over-delegation of law-making authority to executive branch administrative agencies. Of course, enhanced sensitivity to the hard facts on the ground and a focus on problem-solving will require the Court to change these judge-made rules. Doing so should be helpful in minimizing the influence of special interests and their lobbies and slow the revolving door between the regulated and the regulating agencies.

However, an engaged Court must look further, into other judge-made rules of deference. Specifically, the Court must reconsider its Political Question and Standing Doctrines. These two doctrines deny judicial review to aggrieved individuals whose rights are damaged by a political branch of government unwilling to change its conduct without judicial nudging. Blind reliance on the precedent of these judge-made rules, designed in and for another era, simply does not provide a solution. The Court's sensitivity-problem-solving priority must include its revamping these two judge-made rules, the most dangerous to human rights.

New and revised judge-made rules required will not take us outside the pages of our Constitution. Rather, they will confirm the reason we have a Constitution and formed a new government, expressed by Thomas Jefferson in the Declaration of Independence. Do not fear. The Court will not become a pseudo-legislative branch nor a pseudo executive branch. But the Court's checks and balances will minimize the legislative and executive branches straying beyond the Constitution's grant of authority as they are doing today.

The above conclusions in no way remove the responsibilities for us to be informed, active, and concerned citizens. Remember, Madison wrote in 1788 in Federalist Papers #51:

> "A dependence on the people is, no doubt, the primary control on the government; but experience has taught mankind the necessity of auxiliary precautions."

The Engaged Court, Madison's "Auxiliary Precautions"

Yes, Madison and political philosophers have pointed out that democracy is dependent on the people. But, as we have pointed out in this book, experience teaches us that Madison was also right when he wrote that we need auxiliary precautions. The auxiliary precaution we need is an engaged Supreme Court.

The engaged Court supplies our needed auxiliary precautions by providing judicial review, discarding its deference to the two political branches when a branch is the culprit.

We do not need a Supreme Court that is a creative activist operating outside the Constitution, as championed by some progressives. Nor do we need a Supreme Court that is a restrained literalist tied to the past while ignoring the context of the present, as championed by some conservatives. We need a Supreme Court that is engaged, honoring the Constitution and Lincoln's *Golden Apple,* the Declaration of Independence. We need a Court that is deeply aware of, and responsive to, the context of the 21st Century and the undue influence of special interests and their lobbies on the political branches, to the detriment of the people.

An engaged Court has as its objective keeping the political branches within their constitutional framework, while securing our rights. An engaged Court focuses not only on the rights specified in our Constitution, but on the Ninth Amendment's unenumerated rights, which should not be interfered with by our government.

An engaged Court has a methodology. It's probative, backgrounded not only with the history of the Constitution, but responsive to today's context and how the Court's determinations affect our rights in practice.

An engaged Court is less dependent on immutable, mechanical judge-made rules of deference, like the Political Question Doctrine and its Baker Factors or the Standing Doctrine and its redressability. Professor Daniel Farber wrote in his 2007 *Retained by the People:* "Good constitutional decisions involve neither the mechanical application of formal rules nor the freewheeling ways of pure politics. They rely instead on judgement and discretion, which by definition incorporates both flexibility and constraints."

The process also requires, as President Theodore Roosevelt put it in his 1908 "Eighth Annual Message" *to Congress*, "a full understanding and appreciation of the new conditions to which the rules are to be applied. What would have been an infringement upon liberty half a century ago may be a necessary safeguard of liberty today."

Today's Democracy of Dollars differs dramatically from that of a Democracy of the People, the republic our Founders founded for themselves and their posterity when the Constitution was adopted in 1789. The Court cannot overlook that factor when it defers to a political branch for a theoretical solution, a solution that in the real-world injured persons are never going to get.

Why? The influence of special interests and their lobbies are too powerful. Among the many examples available, consider:

> According to a 2019 Pew poll, a large majority of Americans think we need stricter gun laws. Public support for tougher gun laws increased to 60% from 52% in just two years. In the wake of the 2018 Florida Parkland mass shooting in which 49 people were killed, President Trump said that it's time for gun control, and he'd work with Congress. But then, the chief executive officer of the N.R.A. called Trump directly. Following that very personal call from a hefty political supporter and lobbyist, Trump changed his mind — without any discussion with the Parkland families who lost their children to gun violence. After the N.R.A. talk, gun controls were no longer on his agenda or the agenda of his political party. Trump's comments, reported by the New York Times, August 2019 in "N.R.A. Gets Results on Gun Laws in One Phone Call with Trump": "A lot of people that put me where I am are strong believers in the Second Amendment, and I am also."

Is the Court both Independent and Political?

The Supreme Court was architected in our Constitution to be independent, shielding judges from the pressures of politics by providing them with lifetime appointments. In 1788 in Federalist Papers #78, Hamilton saw the Court as independent, but he also saw the judiciary as the least powerful of our three branches of government. As Chapter 3 pointed out, the Court lacks power over the purse of the government. Furthermore, the Court has no direct enforcement mechanism for its decisions.

Thus, the opinions of the Court cannot stray too far from the mainstream thoughts and feelings of the people if they are going to have the impact intended.

The separation of the Court from the other branches of government was viewed by the Framers as essential. In Federalist Papers #78, Hamilton wrote, "For I agree, that 'there is no liberty, if the power of judging be not separated from the legislative and executive powers.' And it proves, in the last place, that as liberty can have nothing to fear from the judiciary alone, but would have everything to fear from its union with either of the other departments; that as all the effects of such a union must ensue from a dependence of former on the latter, notwithstanding a nominal and apparent separation, that as, from the natural feebleness of the judiciary, it is in continual jeopardy of being overpowered, awed, or influenced by its co-ordinate branches; and that as nothing can contribute so much to its firmness and independence as permanency in office, this quality may therefore be justly regarded as an indispensable ingredient in its constitution, and, in a great measure, as a civil doll of the public justice in the public security."

In this 21st Century, as pointed out, the Court is seated too closely in "union" with the two political branches, particularly with the executive branch.

The Court's Political Significance as an Institution

In "Decision-Making in a Democracy: The Supreme Court as National Decision Maker," Yale Professor Robert A. Dahl wrote in 1957, "To consider the Supreme Court of the United States strictly as a legal institution is to underestimate its significance in the American political system."

The Supreme Court is petitioned with about 7,000 requests to hear cases each year. From the thousands of requests, it typically hears 100-150 cases. Year after year, among the few cases it selects to hear, the Court is called upon to decide cases of human rights where the Constitution provides no clear answer. Dahl points out that most of these cases involve controversial questions about alternatives — questions about abortion, gun control, segregation, or the reach of economic regulation. The setting for the Court's consideration of these kinds of issues is always political.

Dahl adds, "Moreover, they are usually cases where competent students of constitutional law, including the learned justices of the Supreme Court themselves, disagree; where the words of the Constitution are general, vague, ambiguous, or not clearly applicable; where precedent may be found on both sides; and where experts differ in predicting the consequences of the various alternatives or the degree of probability that the possible consequences will actually ensue."

The most difficult decisions of the Court are policy decisions. Policy decisions are more than legal decisions. Policy decisions always have political overtones. The difficulty Dahl grasps is the reason that Adams and Jefferson – close friends who played major roles in the founding of our country – argued over the meaning of the Constitution and whether the policy of the government should be to provide a strong, active central government, or a weaker, less active central government, focused more on the varied activities of the states. It's the reason that political parties were formed during Adams' presidency to argue that philosophical difference. It's the reason Marshall's *Marbury* decision was artfully crafted to not offend the political party in power, while successfully mapping the validity of judicial review and the Court's future. It's the reason that the Supreme Court ultimately approved Franklin Roosevelt's New Deal legislation. The New Deal program increased the responsibility of the national government to be solution-oriented for America's desperate people. It's the reason behind the Warren Court's *Brown v. Board of Education* ruling that separate but equal education facilities as a constitutional principle was racist and should be abandoned.

Early in Ronald Reagan's presidency, conservative law students at Yale formed the Federalist Society, in protest to the activism of the Warren Court, supporting a return to a more fundamentalist interpretation of the Constitution. By the time Reagan's second term began, more than half of the Justice Department employees were members of the Society. Barry Friedman reports in his 2009 *The Will of the* People that Ed

Meese, Reagan's Attorney General, spoke at the July 1985 meeting of the American Bar Association, touting the idea that the Constitution must be interpreted by "a jurisprudence of original meaning."

In his speech, Meese said, "The Court is what it was understood to be when the Constitution was framed – a political body. The judicial process is, at its most fundamental, a *political process."* Meese explained that the Court was the place "wherein public deliberations occur over what constitutes the common good understood under the terms of a written Constitution." Reagan's Justice Department prepared an originalist handbook, which Friedman says contained "Orwellian doublespeak," in its asserting that the Constitution remains timeless and fixed, though its provisions could be applied in ways to meet the evolving, changing circumstances of the American society. Friedman concludes that originalism has the same problem as does activism. It allows judges interpretive leeway.

The fictions we live by, that the Court is exclusively legal and that the Constitution's original meaning is easily ascertainable, lie behind the interpretive principle of originalism. If the sole source of the Court's challenging constitutional rights decisions were based strictly on originalism (if such a source can be discovered), without room for judicial interpretation based on our nation's evolving cultural and historical context, the Court's decisions would be sterile. The Court's decisions would provide meaningful and useful answers to but a few of the conflicting policy-related questions the Court must resolve. Could the late Justice Scalia – the champion of originalism – have opined that a person's rights to carry guns include AR-15 semi-automatic rifles, when the only rifles the Framers could have been considering were single shot, front-loaded muskets, if his decision was solely based on originalism?

And why did Scalia's selection of his supporting facts overlook a prime reason behind the Second Amendment when he wrote his opinion about the constitutionality of carrying guns? History tells us that the prime reason the Second

Amendment was included in the Constitution was because the southern states were in fear of the northern states' antislavery positions. Southern states had militias with guns to catch runaway slaves, and they didn't want the northern states to be able to legislate that right away from them. So, they insisted on the Second Amendment to protect their slave-catching rights. Scalia's decision was a decision of policy, and, as we all do, he selected facts and utilized interpretations that supported the policies that he and four other conservative justices agreed should apply. Those policies, however, were influenced by the discussions between the Court's nine judges, which included four different-thinking liberal judges who wrote dissenting opinions. The result: The decision did not take away the right of governments to regulate gun control and was closer to being in sync with the voice of the people, had the Court not had diversity.

The Importance of 5-to-4 Court Decisions

In a dissent, Oliver Wendell Holmes once wrote, that our Constitution "is made for people of fundamentally differing views." In today's contentious politics, when life's blessings are distorted by insistence that "I am always right and you are always wrong," it's easy to overlook the power of sharing and gaining from each other because of our differences. Our creator didn't make about a third of us conservatives, a third of us liberals, and the balance of us independents without reason. Working out solutions by compromising among differing viewpoints is not only healthy, it's what makes a problem-solving democracy work. Policy decisions always involve a variety of beliefs and opinions. It is for that reason that a balanced court is essential for a diverse population. Five to four decisions flush out responsible decisions much better than a Court of like-minded judges with the same political leanings could ever do.

Without the give and take in judicial decision making, decisions become groupthink decisions, poorly thought out, too frequently unquestioned and not reexamined. Groupthink discourages creativity and individual responsibility. Groupthink decisions are fatal in the boardrooms of corporations, in the executive offices of business and government, and in the ivory tower of the Supreme Court.

The Bay of Pigs fiasco during the Kennedy administration and the Gulf Wars during the Bush administration provide studies in groupthink – a way of thinking every organization and government should avoid. Extreme loyalty and like-thinking do not produce sound decisions. In Chapter 7, we pointed out that Washington and Lincoln, our two greatest Presidents, chose cabinet members with differing views so that their efforts as President could better serve our nation. Each sought out the give-and-take and different views of their cabinet members. Each was a good listener. Serving our vast diversity can never be accomplished by political homogeneity, certainly never in the Supreme Court charged with being the fiduciary for all the people.

Shifting Court Balance

Balancing a court means that sometimes 5-to-4 decisions are conservative, sometimes liberal, and sometimes mixed. Unwillingness to accept the value of the give and take, so important for sound decision making, is the reason Vice President Mike Pence expressed his disappointment in Chief Justice Roberts joining liberal judges in several 2020 decisions, including abortion and LGBTQ rights. Pence saw the conservative administration's appointments of judges as the creation of lifelong unelected political allies who could amend the Constitution by distorted judicial opinions favoring his politics. He sees their decisions as group-think decisions, reflecting the unquestioning judicial loyalty to his political party over the responsibility of the Court to all the people. He misses the point that sound judicial policy tuned to the voice of the people requires judgment that goes beyond political party affiliation. Judicial independence provides judges, regardless of their political leanings, with the opportunity to reflect on our country's evolving spectrum of values and requirements. That makes for one of the Court's most vital checks and balances tools.

Mitch McConnell, the Republican majority head of the Senate, also misses the point that balance is healthy for democracy. When Obama was President, he nominated Merrick Garland, a highly qualified person, to the Supreme Court. McConnell refused to schedule confirmation hearings. He expressed a goal of "permitting" the next president to decide, since Obama was in his last year.

A Court of judges with close ties to a party in power does not represent the people any more than Congressmen elected by gerrymandering do. However, McConnell's approach does have the potential to enhance the power of his political party and the special interests it favors.

Similar court packing took place during the late 1800s, the Gilded Age. Barry Friedman tells us in his 2009 *The Will of the People,* that during this growth period of the country following the Civil War, moneyed interests, particularly the railroads, were interested in the Supreme Court and federal judiciary blocking states "interfering" with their expansion.

As a result, "moneyed interests withheld contributions to the Republican Party desperately needed to ensure Garfield's victory in the 1880 election until they were assured Garfield would put the right men on the court." He appointed Rutherford Hayes, who had close ties to the railroad industry. Hayes won Senate approval by one vote. For the next two decades, "businesses got the judges it wished." That's why the Court decided that corporations were persons with federal court access and many of the constitutional rights designed for individuals, as I pointed out in the *Preface*.

However, this strong-arm approach to manning the Court to reflect the will of business was ultimately replaced by Franklin Roosevelt's strong-arm version during the Great Depression of the 1930s, with the Court ultimately reflecting an entirely different set of beliefs. The right to judicial review of state laws and court decisions that interfered with interstate commerce was well established in the Gilded Age.

In the 1930s, the Court's conservative judges' judicial reviews blocked New Deal legislation. Their judicial review became a thorn in Roosevelt's plans for national recovery. Businesses championed judicial review to preserve their freedom from the interference of social laws, like minimum wages and work hours, and unions and employee benefits. The people suffering through the depression, in need of solutions, saw it differently. The Court's judicial review was seen as nine old men interfering with the will of "100 million people." As Friedman put it in *The Will of the People,* judicial reviews provided business's salvation from "the passions of the people."

Critical of the Court, Roosevelt said in his 1936 campaign address, "The Nation looked to Government, but the Government looked away." Despite the pressures of business lobbying and publicity campaigns, Roosevelt won the election in a landslide. The people had lost faith in the judiciary that blocked Congress's efforts to provide relief to suffering multitudes during the Great Depression. The voice of the people backing Roosevelt ultimately influenced the opinions of the Court. The Court reversed itself and began to support New Deal legislation.

Over the decades, with our government alternating between liberals and conservatives being in charge, the appointment of judges should achieve a reasonable balance. Based on judges' retirements and deaths, a president typically appoints one or two judges during a four-year term. Appointed judges reflect the views of the President making the appointment. To reflect the voice of a diverse people, balance over time is essential. Both packing the Court and the Senate's refusing to confirm justices that are politically aligned with the President when the Senate is controlled by a different political party does a great disservice to our country. Either party picking judges based on their political party leanings, while minimizing in-depth consideration of their legal competency, also does a great disservice to our country.

However, the constitutional system which delegates appointment of judges to the President, and confirmation responsibility to the Senate cannot escape its political overtones. Nor can it escape the humanity of judges, who like the rest of us, have value systems, including moral and political beliefs that shape their conduct and decisions. The constitutional system balances and controls these effects through periodic replacement of judges by Presidents from different political parties. Politics distorts the process through packing the courts with judges of a like mind with the party in power while discarding the interests of people with differing political views.

Beliefs, Policy Decisions and Judge-Made Rules

Policy questions are frequently involved in the Court's decision regarding whether one of its judge-made rules applies in a case or controversy. The decision whether a judge-made rule applies is a product of judicial belief as much, if not more, than it is a product of factual analysis and the inflexibility of the Constitution. If that were not true, the two gerrymandering cases we presented in Chapter 6, *Baker* and *Rucho,* would not have come to opposite conclusions about the application of the Political Question Doctrine. The Warren Court saw the doctrine as not applying to a gerrymander in *Baker*. The Roberts Court in *Rucho* concluded that it did. Neither decision was unanimous. Baker had two dissents. Rucho had four dissents. If you added the differing views from lower court judges, the judicial decisions probably ended in ties.

The irony of the two decisions, as pointed out in Chapter 6, is that *Baker* enjoyed strong public support while *Rucho* lacked public support, though it had political support that criticized *Baker. Rucho* had the support of the in-power, political "elite," as Professor Dahl called it in his 1957 "Decision-Making in a Democracy: The Supreme Court as National Decision Maker."

In coming to their differing conclusions, each Court relied on facts that supported the conclusions of the Court's judicial majority. In Chapter 6, we touched briefly on the moral foundations, the belief systems that we employ to make our decisions. How we feel and think about one or more of the six moral foundations affecting us, and the decision we are contemplating, influences the facts we rely on in making our choices. Our factual choices support the moral foundations we prioritize. (Think Scalia and AR-15s.) Rarely is this a conscious decision. We believe first, and then "rationally" select facts that support our beliefs.

When decision-making, Judges are like the rest of us, except judges use the structures of legal syllogisms to organize their facts with the cloak of irrefutability. In his 1894 Harvard Law Review Article, Justice Holmes wrote the illusion of certainty in legal syllogisms "made legal reasoning seem like mathematics."

In this book, we have discussed how politics induces instability in the fourth branch of our government, the administrative agencies. Executive agency heads and agency policies change as political leaders and their policies shift from election to election. Although each party diligently does its best to preserve its power, with our nation balanced between liberals, conservatives, and independents, the idea of perpetual power for either political party is not realistic, nor would it be wise for our nation with its diversity of people and their varied interests and objectives.

We have noted that federal judges, including Supreme Court judges, are appointed by the President, and confirmed by the Senate. Presidents, whether conservative or liberal, select judges with supporting political beliefs. In the long run, this system has the effect of shifting the political balance of the Court over time from liberal to conservative and then conservative to liberal. The change is slow, as judges retire and are replaced. But the change does occur, even after a political party in power does its best to pack the court with political think-a-likes. Furthermore, the lifetime appointments of judges have been helpful in moderating political leanings over time and in confirming a judge's understanding that, for the Court to maintain its strength and influence, the Court's political neutrality must be preserved.

But the influence of underlying political beliefs on policy-related, controversial judicial decisions is obvious in the Court's decisions. Dahl points out that, despite the Court's independence, it is unrealistic to believe that a Supreme Court whose justices are appointed by a President from a pool of like-minded judicial candidates would in the long run approve policies "substantially at odds with the rest of the political elite."

Similar facts were the basis of criticism in Caplan's Phi Beta Kappa magazine article cited in Chapter 7, where we wrote that, "The *American Scholar*, shocked the academic world with its 2015 cover, a picture of the five conservative judges on the Roberts Supreme Court, overlaid with this title: *Company Men: Free Speech Goes to the Highest Bidder*."

Similar facts were also behind Judge Richard Posner's August 1999 sentiments, expressed in his New Republic article, "Appeal and Consent:" He wrote that when the constitutional issue is clear, judicial review is not necessary since any violation of the Constitution would be obvious and would be recognized by the people. But:

> "When the Constitution is unclear, judicial review is likely to be guided by the policy preferences of the judges rather than the Constitution itself.... [C]onstitutional interpretation in doubtful cases (the only cases likely to be litigated) is bound to be creative and discretionary rather than constrained and interpretive."

Judicial Diversity: for Liberals, Conservatives, Independents

Is there no hope to balance and counter judges' personal political bias? There is both hope and reason. Furthermore, the voice of the people, the subject of the next chapter, is of paramount influence.

It is in the interest of conservatives and liberals alike for the Court to reconsider its use of its rules of deference, particularly those rules that deny judicial review to individuals harmed by a political branch of government. The use of judge-made rules which reflect the mindset and the political leanings of the judges making the selection have the potential to produce judicial instability. The instability is not as quick and chaotic as the fourth branch of government experiences with replacement agency heads and changing agency policies with every change in political control. The Court's allegiance to stare decisis does provide stability. Thus, when earlier decisions of the Court conflict with deeply held judicial beliefs of a group of like-minded justices, judicial stability is present when stare decisis is honored. The two gerrymandering cases reflect that sort of instability that can occur over a relatively short period of time, some 4 or 5 decades when stare decisis is ignored.

When the Court, whether its majority be liberal or conservative, decides that the Court should not provide judicial review because of the Court's deference to a political branch, there is no judicial record based on facts for either the Court or the public to consider. There is no give and take between justices with differing points of view as to what is right or wrong. There is no solution.

The individuals injured, whether conservative or liberal, are still injured. In the gerrymandering cases, one was a Republican state injuring Democrats, and the winners were Republicans. In the other state, it was the opposite. That is not a healthy way for the fundamental rights of people to be determined. Voting is not a craps game where the house has loaded the dice. For democracy to thrive, each person must be encouraged to vote and must vote enthusiastically – not fail to vote because of despair.

As Bradford Hatcher put it in his 2016 "Notes for the Next Constitution," "Just as a garden is a better place without monoculture, the world is a better place without homogeneity, provided that we can outgrow our ancient xenophobias."

Without the give and take, and compromise provided by political diversity, our rights run the risk of being squelched from the political philosophy of the party in power, or by the party next in power. Certainly, the alternative to judicial review – deference to the political branches serving special interests before the people – does not faithfully reflect the majority or protect the minority or speak with the voice of the people. Each of us would be better off, and both political parties would be better off, if the Court fulfilled its constitutional purpose by providing judicial review. When the Court comes to that realization, the Democracy of the People can thrive. And the standing of the Court will be Supreme.

The Real World

The discussion just presented is jurisprudential, the way things ought to be. We live in the real world, driven by short-term reasoning and short-term objectives. The result: Political power to shape the here and now has priority.

Today legislation is controlled by the special interests who are happy with delegation by Congress to the executive branch and the Court's minimal interference through its judge-made rules of deference. If the court reactivates judicial review in earnest, there most likely will be a political movement championed by special interest lobbies to block that effort. There was when the tobacco industry opposed smoking bans. There was when the fossil fuel industry opposed pollution controls and clean energy. The buzz words of such a movement would probably be built around the idea that judicial review is the Court's way of stealing the right to decide from the American people. Unfortunately, in the Democracy of Dollars, it is not the voice of the people that prevails.

Ironically, in the Gilded Age, the power of money shaped the appointment of judges favorable to providing judicial review by overturning state laws that conflicted with economic objectives of the railroads and other expanding businesses.

In the 21st Century we have the opposite. Moneyed interests fund reelections that align the political branches of government with the wishes of special interests, regardless of what is best for the American people. 21st Century moneyed interests do not need judicial review to interfere with the system as they did in the Gilded Age. Delegation to the executive branch works well for them. Congress and the White House pretty much do their bidding. Through the swinging door between regulated industries and the regulatory agencies, the White House employs regulated company executives and their lobbyists to lead and operate its administrative agencies. Then, when the door swings back, and the regulatory rules have been shaped to their advantage, the executives and lobbyists return to the prior positions. By its deference, the Court offers little protection for the rest of us. Thus, efforts to increase judicial reviews are met with elitist hostility from those in power. Systemic change is not the friend of those in power.

In 1962, in his *Least Dangerous Branch,* Yale Professor Alexander Bickel described judicial review as "countermajoritarian." When the Court declares a law as unconstitutional, it is acting against the decisions of the people's elected representatives. However, the impact of the growing Democracy of Dollars was not as visible in 1962 as it is today. With today's laws – particularly the offerings of the fourth branch, the administrative agencies – skewed by special interests with little or no input from the people, his concern no longer represents reality. Today, when the Court invalidates congressional or administrative agency actions by judicial review, it is more likely to be expressing the voice of the people rather than opposing it. The tyranny the Court is thwarting is the tyranny of special interests, not the majority. But Bickel's writings have been a strong influence among conservative members of the Supreme Court and scholars who favor judicial deference over judicial review.

Always a political threat by those benefitting from minimal judicial reviews is Article III, Section 2 of the Constitution. That section grants Congress the right to grant exceptions to appellate review. However, over the 230 plus years of our constitutional government, with few exceptions, primarily during the Civil War Reconstruction era, the Court's constitutional grant of authority for judicial review has remained intact. However, threats have been made in recent times, both to the Warren Court and the Rehnquist Court. And during the George W. Bush administration, Congress stripped the Court's authority to hear cases from a Guantanamo detainee through its Military Commissions Act of 2006. The legislation stripped detainees of their right to a writ of habeas corpus —

the right of a detained person to be brought before a court for a hearing on his or her detention. However, a writ of habeas corpus is a basic constitutional right. The Court ruled 5 to 4 that Congress's Act was unconstitutional.

On September 18, 2020 liberal Justice Ruth Bader Ginsburg, the Supreme Court's second woman justice, died. Her death occurring during the final months of the 2020 presidential campaign between Republican Donald Trump and Democrat Joseph Biden raises the question: *Should the Court be "Supreme?"*

Among Trump's campaign promises is his promise to politicize the Court's majority with judges supporting a politically conservative judicial point of view at the expense of all other points of view. He claimed his appointing a conservative judge as Ginsburg's successor before the November 2020 election is vital to his political base. In contrast, Biden championed Senate Majority Leader McConnell's 2016 message, when the Republican-led Senate refused to approve Obama's judicial selection. McConnell then theorized that with the election near at hand, the winning presidential candidate representing the "people's choice," should be able to make the appointment.

A few political commentators and judicial scholars are again debating whether it is appropriate that our government's judiciary branch should hold checks and balances over the legislative and executive branches. They argue that no other democratic nation appoints judges for life and grants them the authority our Constitution endows on the Supreme Court and the federal judiciary.

In a Democracy of People, the people's representatives in government, generally, can be trusted to represent all the people. But in a Democracy of Dollars, an oligarchy where a government of the few operates for the benefit of a privileged few, the same level of trust cannot be validated.

Within a week following Ginsburg's death, three Democrat Congressmen introduced *The Supreme Court Term Limits and Regular Appointments Act.* The proposed bill limits the term of each Supreme Court justice to 18 years. The bill also limits a

President to nominating two justices during a four-year term. Respectful of the Constitution's requirement that justices be appointed for lifetime, the bill provides that after an 18-year term, a justice is classified as "senior." A senior justice then rotates to lower federal courts for the remainder of his or her lifetime. California Congressman, Ro Khanna, one of the bill's sponsors, said, "It would save the country a lot of agony and help lower the temperature over fights for the court that go to the fault lines of cultural issues and is one of the primary things tearing at our social fabric."

For some time, conservative and liberal legal scholars have supported the idea of term limits for justices. Whether the Constitution's lifetime appointment requirement can be met by the proposed judicial rotation is an issue that will have to be decided. But the proposal has merit in the context of today's Democracy of Dollars, which politicizes judicial appointments to secure unelected judges as ultimate political allies, not independent umpires forcing all of us to play by the rules.

Today's politicization has the power to destroy the Court's independence and the usefulness of its constitutional checks and balances. Another question: Will term limits meet Lincoln's concern, expressed in his 1861 first inaugural address? He said:

> "At the same time the candid citizen must confess that if the policy of the Government upon the vital questions affecting the whole people is to be irrevocably fixed by the decisions of the Supreme Court, the instant they are made in ordinary litigation between parties in personal actions, the people will have ceased to be their own rulers, having to that extent practically resigned their Government into the hands of that eminent tribunal."

Lincoln's concerns were considered in a March 9, 1861 New York Times letter to the editor, with NYT's response concluding: "Until the laws are changed in a constitutional manner, as a matter of course, the decisions of the Supreme Court are binding in regard to them."

Regardless of political beliefs, the frailties of our system, political party court packing, term limits or other congressional proposals to rein in the authority of the Court, we must not forget it is the American people that are the intended beneficiaries of our Constitution. Over the decades, the American people have jealously guarded the idea that an independent Supreme Court and federal judiciary are essential as protectors of our natural and constitutional rights, untrampled by politics. Friedman points out in his 2009 *The Will of the People* that the American people see the Constitution as a "problem-solving document." If the Constitution is a problem-solving-document, so must be its three branches of government operating within the scope of their constitutional authority. An independent Court, with justices, though politically appointed, that rises to the occasion and is governed by the Framers' idea that an independent judiciary is where we need to end up is essential.

Judicial Review: Shaping Political Branch Homework

In her October 12, 2020, hearing before the Senate Judiciary, the Supreme Court presidential nominee Amy Coney Barrett vowed to apply the law "as written." She said that she believed that the courts were not designed to solve every problem or right every wrong in our public life." She added, "The political decisions and value judgments of government must be made by the political branches elected by and accountable to the people. The public should not expect courts to do so, and courts should not try."

Her expressions about the role of the Supreme Court and the federal judiciary are like those of Judge Hurwitz in his *Juliana decision.* These views express a "hands off" approach of a conservative Supreme Court. Hands off means less, not more, judicial review.

As we reflect, I wonder how today's conservative court

would have decided *Brown v. Board of Education.* Would black children today have to be satisfied with "separate but equal" education facilities, or would all our education facilities be available to them? Would cruel and unusual punishment still reflect 18th Century standards? Would the Court have decided that marital couples have an inherent right to privacy?

Consider the following from the Supreme Court webpage:

> "The Court and Constitutional Interpretation," includes a discussion of judicial review, including: "Hamilton had written that through the practice of judicial review the Court ensured that the will of the whole people, as expressed in their Constitution, would be supreme over the will of a legislature, whose statutes might express only the temporary will of part of the people. And Madison had written that constitutional interpretation must be left to the reasoned judgment of independent judges, rather than to the tumult and conflict of the political process. If every constitutional question were to be decided by public political bargaining, Madison argued, the Constitution would be reduced to a battleground of competing factions, political passion and partisan spirit."

In 2015 in *Ecolinguistics*, Arran Stibbe reminded us that, "politicians are people too." Although it would be nice to be able to assume that politicians are fulfilling their role of looking after all of us and society, that thought is not realistic. Particularly in today's Democracy of Dollars. There is too much evidence that too many politicians are willing to sacrifice the public good. Stibbe adds, "Policy is not made by a benevolent king but by real people with their own all-too-human desires."

Despite a conservative Court's desire not to set policy, judicial review must play a dominant role. A solid, evidence-driven judicial review requires the political branches to do their homework, justify their actions or inactions, and respect the rights of people our government was formed to protect. Denying judicial review denies people their constitutional right to present the facts and science that demonstrate the wrongs the political branches are charged with correcting. The checks and balances role of the Court is a "fact-checker" role. The Court may not see its role as dictating to the political branches that it must follow a road the Court believes to be a better choice.

But "checks and balances" has a meaning the Court cannot set aside. Checks and balances are intended to be the counterbalancing influences so that no single branch of government can control the government. Without checks and balances, today's Imperial Presidency, linked to special interests, dominates and controls our political lives. We the people are little more than compliant consumers.

Thus, a conservative court has absolutely the same responsibility to each of us that a liberal court would have: It must be an engaged court. An engaged court does not live outside the Constitution. But it assures the political branches don't either, as the political branches do in a Democracy of Dollars.

In 2019 Vanderbilt Law professor Suzanna Sherry pointed out in "A Summary of Why We Need More Judicial Activism," "Judicial review is not judicial supremacy. Judicial review allows courts an equal say with the other branches...." Agreeing with Hamilton and Madison, she writes, "[O]ur constitutional history confirms that the founding generation — the drafters of our Constitution — saw a real need for a strong bulwark against majority tyranny." She defines "judicial activism" as the Court's invalidation of "the government action it is reviewing." She concludes, "Finally, an examination of constitutional *practice* shows that too little activism [too little judicial review] produces worse consequences than does too much. If we cannot assure that the judges tread the perfect middle ground (and we cannot), it is better to have an overly aggressive judiciary than an overly restrained one."

Thus, a conservative Court that minimizes its judicial review role, particularly when political branches cause harm to our fundamental rights, is an abrogation of the Court's fundamental responsibility. The Court, liberal or conservative, must insist the political branches do their homework.

Will the Court Rise to the Occasion?

IIn Chapter 8, we closed our discussion of the Justinian Code and the Ninth Amendment, with the question of whether the Supreme Court would affirm its role as guardian of our unalienable rights. The "oughts" of the law expressed in this chapter, and raised in this book, raise a similar question.

> Will the Supreme Court continue to defer to
> the political branches, or will it mend its ways?

Ultimately, I believe the answer is that somehow the Court will rise to the occasion. But the process will not be quick. It is most likely going to be messy. It will require perseverance of legal advocates and their troubled clients. And the Court's response will be shaped by the voice of the people in the 21st Century as it has been in the past, from the days of the Marshall Court, through Franklin Roosevelt's time and the Great Depression, and later, during the times of the civil rights movement and one of the Court's most important decisions, Brown v. Board of Education.

In August 2020, Our Children's Trust celebrated its tenth anniversary. OCT's *Juliana* case has been in the courts for at least five years, without a hearing on the merits or a final resolution. OCT's anniversary web page includes a message from Alex, one of the gutsy-kid plaintiffs. Alex is now 23. His message: "We're in it for the long haul." That's what it takes: the long-view and perseverance to right an embedded legal wrong.

None of OCT's U.S. cases have yet achieved final, favorable resolution. But that hasn't diminished OCT's resolve, nor the resolve of the gutsy kids, its plaintiffs. OCT is now active in all 50 states and 13 countries. Its efforts are accelerating, not diminishing.

Yet, the courts, federal and state, continue their habits of deference. They deny judicial hearings and reviews. They deny the rights of the youth plaintiffs, which has the effect of supporting the political branches causing their harm. The political branches of government, recipients of the judicial blessings, continue their willful blindness and their favoring of special interests, which contribute to the unconstitutional injury suffered by the youths.

The continued tenacity of gutsy kids – now mostly young adults – and organizations like OCT are necessities if their rights to a healthy environment, clean air and water, are to prevail over the pressures of special interests. As pointed out, their tenacity will most likely be linked to a series of dissenting opinions that ultimately become the law of the land, as dissenting opinions regarding other rights have in the past. The same persistent effort will be necessary to correct the denial of meaningful voting rights that come from gerrymandering. Similarly, dogged tenacity will be essential before the Court gives appropriate recognition to our Ninth Amendment's unenumerated rights which have, for the most part, been unheard.

If the Supreme Court and the rest of the judiciary are to reach their rights-protecting destiny envisioned by the Founders, public influence – a strong, continuing message from the people – will be necessary.

After all, "Judges read newspapers, just like everybody else," Justice Stephen Breyer remarked in a 2015 *92*Y chat with Harvard Law professor Noah Feldman.

And the late Chief Justice William Rehnquist once said, "No judge worthy of his salt would ever cast a vote in a particular case simply because he thought the majority of the public wanted him to vote that way, but that is quite a different thing from saying that no judge is ever influenced by the great tides of public opinion."

Commenting on Rehnquist's remarks, in 2017's *Routledge Handbook of Judicial Behavior*, Peter K. Enns and Patrick C. Wohlfarth, contributing authors, wrote: "Rehnquist's statement underscores the potential importance – analytical challenges – of the study of public mood as a meaning determinant of

Supreme Court decision making.

Although justices' collective policy preferences surely influence Court policy output, as the late Chief Justice suggested, the Court may not be free to ignore the prevailing sentiment of the mass public." Now, to the *Voice of the People*.

Public opinion sets the bounds to every government, and is the real sovereign in every free one.

James Madison, Founder and President

Public sentiment is everything. With public sentiment, nothing can fail; without it, nothing can succeed.

Abraham Lincoln, President

You cannot get through a single day without having an impact on the world around you. What you do makes a difference, and you have to decide what kind of a difference you want to make.

Jane Goodall, Anthropologist

Chapter 10 – The Voice of the People

When We Crow Like a Rooster

In this book, we concentrate our focus on both the importance and the difficulty of our return to be a Democracy of People. We have pointed out that today's Democracy of Dollars is in fact an oligarchy. This oligarchy is the result of the three branches of our government failing in the performance of their constitutional responsibilities. Congress has over-delegated its legislative powers and responsibilities to the executive branch. The Supreme Court and the federal judiciary have, for the most part, stood idly by, deferring to Congress's delegation, and the resultant unfettered power-grab by the executive branch. Today we live in what we have kindly called in Chapter 7 *Era of Presidential Administration*. It is, however, the *Age of the Imperial President* – the age our Framers sought to avoid. A few of the Imperial Presidential powers we have touched on that must be reined in include:

- Presidential appointment of "acting" administrative agency heads, avoiding the constitutional requirement of Senatorial vetting and approval of agency leadership.

- Presidential abuse of Congress's delegation of emergency powers in the pursuit of political objectives unconnected with true emergencies.

- Presidential abuse of executive orders issued to regulate outside the scope of the President's constitutional and statutory authority.

- Presidential shift in the use of funds from programs approved by Congress to programs favored by the President that are not approved by Congress.

- Presidential firing of independent inspector general personnel investigating the executive branch, as intended by Congress, replacing them with political appointees who turn a blind eye to presidential actions that violate executive branch constitutional and statutory authority.

- Presidential appointment of lobbyists and business executives from regulated businesses to regulatory posts in administrative agencies.

- Presidential abuse of the fourth branch of Government, the administrative agencies, changing their purpose from regulation that benefits the people to regulatory waivers and non-enforcement of regulations to favor the regulated.

- Presidential refusal to respect and comply with Congress's oversight responsibilities.

Of course, the list is not complete, nor does it cover every point we discussed in the book. But the list is illustrative.

We also pointed out that it is nearly impossible to change the way our government now operates through its unelected fourth branch. However, we can begin to mitigate the damage. We can limit unfettered delegation by Congress and unfettered deference by the Court. We can reduce the influence of special interests. We can encourage people to vote in federal, state, and local primary and general elections, limiting the election-dominance of extremists. We can, over time, return us to a Democracy of People. We agree with Madison's advice, repeated in this book:

> "A dependence on the people is, no doubt, the primary control on the government; but experience has taught mankind the necessity of auxiliary precautions."

We the people must assert control. But in today's Democracy of Dollars, we cannot do it alone, short of another revolution. The Supreme Court and the federal judiciary fulfilling their checks and balances responsibilities are our "auxiliary precautions," necessary to launch us on our way.

The Court's deference to the political branches when our rights are at stake and a political branch as the offender is, as we pointed out, like Farmer Brown telling his hens to make their peace with the Fox that invaded the henhouse. Obviously, this system is not working, nor is it fulfilling the purpose of our Constitution in the protection of our unalienable rights, as Jefferson wrote in the Declaration of Independence.

Contrary to what is happening in today's Democracy of Dollars, what we need to do is to refocus our government to keep the Fox out of our henhouse. What we need, as Thoreau wrote in *Walden,* is to crow like a rooster to arouse the sleeping among us to action. Kayann Short wrote in her 2015 "Like Roosters":

> "Today, social networking provides roosters more perches from which to crow than in Thoreau's time. That may not make it easier to be a rooster – the risks of raising an unwelcome alarm will always exist – but more roosts means more roosters crowing together about the big things we're facing like climate crisis, violence in communities and nations, and an ever-deepening gap between the have-mores and the have-lesses."

It's when we crow together the voices of the people become the *Voice of the People*, strong and clear enough to exert change. It's when we collaboratively combine our individual efforts that the possibility of change can occur.

Our crowing together can wake up our Court to the reality of the world the Court helped create, the Democracy of Dollars. Pointed out in Chapter 2, solutions will make progress when the third branch of government – the "politically independent" Supreme Court and the federal judiciary – becomes hands-on sensitive to today's Era of Presidential Administration. With that sensitivity, the Court will be able to visualize how this Era's context stripped the American people of key constitutional rights our Framers confirmed are reserved for us, the people.

Barry Friedman's 2009 The Will of the People traces the power of public influence from the days of the Marshall Court into the 21st Century and the Rehnquist Court. The Rehnquist Court preceded today's Roberts Court. Friedman observes that when the Court has ignored public opinion, it has done so at its peril. Only rarely does the Court stray far from mainstream thought.

The Court Wants to Hear Our Voice

Sandra Day O'Connor, a moderate Republican, was

appointed to the Supreme Court in 1981 by Ronald Reagan. She was the first woman appointed to the Court. She received unanimous approval in the Senate. During her 25 years on the Court, she was able to pull together both conservative and liberal court members on a variety of contentious issues. Her 1992 opinion in Planned Parenthood of Southeastern Pa. v. Casey, confirming a women's rights to abortion, based on the fundamentals of the earlier Roe v. Wade abortion rights decision, is perhaps one of her most memorable.

Important to us is the following excerpt from her opinion about the source of the Supreme Court's authority:

> "Our analysis would not be complete, however, without explaining why overruling Roe's central holding would not only reach an unjustifiable result under principles of stare decisis, but would seriously weaken the Court's capacity to exercise the judicial power and to function as the Supreme Court of a Nation dedicated to the rule of law. To understand why this would be so it is necessary to understand the source of this Court's authority, the conditions necessary for its preservation, and its relationship to the country's understanding of itself as a constitutional Republic."

> "The root of American governmental power is revealed most clearly in the instance of the power conferred by the Constitution upon the Judiciary of the United States and specifically upon this Court. As Americans of each succeeding generation are rightly told, the Court cannot buy support for its decisions by spending money and, except to a minor degree, it cannot independently coerce obedience to its decrees. The Court's power lies, rather, in its legitimacy, a product of substance and perception that shows itself in the people's

acceptance of the Judiciary as fit to determine what the Nation's law means and to declare what it demands."

"The underlying substance of this legitimacy is of course the warrant for the Court's decisions in the Constitution and the lesser sources of legal principle on which the Court draws. That substance is expressed in the Court's opinions, and our contemporary understanding is such that a decision without principled justification would be no judicial act at all. But even when justification is furnished by apposite legal principle, something more is required. Because not every conscientious claim of principled justification will be accepted as such, the justification claimed must be beyond dispute. The Court must take care to speak and act in ways that allow people to accept its decisions on the terms the Court claims for them, as grounded truly in principle, not as compromises with social and political pressures having, as such, no bearing on the principled choices that the Court is obliged to make. *Thus, the Court's legitimacy depends on making legally principled decisions under circumstances in which their principled character is sufficiently plausible to be accepted by the Nation.*" [emphasis added]

The Silent People

The voice of the people has been noticeably silent regarding the judicial deference problems we addressed in this book. In his 2009 *The Voice of the People*, Friedman describes the healthy judicial review process as a three-step process: decision, reaction, and, ultimately, correction. Without the reaction of the people, there is less likelihood of meaningful judicial correction.

We have pointed out there have been rumblings against the Court's deference to Congress's delegation of its exclusive constitutional legislative authority to the executive branch. These rumblings by Justice Gorsuch and a few other conservative judges are an early indication that the Court is considering a more active role for judicial review regarding legislative delegation to the executive branch and the power of administrative agencies to set their own, unsupervised course.

Surprising to me, is how the liberal members of the Court seem less inclined to interfere with congressional delegation or administrative rulemaking. This indicates to me that the Court, particularly its liberal members, has not grasped the 21st Century Democracy of Dollars' destructive effect left in the wake of unsupervised political-branch alignment with special interests.

Nor has the Court picked up on the disruptive effect on our democracy of the turnover within administrative agencies brought about by their responding to whatever are the current wishes of the political party in power. The voice of the people has not been heard in this debate about the loss of constitutional checks and balances in any serious fashion.

With the Court's deference to political branches in cases and controversies regarding the rights of individuals damaged by political branch collaboration with special interests, there is also a noticeable silence. The voice in opposition comes from the hark of liberal members of the Court. However, the Court's conservative members seem perfectly content with the Court's deference even when they are aware of the harm to the people. We repeat from Court of Appeals Judge Hurwitz's 2020 opinion in *Juliana*:

> "We do not dispute that the broad judicial relief the plaintiffs seek could well goad the political branches into action..... We reluctantly conclude, however, that the plaintiffs' case must be made to the political branches or to the electorate at large, the latter

of which can change the composition of the political branches through the ballot box. That the other branches may have abdicated their responsibility to remediate the problem does not confer on Article III courts, no matter how well-intentioned, the ability to step into their shoes."

Similar language was written by Chief Justice Roberts in the Supreme Court's Rucho gerrymandering decision. The Court has not accepted the fact that, when it comes to protecting our unalienable rights, the Court is the last bastion of hope for the people. Simply put, the Court's approach is out of touch with 21st Century reality: Deference is the ultimate denial of remedies.

Throughout our history, during stressful times, the people have looked to the Court as the protector of their rights. Chief Justice Marshall grasped that responsibility when he wrote in 1803:

"The very essence of civil liberty certainly consists in the right of every individual to claim the protection of the laws, whenever he receives an injury. One of the first duties of government is to afford that protection."

On this point, this book has shown that the 21st Century Court is failing in its mission. Its ivory-tower, phonograph-like, mechanical deference approach has been devoid of realistic consideration of the context in which its decisions are being made. Borrowing from Theodore Roosevelt in his Eighth Report to Congress, the Court lacks "a full understanding and appreciation of the new conditions to which the rules are to be applied." Paraphrasing Franklin D. Roosevelt's 1936 Madison Square Garden acceptance speech:

The people looked to the Court, but the Court turned away.

Surprisingly, the voice of the people has been but a

whisper, on the tongues of organizations like Our Children's Trust, ACLU and the National Democratic Redistricting Committee, but otherwise nonexistent.

This silence is a concern for each of us.

Building the Movement

America's 2020 Mindset, Ready for Change

Despite the silence, a September 2020 Pew Research Center Poll concludes that the "Majority of Americans say significant changes are needed in the 'fundamental design and structure of American government.'" Of those polled, less than 36% of Democrats and Republicans believe elected officials face serious consequences for misconduct. They also don't believe our government is open and transparent, the tone of political debate is respectful, campaign contributions do not lead to greater political influence, judges are not influenced by politics, or that people agree on basic facts. Pew concludes, "In assessing the state of U.S. democracy, Americans continue to give their country negative ratings for living up to several key democratic ideals and principles." The trend from Pew's 2018 poll is downward. Discomfort with the way things are is higher among the young, those under age 30.

Thus, we don't have to create the moment for change; we are living the moment for change. Americans are ready for a movement that leads us away from today's Democracy of Dollars and returns us to our Democracy of People.

Our Movement's Objective: Reestablish Our Democracy of People

The objectives we seek: Our ultimate objective is to rid ourselves of the Democracy of Dollars and return us to a Democracy of People.

This objective will not be achieved as long as the Supreme Court and federal judiciary defer to the two political branches of government instead of providing judicial review under the circumstances we have described in this book. Achieving our objective will minimize and reverse the damages wrought by today's Democracy of Dollars, putting us on course to reestablish ourselves as a Democracy of People.

The Arc of Change

The Brennan Center for Justice's 2015 report, "Legal Change: Lessons from America's Social Movements," is an anthology, pertinent to our mission. Keesha Gaskins authored the anthology's chapter, A 21st Century Model for Change, which begins: "I would first like to outline the trajectory, or the "arc of change," of a movement. An arc of change must have three elements: (1) a public awakening to a problem, (2) a change in the law or legal parameters, and (3) a cultural and behavioral reformation, where the actions and attitudes by both individuals and institutions change to conform to both the letter and intention of the law. Some arcs are relatively short, others take decades."

Successful movements, Gaskins points out, have historically been "counter-majoritarian, organized around specific goals where populations that constituted a numerical minority sought concessions from the larger power structure." Those strategies most likely will not work in the 21st Century, steeped in diversity, fragmented partisan allegiances and identity politics. The 21st Century challenge is to engage a "significant majority" from a people that is "often politically, socially, and culturally divided."

Gaskins discusses "four distinct challenges for social change movements focused on reforming public policy in the United States today":

1) Harnessing *disruption*: Shifting the current distribution of power from special interests and their lobbies to the people. To reach this objective, Gaskins advises, there must be a "clear demand for meaningful, discrete change."

1) *Maximizing Digital Age Opportunities:* Although the digital age allows movements

without geographic limitations, "policy reform and political infrastructure remain geographically fixed." Thus, successful movements begin decentralized, led bottom-up, even when coordinated top-down. Gaskins also recommends that interested corporations be recruited to "participate in public deliberation." She concludes, "corporations can lead trends," and "push governments."

2) *Elevating Injustice Issues:* Although we touched only lightly on these issues in this book, the evidence points to the fact that racial and cultural minorities are the most frequently injured by the Court's deference. Partisan gerrymandering is tied closely to racism. Climate change and global warming has the most damaging effect on those least able to care for themselves. Gaskins writes, "courts are less sympathetic to cases of historical and structural discrimination or economic inequality that results in unequal opportunity and disparate outcomes." Gaskin adds that the courts' indifference "leaves a significant gap that must be addressed by social movements."

3) *Improving Intergenerational Communication:* There are clearly differences in communication styles between generations. Effective, repeated communication between generations is essential in a movement intended to last. Achieving this result must be "purposeful with clear goals." Thus, the messaging tools and language must be purposefully chosen.

The final chapter in the Brennan Center's anthology is titled *How Does Legal Change Happen?* The authors, NYU law professors, converse about the Court and public opinion. Michael Waldman begins with "you have to win in the court of public opinion before you win in the court." Barry Friedman responds that if we want lasting change, there has to be a "relationship between public opinion and your goals. Nothing you achieve in any form is likely to endure, unless you can bring the public along with you." Helen Hershkoff adds, "The public speaks through multiple voices at different times." To persuade the public, "you need different levers, and you need to secure support along many different channels" to accomplish serious reform in politics or in society.

Do courts make policy? Hershkoff answers, "I think that courts have engaged in policymaking of a first order nature from the beginning, and that this role is consistent with their common law authority. The court shifts policy and directs policy in so many ways..."

The professors then wrestled with the questions about the kinds of organizing and messaging. Kenji Yoshino spoke about the importance of messaging, understanding how the messaging words are perceived by the public and are educating the public "to help individuals understand there is much more similitude than differences [between people]." Friedman adds, "it is important to speak in the public sphere about things that it might not be appropriate to speak about in the court, and yet it's not that courts don't hear it – and in fact, it penetrates." He adds that arguments that start as "off-the-wall" public arguments can become "on-the-wall" legal arguments, concluding that when arguing issues in court, you're arguing in other places, "articulating your positions in ways that appeal to common sensibility."

The Will and Voice of the People: A Myth or a Jazz Band?

The voice of the people embodies the will of the people. In his 2018 *The Will of the People: A Modern Myth*, Albert Weale, emeritus professor of political theory and public policy at University College London, argues that, in these contentious and diverse times, there is no such thing as a unified will of the people. Weale writes: "As a citizen of a democratic country you know you are in trouble when a political party – any political party – claims to embody the will of the people!" After concluding that the idea of a will of the people is myth, he continues, "Paradoxical as it might seem, that view all too often has the effect of putting more power into the hands of the executive." Which, of course, is what deference by the Court does in our Democracy of Dollars – puts the power our Constitution meant to be in the hands of the legislative branch and the judicial branch into the hands of the President. It is the Court's failure to recognize the myth underlying the effects of its deference in these contentious times that is the source of its willing subordination of its responsibilities to the political branches, particularly the executive branch.

Weale concludes that the will of the people is a myth because of the diversity of peoples and the difficulty in finding compatible ways to combine their varying points of view. People are a plurality. And it's difficult to convert "the plural to a single."

In 1957, in "Decision-Making in a Democracy: The Supreme Court as National Decision Maker," Professor Robert A. Dahl wrote, "policy at the national level is the outcome of conflict, bargaining, and agreement among minorities, the process is neither minority rule nor majority rule but what might be better called minorities rule, where one aggregation of minorities achieves policies opposed to another aggregation."

As pointed out in Chapter 2, the United States has been described by Colin Woodard in his 2012 *American Nations: A History of the Eleven Rival Regional Cultures in North America,* as a country that houses eleven different nations, each with different geography, different cultures, different priorities, and differing, fundamental values. The differing cultures, priorities, and values must be compromised within our system of government to assure the ultimate long-term success of what the late Supreme Court Justice Oliver Wendell Holmes called in his 1919 *Abrams v. United States* dissent the American "experiment."

Fundamentally, Woodard's book is about how America functions under Dahl's "minorities rule." When the "minorities rule" prevails, the voice of Weale's "plural" converts to "single." Weale concludes:

> "The voice of the people has to be distilled from the voices of the people. The wills of the many have to become one."

As a metaphor, I think of the voice of the people as being like the music of a New Orleans jazz band, its musicians each engaged in polyphony, improvising separately as if they were solo players, yet syncopating in melodic harmony. However, in the Democracy of Dollars, there is no effective coalition of minorities, as Dahl or Weale envisioned. There is no New Orleans jazz band. There is only disfunction. Our political branches financial lock to special interests blocks out contrary voices. Public interest groups, like Our Children's Trust or ACLU, have no alternative but to turn to the Court for remedies. When that occurs, judicial intervention is a necessity to restore constitutional checks and balances.

Who Speaks for the People?

In Chapter 1, we posed a question that remains unanswered. In today's Democracy of Dollars: *Who speaks for the people?*

When the Constitution was written, the Framers had the objective that Congress, whose House members were elected by the people and Senate members were appointed by state legislative bodies, would speak for the people. In Federalists Papers #10 Madison wrote that the operation of our government, being delegated to a "small number of citizens elected by the rest," refine "and enlarge the public views, by passing them through the medium of a chosen body of citizens, whose wisdom may best discern the true interest of their country, and whose patriotism and love of justice will be least likely to sacrifice it to temporary or partial considerations. Under such a regulation, it may well happen that the public voice, pronounced by the representatives of the people, will be more consonant to the public good than if pronounced by the people themselves, convened for the purpose."

Unfortunately, Madison erred, for our elected representatives have amalgamated themselves with special interests who bought their way to the head of the line. The "wisdom" of our representatives in government is of little value to dispossessed people.

Chapter 6 raised the question, "What is the role of political parties?" The chapter provided the text-book answer: Political parties are "democracy's organizers, simplifying candidate selection and the process of voting." Political parties organize us into groups "with common objectives." However, there is a 21st Century flaw in that reasoning. With but a small percentage of eligible voters participating in primary elections, extremists have come to dominate political party candidates. These extremists do not speak for most of the people. The majority tend to be centrist in their political thinking.

Thus, in our Democracy of Dollars, as long the percentage of people voting remains low, neither Congress nor our political parties represent the will of the people, nor truly speak for the people.

Who will speak for the people?

We must. We can no longer be the silent people. Without a concerned, knowledgeable and active people today's Democracy of Dollars will continue to prevail, and we will never again be a Democracy of People. We must, as Thoreau put it, become roosters crowing for change.

Yes, we each have separate voices. But, the voices of the many must sync for the common good as well as for our individual liberty. We cannot have one without the other. As I wrote earlier in this chapter, we must harmonize our individuality like a New Orleans jazz band. It is that sort of harmonic unity that provides the unity we need to thrive as a nation.

George Washington was clear on that point in his 1796 farewell address, his letter to Congress and the people. He wrote about life's "disorders and miseries" that motivate us "to seek security and repose in the absolute power of the individual; and sooner or later the chief of some prevailing faction, more able or more fortunate than his competitors, turns this disposition to the purposes of his own elevation on the ruins of liberty." The adverse result, Washington reasoned, was to put in place "of the delegated will of the nation the will of a party, often small but artful and enterprising minority of the community; and, according to the alternate triumphs of different parties, to make the public administration the mirror of the ill-concerted and incongruous projects of faction, rather than the organ of consistent and wholesome plans digested by common counsels and modified by mutual interests."

In her "The Road from Serfdom" chapter in *The American Crisis* anthology, Danielle Allen wrote, "In Washington's view, public liberty depended on a process of mutual consultation — adjust the interests of various parties in relation to one another. … Washington believed that the business of government — of 'public administration' — was to get important things done, that getting things done depended on compromise, that compromise was enabled by a commitment to unity, and that deciding what needed to be done required a long view of the public interest."

Allen concluded, "Compromise is what allows us to stay together in the space we share; discard it, and we're all condemned to our own private Bosnias." Politics is not about "the winners make policy and the losers go home" as it is in 21st Century politics. Rather, politics is about the winners deserving "a leadership role" in leading us to the creation of Washington's "consistent and wholesome plans digested by common councils and modified by mutual interests."

In the *Epilogue,* as we address the lessons from the 2020 election and the failed coup d'état, we have more to say about balancing individual liberty and the common good.

Where Our Unfinished Work Begins

A few months ago, I gave a talk to an environmental group in Florida, *On Becoming a Difference Maker*. The talk began with a discussion about the value of "dirty-hands, wet-feet" learning – hands on experiences that convert looking into seeing. The discussion ended with a story about my favorite humanitarian and philosopher, Albert Schweitzer. Schweitzer was also a medical doctor, devoting his life to his mission hospital in Africa. He was a prolific writer. In 1923, he published the first two of a planned four-volume set of books, *The Philosophy of Civilization.* Only the first two volumes were published. When Saturday Review editor Norm Cousins interviewed Schweitzer in the 1960s at his hospital compound in Lambaréné for his biography of Schweitzer, he asked the great man why he never completed his last two volumes. Schweitzer replied simply, *"My life is my argument."*

During the Q & A following my talk, a young lady asked me what specific recommendations I could offer to answer Schweitzer's challenge. I replied that how each of us meets Schweitzer's challenge will be different. We each have different talents and varying interests. What we need to do is link ourselves to causes that mean the most to us, to causes that can value the talents we have to offer. Astronaut Amelia Wren once said, "You don't change the world by looking at it. You change it through the way you choose to live it." We introduced this chapter with Jane Goodall's advice:

> "You cannot get through a single day without
> having an impact on the world around you.
> What you do makes a difference, and you have
> to decide what kind of a difference you want to
> make."

I urge each reader to personally accept Schweitzer's challenge: *My life is my argument.* By so doing, each of us, in some very personal way, becomes involved in returning us to a Democracy of People. By so doing, we will keep the Fox out of our henhouse. Like musicians in a New Orleans jazz band, our individual voices will harmonize with others and will collectively become the *Voice of the People.*

The "Me's" collaborate to become "We." The *We* of *We the People,* the opening stanza of our Constitution. And, together, we crow like a rooster.

I agree to this Constitution with all its faults.... I believe, further, that this is likely to be well administered for a course of years, and can only end in despotism, as other forms have done before it, when the people shall be so corrupted as to need a despotic government, being incapable of any other.

Benjamin Franklin

Constitutional Convention 1787

In the big lie there is always a certain force of credibility; because the broad masses of a nation are always more easily corrupted in the deeper strata of their emotional nature than consciously or voluntarily; and thus in the primitive simplicity of their minds they more readily fall victims to the big lie than the small lie, since they themselves often tell small lies in little matters but would be ashamed to resort to large-scale falsehoods. It would never come into their heads to fabricate colossal untruths, and they would not believe that others could have the imprudence to distort truth so famously.

Adolf Hitler

Mein Kampf 1925

Epilogue

Takeaways from the 2020 Presidential Election and the Failed Coup d'État

Definitions:

Coup d'État: An organized effort to effect sudden and irregular (e.g. illegal or extra-legal) removal of the incumbent executive authority of a national government, or to displace the authority of the highest levels of one or more branches of government. (The University of Illinois Cline Center *Coup D'État Project* definition.)

Insurgency: An active revolt or uprising.

Introduction

I pointed out in the *Preface* of this book that the examples used in the book have, for the most part, been the products of the Trump administration. However, I cautioned that the systemic problems our 21st Century Democracy of Dollars creates for us, the American people, are not, in their fundamentals, the exclusive products of one political party or president. They are fundamental to a contaminated system of government. Both parties have, in their own ways, infected our constitutional democracy over time.

In fact, I had started working on *Democracy of Dollars* before Trump was elected President. However, its writing occurred during Trump's presidency, and his administration provided a fertile ground to illustrate the problems that concerned me.

I completed *Democracy of Dollars* ("DOD") in the late fall of 2020. DOD was scheduled for release in November, about the time of the presidential election. I did not contemplate an epilogue. What happened during the months following the November 3, 2020 presidential election — the false election claims made by the President that the liberal one-third of America, the Democrats, foisted a massive election fraud, thereby stealing the 2020 presidential election from the "rightful winner," Donald Trump, and those Americans who voted for him, which led to the attempted coup d'état aimed at overturning the election — added a challenging context for those among us who take the recommendations we make in Chapter 10, *The Voice of the People*, seriously. Thus, this *Epilogue* became a necessity.

As a result, DOD's release was further delayed, initially until January 20, 2021, the Presidential inauguration day; and later, because of the aftermath of the attempted coup, until Biden was settled in office. These events have warped the context we Americans will operate in as we resuscitate our fragile and damaged democracy.

False claims of a stolen election, preached by Donald Trump dozens of times each day and night during his presidency, particularly in his 2020 campaign and post-election tweets and talks, were accepted by his followers as gospel — driving a saber into our common hearts, severing our country into warring camps, creating wounds not only to our democracy but to our human relationships that could take years to heal.

What happened is more than a harbinger of what could happen. It is a product of the here and now. It is the product of a once proud Democracy of People now driven by conspiracy theories and untruths, overlaid with the power of money. It is the product of our democracy morphing into despotism, as Benjamin Franklin warned us in 1787, at the Constitutional Convention.

It is what happens when we have an *Imperial President* who propagandizes, and as Hitler predicted a century ago in *Mein Kampf*, wins because too many Americans become enamored by his "big lie." Paraphrasing Hitler, the President's lie was too big, and it came from a leader too powerful, for too many of us to think it could be false.

Yes, we all should have recognized that what was being said lacked veracity. But, too many of us were lulled to sleep by Trump's operating behind a comfortable façade touting constitutionalism and democratic ideals — like Make America Great Again, Drain the Swamp, Deconstruct the Deep State[1]. Trump cleverly masked his authoritarianisms, blinding too many of us by claiming his looming coup d'état was just for us.

However, his agenda was not about bettering us, but about his own self-aggrandizement, his usurpation of power and the perks it provided him and his insiders. His prime accomplishments as President did little to match his campaign promises.

In writing about the dangers of an oligarchy led by its Imperial President, I wrote in Chapter 6:

> "In *Madison's Nightmare: How Executive Power Threatens American Democracy*, Peter M. Shane wrote in 2016, '[T]he growing concentration of executive power and the campaign for party predominance have produced an era of aggressive presidentialism, a theory of government and a pattern of government practice that treat our Constitution as vesting in the President a fixed and expansive authority largely immune to legislative control or judicial review.'"

Shane was right on.

Trump proved to be a master in the use of falsehoods to promote himself and his form of "presidentialism." Fact-checkers concluded that in his four years in office he fed us, primarily in tweets, over 30,500 false or misleading claims — an average of 6 claims per day his first year. 16 per day his second year, 22 per day the third year and 39 per day his final year[2]. The irony of the 21st Century's brand of online communication, particularly Twitter and Facebook, is that on the internet, "Falsehood flies, and the Truth comes limping after it," as Jonathan Swift wrote some five centuries ago. After examining 126,000 rumors spread by 3 million people on Twitter over a decade, MIT researchers reported in a Science Magazine study, "The spread of true and false news online:"

> "Falsehood diffused significantly farther, faster, deeper, and more broadly than the truth in all categories of information, and the effects were more pronounced for false political news than for false news about terrorism, natural disasters, science,

urban legends, or financial news…. [H]uman behavior contributes more to the differential spread of falsity and truth than automated robots do."[3]

In Chapter 7, I pointed out that Justice Kagan championed the 21st Century's *Era of Presidential Administration* as a necessity to deal with today's complexities and the leadership expectations of the American people. As Madison was wrong in his assumptions that our Constitution could balance the pressures of factions, Justice Kagan was wrong in assuming that today's Era of Presidential Administration, promoted by excessive delegation from Congress to the executive branch and encouraged by Supreme Court deference, would avoid the pitfalls of a President who became an *Imperial President*.

University of California Law Professor Dan Farber expressed similar, but gentler, sentiments in his January 12, 2021 blog, "Rethinking Presidential Administration." Farber points out, "The President and the higher staff care only about the President's policy and political agendas. From their perspective, the law actually passed by Congress only matters to the extent it might let courts get in the way of those other agendas…. Thus, presidential administration is partly a necessity and partly a good thing. But there can be too much of a good thing, and [the president's] centralized control of regulations is one of them."[4]

Perhaps, Justice Kagan was too idealistic about human nature, as was James Madison, who in 1788 (before there were political parties, billion-dollar elections, Twitter, Facebook, or QAnon conspirators), saw the American people as the unfailing virtuous electors of congressmen and presidents who would, as a result, likewise be virtuous. Madison wrote:

> "I go on this great republican principle, that the people will have virtue and intelligence to select men of virtue and wisdom. Is there no virtue among us? If there be not, we are in a wretched situation. No theoretical checks — no form of government can render us secure…. If there be sufficient virtue and intelligence in the community, it will be

exercised in the selection of these men."[5]

November 3, 2020: The Insurgency Begins

As America's presidents in the past have done when a foreign country's leader refuses to accept election results and step down in favor of the popular vote winner, President Trump had a strong reaction to the 2018 election of Venezuelan dictator-president Nicolás Maduro. Maduro, the Trump administration claimed, "fraudulently manufactured" his May 2018 presidential election victory. Trump quickly imposed sanctions on Venezuela's oil and its government bonds. He recognized Juan Guaidó, Maduro's opposition, as Venezuela's legitimate president. Trump also condemned Maduro's "usurpation of power" and said he was considering military action[6]. On September 4, 2020, Trump's Secretary of State, Mike Pompeo, put out a Press Statement following Trump's Executive Order 13692, which imposed additional Venezuelan sanctions. The Press Statement closed with "the United States reaffirms its commitment to promoting accountability for all those who seek to rob Venezuela of its democratic future. We stand with interim President Guaidó in his effort to restore a democratic Venezuela."[7]

Pompeo also spoke out in October 2020 against dictator-president Aleksandr G. Lukashenko's "landslide" August victory in Belarus, calling the election a "fraud," adding: "We've opposed the fact that he's now inaugurated himself. We know what the people of Belarus want. They want something different."

Similar election tactics have recently been employed by other presidential dictators, like Robert Mugabe of Zimbabwe and Slobodan Milosevic of Serbia — and, in 2021, in a military coup in Myanmar, which resulted in an overthrow of a democratically elected government. Tactics include refusal to "concede defeat" while "hurling unfounded accusations of election fraud." The strategies also include denouncing the press, as well as opponents[8].

Then came November 3, 2020. The day for America's 58th presidential election. It was Trump's turn.

Biden won 81 million popular votes — the most votes in American history — and 306 electoral college votes. Trump won 74 million popular votes — the second most votes in American history — and 232 electoral college votes. The counties Biden won had 67 million more Americans living in them than the counties Trump won[9].

Despite the *Voice of the People* giving 7 million more popular votes and 74 more electoral votes to Biden, Trump refused to concede the race or accept the results. Three weeks after the election, Trump announced (tongue-in-cheek, as it turned out) that if the electoral college declared Biden the winner, he'd leave the White House. But he added, "If they do, they made a mistake. It's going to be a hard thing to concede…. I don't know what is going to happen. I know one thing: Joe Biden did not get 80 million votes."[10]

The date for the electoral college to cast its ballots was December 14, 2020.

Set on influencing states' certifications of election results to be presented to the electoral college, after the November election, Trump immediately ramped up his claims unsupported by evidence of widespread voter fraud in swing states won by Democrats, primarily by mail-in ballots.[11] The key swing states that went for Biden included Wisconsin, Georgia, Arizona, Michigan, and Pennsylvania.

Trump's claims of mail-in ballot fraud defy logic. There were no separate presidential ballots for the November 2020 election. The same ballots casting votes for Biden or Trump also cast votes for congressional, state and local elections. In those elections, the Republicans, on the same ballots that voted for Biden, made gains while Trump lost support.

Changing a vote from Trump to Biden on a ballot, while leaving all the other Republicans in winning positions, does not appear to be sensible vote stealing. Nor does programming voting machines under multi-state systems to vote all candidates but the President as cast by the voters while changing only the presidential votes. Skimming off only the votes for the President seems contrary to anyone wanting to steal an election. If an election is to be stolen, the thief would want a winning, supporting cast in Congress as well as among state and local officials. And the theft wouldn't focus on only a handful of jurisdictions. It would also be particularly difficult to succeed with the theft when the votes are counted by teams of Republicans and Democrats working together.

However, this view was not shared by Trump supporters. Andy Biggs, an Arizona Republican, won his congressional race handily. His winning and Trump's Arizona loss were, for him, evidence of fraud. He told CNN he didn't dispute his own race, but, he said, "I dispute the presidential election results." He told CNN that coupling his victory with a Trump loss was "almost inexplainable." How could he and other Republicans do well while Trump lost? Yes, across the nation the Republicans did quite well. But in the election the *Voice of the People* called out to the Republicans to change their leadership. That's why their leader, Donald Trump, lost big. From the Democrats point of view, the rest of the election results left Biden without the deep Congressional support he would want and would expect from any group of thieving liberals[12]. If anything, Biggs' point is indicative of the lack of fraud.

Another indication of the lack of fraud is in what was claimed: a multistate conspiracy to change recorded votes. Such an effort would have had to involve hundreds, if not thousands, of people coordinating the events over time from places distant from each other. There would have had to be communications between the conspirators — calls, emails, meetings. In his *Nature of Conspiracy Theories,* Professor Michael Butter wrote, "[A] given conspiracy would logically become public on the grounds of size alone." Butter concludes, "[C]onspiracist thinking rests on a false understanding of social processes.... [T]he extensive scenarios put forward by conspiracy theorists are inconsistent with reality."[13]

As the election result became known, with Trump losing, Trump and his followers quickly filed dozens of lawsuits against the swing states that voted for Biden to throw out mail-in votes and, in some cases, early-voting results. A Trump legal advisor, Harmeet Dhillon, called openly for the Supreme Court's help. On Fox Business Network's Lou Dobbs Tonight,

Dhillon said, "Meanwhile, we're waiting for the United States Supreme Court, of which the president has nominated three justices, to step in and do something. And hopefully Amy Coney Barrett [Trump's last pick] will come through and pick up."[14] So much for Court's role as an independent umpire assuring all Americans that everyone in government is playing by the rules.

Trump's court-room success, however, was less than stellar. The courts, including those Trump populated with conservative judges, did not support his version of winning. The Associated Press reported: "Judges have heard the cases and have been among the harshest critics of the legal arguments put forth by Trump's legal team, often dismissing them with scathing language of repudiation. This has been true whether the judge has been appointed by a Democrat or a Republican, including Trump himself."[15]

Over 60 vote-irregularity lawsuits were filed by Trump and his hard-core followers. There was but one victory. A Pennsylvania court agreed that a small number of ballots, which were not included in the state's election totals, should not be counted[16].

Losing in the courts, Trump called upon swing state Republican governors and legislators to decertify elections and direct their state electoral college members to cast their ballots for Trump[17]. None of Trump's efforts to change the election results succeeded. As Georgia's Secretary of State put it, calling for state legislative sessions to overturn election results amounts to "nullifying the will of the people."[18] Chris Christie, former governor of New Jersey and a Trump ally, called Trump's legal team "a national embarrassment." Maryland's Republican Governor, Larry Hogan, added that the United States is "beginning to look like we're a banana republic."[19]

The problem, however, is not merely cosmetic. It is not a matter of what we were beginning to look like. It is a matter of what we are in danger of becoming.

V-Dem, an independent research organization headquartered at the Department of Political Science, University of

Gothenburg, Sweden, released its global "Democracy Report 2020" before the November presidential election. V-Dem's findings about the United States were not surprising nor pleasant. The United States, the report concluded, is undergoing a "substantial autocratization" — a loss of democratic traits. The acceleration increased precipitously during the Trump administration.

More shocking, however, was V-Dem's conclusion that only 20% of the countries that undergo substantial autocratization can avoid "succumbing to full-blown autocracy." Globally, national autocracies are now in the majority. They include 92 countries housing 54% of the world's population. Autocratizing nations, like the U.S., house 35% of global population. That leaves 11% of the world's population with true democracies, and, though we think of our DNA as being "democracy," America is no longer a member of that select group! V-Dem concluded:

> "The United States — former vanguard of liberal democracy — has lost its way…. The United States of America is the only country in Western Europe and North America suffering from substantial autocratization."[20]

In a Washington Post article about the V-Dem report, Michael Coppedge, a V-Dem chief investigator, is quoted as saying, "Executive respect [in the U.S.] for the Constitution is now at the lowest levels since 1865. Corruption in the executive branch is basically the worst since Harding."[21]

December 7, 2020: Trump Hints at "Big Things Happening"

A week before the electoral college was scheduled to meet, at his December 7, 2020 press conference, in response to a question about his chances of overturning the election, President Trump answered:

> "Well, I think the case has already been made. If you look at the polls, it was a rigged election. You

look at the different states. The election was totally rigged. It's a disgrace to our country. It's like a third-world country — these ballots pouring in from everywhere, using machinery that nobody knows ownership, nobody knows anything about. They have "glitches," as they call them. Glitches. The glitches weren't glitches. They got caught sending out thousands of votes — all against me, by the way. No, this was like from a third-world nation. And I think the case has been made. And now we find out what we can do about it. *But you'll see a lot of big things happening over the next couple of days.*"[22] [emphasis added]

December 7, 2020 was our nation's 79th *Pearl Harbor Day* — the day that President Roosevelt described seventy-nine years ago as a day that would "live in infamy" — the day in 1941 Japan made its sneak attack on Pearl Harbor in Hawaii, bringing us into World War II. December 7, 2020 was also the day that Trump and his clan took their next step in his coup d'état. It, too, is a day that will live in infamy.

December 8, 2020 was the presidential election's *Safe Harbor Day.* The Electoral Count Act of 1887 provides that when there are disputes in a state over election results that are resolved at least six days before the electors are scheduled to vote, the results are conclusive and must be counted by Congress[23]. December 8 is the sixth day before the electoral college vote. Thus, Trump and his followers filed their "big-things happening" lawsuit on December 7, 2020, the day before the Safe Harbor Day clock ran out. The suit was filed by a devoted Trump supporter, Texas Attorney General Ken Paxton, directly with the Supreme Court claiming unlawful election results in Pennsylvania, Georgia, Wisconsin and Michigan in the 2020 election adversely affected Texas.

Legal scholars and others were immediately critical of Paxton's lawsuit. Georgia's deputy secretary of state called the claims "false and irresponsible." Michigan's attorney general called the lawsuit a "publicity stunt beneath the dignity" of Paxton's office. Wisconsin's attorney general said the whole thing was "genuinely embarrassing." A Georgetown law professor, Paul Smith, who has argued cases before the Supreme Court, called the case "wacko." He also said that Texas had a "standing" problem: "It's totally unprecedented, the idea that one state would, at the Supreme Court, claim that other states' votes were cast the wrong way — that's never happened. What is the injury to the state of Texas because Pennsylvania votes were cast for Mr. Biden instead of Mr. Trump? There is no connection there." UC professor Rick Hasen said the lawsuit was "utter garbage... [A state] has no say over how other states choose electors."

Paxton claimed that Texas had *standing* (the subject of Chapters 4 and 5 of this book) because Texas has an interest in which party controls the Senate. Paxton's idea, apparently, is that Texas, a red state, has a constitutional right to have the country governed by Republicans. He wrote in his brief, "While Americans likely care more about who is elected President, the States have a distinct interest in who is elected Vice President and thus who can cast the tie-breaking vote in the Senate."[24]

The legal scholars and others may view Paxton's effort as garbage, but it didn't stop 17 Republican states, led by Missouri, from petitioning the Supreme Court for permission to file a friend of the court brief (an *amicus* brief) supporting Paxton's effort[25]. The rationale, stated in the motion:

- "In the context of a Presidential election [state actions] implicate a uniquely important national interest [because] the impact of votes cast in each State is affected by the votes cast for the various candidates in other states."

- "States have a strong interest in ensuring that the votes of their own citizens are not diluted by the unconstitutional administration of elections in other States. When non-legislative actors in other States encroach on the authority of the 'Legislature thereof' in that State to administer a Presidential election, they threaten the liberty, not just of their own citizens, but of every citizen of the United States who casts a lawful ballot in the election — including the citizens of *amici* states."

- "States have a strong interest in safeguarding against fraud in voting by mail during Presidential elections."[26]

Several Republicans supported the Texas litigation. Sixteen Georgia state senators backed the lawsuit. Congressman Mike Kelly from Pennsylvania pushed to have his state's election results declared illegal[27]. Louisiana Republican Congressman Mike Johnson solicited other Congressmen to join in a friend of the court *amicus* brief[28]. He was successful. One hundred-forty of the House Republicans signed on to his brief supporting Texas's lawsuit. The brief states:

"This brief presents [our] concern as Members of Congress, shared by untold millions of their constituents, that the unconstitutional irregularities involved in the 2020 presidential election cast doubt upon its outcome and the integrity of the American system of elections."[29]

Trump also filed a motion to join the lawsuit[30]. Kirby Wilson, writing for the Times/Herald Tallahassee Bureau about Florida's joinder in the lawsuit, quoted Stetson University College of Law professor Ciara Torres-Spelliscy:

"The states have 50 different election laws. I doubt the Supreme Court wants to open Pandora's box of allowing states to sue each other because they don't like how another state is running their election. I expect the Supreme Court justices to reject this effort to undermine the will of millions of American voters."[31]

On November 8, 2020, Washington Post's Editorial Board

gave us an early warning of Trump's "end game," described by Trump's legal advisor, Jenna Ellis:

"Have Republican lawmakers in control of swing states, like Pennsylvania, Michigan, Wisconsin and Georgia, grant their electoral college votes to Trump despite Biden's winning the popular votes."

The Editorial Board wrote: "Rudolph W. Giuliani, Mr. Trump's lawyer, is also talking up what would amount to a coup." If Giuliani is successful in preventing enough of the swing states from certifying their votes by December 14, 2020, "the election could be thrown into Congress." Article II, Section 1 of the Constitution provides for such a contingency. It happened in 1803, Jefferson's election (discussed in this book), in 1825 and in 1835.

The House of Representatives would select the President. However, our Constitution's 12th Amendment provides that when the House elects the President, a House majority vote does not determine the outcome. The vote is by states, with each state having but one vote. Although the Democrats represent more people and are the House majority, the Republicans represent more states, 27 to 20, with 3 states being evenly split between the two parties. Thus, the House Republicans would prevail in the presidential election, which is what Trump hoped would happen[32].

The Editorial Board concluded: "Indeed, the president's lies about widespread fraud have persuaded half the Republicans to believe that Mr. Trump 'rightfully won' the election." Several Republicans in the House apparently also shared that view. Thus: "Mr. Biden will enter office with a massive chunk of the country believing he, in fact, stole the election, when it is Mr. Trump who is trying to do just that. These people will not just preemptively reject their next president, but also doubt the democracy in which they live."

The Board was also concerned that Trump's tactics may set a dangerous precedent for future presidential elections, turning what historically have been "pro forma matters of election administration to become partisan weapons."[33]

As I worked on the beginning draft of this *Epilogue* on December 7, 2020, a Washington Post article flashed into my inbox at 4:35 AM, "Armed protesters alleging voter fraud surround the home of Michigan's secretary of state." The article begins:

> "Michigan Secretary of State Jocelyn Benson had just finished wrapping string lights around her home's portico on Saturday evening and was about to watch 'How the Grinch Stole Christmas' with her 4-year-old son when a crowd of protesters marched up carrying American flags and guns."

The protesters shouted accusations that Benson ignored Trump's claims of widespread voter fraud and chanted "Stop the Steal."[34]

That was but the beginning.

January 6, 2021: The Attempted Coup d'État

The events that took place next will fill volumes written by legal scholars. The Supreme Court rejected the Texas lawsuit. The electoral college met and cast its votes for Biden, in accordance with the election tallies. Neither was enough to stop Trump's "crusade against American democracy." Luke Mogelson wrote in his New Yorker article, "Among the Insurrectionists:"

> "[A]fter a relentless deployment of propaganda, demagoguery, intimidation, and fearmongering aimed at persuading as many Americans as possible to repudiate their country's foundational principles – a single word sufficed to nudge [Trump's] most fanatical supporters into open insurrection."

The word was "Bullshit," Trump's caricature of the massive voter fraud he claimed in his speech to the crowd of his supporters assembled on January 6, 2020 near the Washington Monument[35]. January 6th was the date that Congress, presided over by Vice President Mike Pence, was in session to accept the votes of the electoral college, finalizing the election of Joe Biden as President.

Trump had failed in getting swing-state governments to change their electoral ballots in his favor. The courts had found his claims, filed in more than 60 lawsuits, to be without merit. He pressured Vice President Mike Pence to countermand his Constitutional responsibilities, stated in Section 1 of Article II, and Amendment 12, of the Constitution to "open all the [state electoral college] certificates" so that the votes can be counted. He wanted Pence to reject the electoral college votes, send the election back to the states, and, if that failed, then to Congress for deciding. That too was a failure.

Trump's speech, motivating his fired-up devotees to march on the Capitol, was his final attempt to overturn his lost election. Neither the speech nor the assembly nor the walk to the Capitol was spontaneous. Contributions from wealthy Trump donors funded the rally, which was planned by members of the Trump team. Eight Trump campaign officials were listed on the rally permit[36].

"We're going to have to fight harder," Trump said. "We're going to walk down to the Capitol, and we're going to cheer our brave senators and congressmen and women. We're probably not going to have to be cheering so much for some of them — because you'll never take back our country with weakness. You have to show strength."

Before Trump finished his speech, a spectator shouted, "No weakness!" And the crowd screamed, "We're storming the Capitol."[37]

And storm the Capitol the mob did, overwhelming the Capitol guards, driving the members of Congress and Vice President Pence into hiding. Five people died, including a Capitol guard. Finally, the Capitol was cleared, Congress reconvened, and the electoral college votes cast were counted. Biden was confirmed as our 46th President.

Trump's speech was the ultimate, but not the only, potentially inciteful rally speech. At the rally Madison Cawthorn (Representative, North Carolina) claimed the election was a fraud perpetuated by the Democrats and urged the crowd to fight. The Washington Post reported that other

Republican Representatives — Andy Biggs (Arizona), Marjorie Taylor Greene (Georgia) and Mo Brooks (Alabama) — also spoke at rallies supporting Trump's claims.

House Speaker Nancy Pelosi warned in her January 15 news conference, "If in fact it is found that members of Congress were accomplices to this insurrection, if they aided and abetted the crimes, there have to be actions taken beyond the Congress, in terms of prosecution for that."[38]

Was the insurgency a coup attempt? The Cline Center at the University of Illinois, which specializes in studying coups, concluded:

> "Using the Cline Center's Coup D'État Project definitions, the storming of the US Capitol Building on January 6, 2021 was an attempted coup d'état: an organized, illegal attempt to intervene in the presidential transition by displacing the power of the Congress to certify the election."

The Cline Center's Coup D'État Project is the world's largest registry of successful and failed coups. Using the Center's definition, a coup d'état must meet these 5 conditions:

1. "There must be some person or persons who initiated the coup."

2. "The target of the coup must have meaningful control over national policy."

3. "There must be a credible threat to the leaders' hold on power."

4. "Illegal or irregular means must be used to seize, remove, or render powerless the target of the coup."

5. "It must be an organized effort."

In reaching its conclusion that the five conditions were met, the Cline Center reasoned that the insurrection was "carefully planned, equipped, and organized themselves for violent action." The rioters had a clear mission: "to usurp congressional authority to certify the election, arrogating control of the transition to themselves or to the executive branch." Their goal was not merely to upset the election process, but to force a change in control of the government[39].

The Wall Street Journal disagreed. After pointing out that the Journal agreed that Trump made false claims about the election being stolen, and that his conduct was "disgraceful," the Journal concludes:

"The assault on the Capitol was a riot, and a violent one, but it wasn't an insurrection."

The Journal's rationale? After the riot, the Capitol was successfully cleared, and Congress was able to return to its chambers "to count the votes."[40]

Republican Senate majority leader Mitch McConnell was blunt when he spoke to the Senate January 19, 2021: "The mob was filled with lies. They were provoked by the President and other powerful people. And they tried to use fear and violence to stop a specific proceeding" — Congress's ratification of Biden's election[41].

My conclusion? The attack on the Capitol was more than a riot. It was a failed coup d'état. The February 2021 congressional hearing on the insurrection also supports that conclusion. Reporting on the evidence presented at the hearing, reporters Wong and Lillis wrote in The Hill that the insurrectionists came to the Capitol with climbing equipment, communicated with hand signals and hand radios, were wearing tactical gear and carrying weapons. The Capitol security officials testified "that is all evidence of a highly coordinated and planned assault."[42] Acting Capitol Police Chief Yogananda Pittman also warned that the Capitol Police continued to be on guard after the January 6th assault as there could be more violence to come. She said, "We know members of the militia groups … have stated their desires that they want to blow up the Capitol and as many members as possible with a direct nexus to [President Biden's] State of the Union…. They want to send a symbolic message to the nation as to who was in charge of that legislative process."[43] She estimated that there were 10,000 demonstrators and about 800 broke into the

Capitol on January 6th.

Impeachment

The House of Representatives impeached President Trump, alleging that he incited the attack on the Capitol. He was tried by the Senate during the week of February 8, 2021. He was acquitted. 67 votes were needed for conviction. 57 votes were obtained, when 7 Republicans voted with 50 Democrats. Many of the 43 Senators voting for acquittal reasoned that the Senate lacked constitutional authority to impeach a president who was no longer in office. Others thought his comments were protected free speech, not directly linked to the actions of the mob.

No impeached President has ever been convicted by the Senate. The closest to being convicted was Richard Nixon, who resigned when confronted by Republican Senators. We must remember that the Constitution's provisions dealing with impeachment and trial by the Senate did not contemplate political parties. Madison saw the Senate as a body of virtuous men, appointed by state legislatures, exercising independent judgment, providing appropriate checks and balances over the chief executive.

On March 7, 1778 Hamilton wrote in Federalist Papers #65 that the nature of the charges brought in an impeachment "proceed from the misconduct of political men, or, in other words, from the abuse or violation of public trust. They are of nature which may with particular propriety be denominated POLITICAL, as they relate chiefly to injuries done immediately to society itself. The prosecution of them, for this reason, will seldom fail to agitate the passions of the whole community, and to divide it into parties more or less friendly or inimical to the accused." Thus, the impeachment risk, as Hamilton saw it was "that the decision will be regulated by the comparative strength of the parties, than the real demonstrations of innocence or guilt." To minimize the risks of political pressure in a time when there were no political parties, Hamilton saw the Senate as the most trustworthy. "Where else but in the Senate could have been found a tribunal sufficiently dignified, or sufficiently independent? What other body would be likely to feel CONFIDENCE ENOUGH IN ITS OWN SITUATION, to preserve, unawed and uninfluenced, the necessary impartiality between an INDIVIDUAL accused, and the REPRESENTATIVES OF THE PEOPLE, HIS ACCUSERS?"

Hamilton's reasoning was, as was Madison's, based on the initial provisions of the Constitutions that had Senators appointed by the legislators of each state rather than by direct election. And, of course, there were no political parties.

What has happened historically is that Senators from the President's political party rarely cast impeachment votes against the President. As Senator Lindsey Graham put it, a Republican vote of impeachment after Trump was out of office would be a vote to destroy the Republican Party[44].

The Trump impeachment, with 7 Republican Senators joining with the Democrats, was the most votes for impeachment by a President's party in the history of our country. Six of the seven are not running for reelection in 2022. Two are retiring. Only Alaska's Lisa Murkowski is up for election in 2022[45]. These Senators, however, are now facing censure and other repercussions from their state Republican parties. Those seeking reelection will most likely be facing far-right Trump supporters in their next elections, as party leaders seek to retain Trump supporters in the Republican political fold[46].

The Founders contemplated the trial before the Senate being somewhat akin to a trial by an independent jury. Half of the Senate jurors were Republicans, mostly Trump supporters. All the jurors were witnesses to, and potential victims of, the insurrection and failed coup d'état. Their impeachment votes set aside their harrowing personal experiences during the insurrection and the effect of the attack on our democratic institutions and supported continued Republican Party power.

A prime example is the vote of Mitch McConnell, who, at the start of the impeachment proceedings, after condemning Trump for his insurrection role, called on Republicans to cast their ballots as votes of conscience. His vote of acquittal with

42 other Republicans was anything but a vote of conscience. He followed the impeachment proceedings with harsh criticism of Trump and his role in the insurrection and coup d'état attempt, saying, "There is no question — none — that President Trump is practically and morally responsible for provoking the events of the day." McConnell's vote was based on his view that the Senate had no power to convict Trump once he was out of office. McConnell wrote a follow-up Op-Ed confirming his position for the Wall Street Journal, "Acquittal Vindicated the Constitution, Not Trump."[47]

The New York Times summed up: The Republicans "could not bring themselves to find [Trump] guilty of sparking the chaos, brutality and darkness that engulfed the Capitol, for fear of potentially offending the Trump supporters Republicans have come to rely on to win elections, and will need again in 2022 if they hope to regain the Senate — a paramount goal of McConnell."[48] And, of course, McConnell did not want his Senate leadership challenged, as it would have been had he voted for conviction. Some say McConnell sees Trump as a danger to the party. But after his criticism of Trump he said, "I'm not assuming that, to the extent the former president wants to continue to be involved, he won't be a constructive part of the process."[49]

Trump's reactions to McConnell's criticism and comments? His statement: "Mitch is a dour, sullen, and unsmiling political hack, and if Republican Senators are going to stay with him, they will not win again."[50]

Proving football coaching legend Vince Lombardi was right when he said, "Winning isn't everything, it's the only thing," McConnell followed up Trump's comments by saying on Fox News that he would "absolutely" support Donald Trump if he was nominated by the Republican Party in 2024[51].

Post Impeachment Commission and Investigations

Following growing bipartisan support for an inquiry into the Capitol insurrection after Trump's acquittal, House Speaker Pelosi announced that Congress would appoint an independent commission to "investigate and report on the facts and causes relating to the January 6, 2021, domestic terrorist attack upon the United States Capitol Complex ... and relating to the interference with the peaceful transfer of power."[52]

A question to be resolved by post-insurrection investigations is whether Trump will face criminal charges for his interference with the 2020 election[53]. In the meantime, civil suits against Trump have been filed. In February 2021, the NAACP and others sued Trump under the 1871 Ku Klux Klan Act for inciting the Capitol riot, conspiring with extremist groups and his attorney to prevent Congress's certification of the 2020 election results[54]. This law suit was followed by Congressman Eric Swalwell's law suit charging Trump, his son and his lawyer with inciting the "attack on the Capitol that terrorized lawmakers...."[55]

As of February 4, 2021, 26 individuals had been charged with conspiracy crimes or assault, 43 individuals have been charged with interference with law enforcement, threats or property crimes or weapons crimes and 107 individuals have been charged with disrupting Congress or trespassing. The New York Times reported that, "At least 21 of those charged had ties to militant groups and militias." In addition, about a dozen charged were QAnon conspiracy theory supporters. Most rioters, however, were there as Trump supporters who had lost faith in our democracy and government. The arrestees came from 40 states and the District of Columbia. Two prominent right-wing groups, the Proud Boys and the Oath Keepers, were involved in the riot, as were a few white-supremacist groups like the Patriot Front. The Times article concluded: "Justice Department officials have said they expect the number of people charged to increase geometrically in the days and weeks to come."[56] And that happened. Subsequently, the rioters were charged with more serious crimes coming out of the insurrection, and more people were charged[57]. As of March 1, 2021, more than 310 people were criminally charged[58].

What will be the effect of the criminally charged Capitol rioters who claim they were acting at the President's direction? Will Trump's call to action provide the rioters with defenses of "no criminal intent?" A criminal defense attorney reasoned: "The president of the United States telling you that it's OK to do something or telling you to do something – that destroys your intent to commit a crime, because the president is telling you it's OK."[59] However, judges are not buying into the idea. In a Washington Post article, "Capitol riot defendants facing jail time have regrets. Judges aren't buying it," U.S. District Judge Beryl Howell is quoted as saying that "if a president could authorize overturning an election, he would be no different from 'a king or a dictator,' and 'that is not how we operate here.'"[60]   Digging into the pages of history, the Nuremberg Court that tried the Nazi war criminals after World War II let no defendant off because he followed the orders of Hitler[61]. An interesting point is Trump's June 26, 2020 Executive Order 13933, which provides in Section 2: "It is the policy of the United States to prosecute to the fullest extent permitted under Federal law, and as appropriate, any person or any entity that destroys, damages, vandalizes, or desecrates a monument, memorial, or statue within the United States or otherwise vandalizes government property." This order followed the destruction of Civil War monuments by Black Lives Matter demonstrators. The order also reminds rioters that the penalty for property destruction is 10 years in jail. It's clearly applicable to the insurrection at the Capitol[62].

On March 5, 2021, the New York Times reported, "A member of the far-right nationalist Proud Boys was in communication with a person associated with the White House in the days just before the Jan. 6 assault on the Capitol, according to a law enforcement official briefed on the investigation." The Times reported in related articles that about a dozen members of the Proud Boys had been arrested in connection with the Capitol riot, and the F.B.I. tracked calls between rioters on mobile devices used within the Capitol during the riot and calls that used cell tower serving the Capitol. The Times also reported that the F.B.I. linked a few Republican lawmakers to organizations that had a role in the insurrection[63].

The coup-attempt's cost to American taxpayers, federal and

state? The Washington Post's take, as of February 6, 2021:

"The total so far is $519 million."[64]

Over time, the independent commission, and the courts, will provide answers to the extent of a president's responsibility for his interference with the peaceful transfer of power and whether any members of Congress have liability for the roles they played in the insurrection. I leave further discussion of the election, insurrection, failed co d'état and the impeachment trial to the memories of those of us who lived during those un-American times, and to the analyses of scholars who will write about these events on the pages of history.

However, there are five takeaways from these historic events worthy of our consideration. These takeaways reflect on the political context that surrounds us and shapes our selection and approach to the projects we must address as we work our way back to becoming a Democracy of People.

> *It's not what you look at that matters,*
> *it's what you see.*
>
> Henry David Thoreau
> Circa 1850
>
> *For there is always light*
> *If only we're brave enough to see it*
> *If only we're brave enough to be it*
>
> Amanda Gorman
> *The Hill We Climb*
> Presidential Inauguration Poet
> January 20, 2021

> *Democracy doesn't happen by accident.*
>
> President Joe Biden
> Munich Security Conference Speech
> February 20, 2021

Five Takeaways

Chapter 10, *The Voice of the People,* closes with a challenge:

> I urge each reader to personally accept Schweitzer's challenge: *My life is my*

argument. By so doing, each of us, in some very personal way, becomes involved in returning us to a Democracy of People. By so doing, we will keep the fox out of our henhouse. Like musicians in a New Orleans jazz band, our individual voices will harmonize with others and will collectively become the *Voice of the People*.

The issues raised in the five takeaways that follow touch on prime challenges that need our attention. The takeaways are a big part of the 21st Century context in which we live. How we solve the issues raised will go a long way in determining whether the United States, once the global leader among democratic countries, will be able to return from the oligarchical cusp of authoritarianism where we are today to a true Democracy of People. We pointed out that, historically, countries which once were democratic, but are now authoritarian, have but a 20% chance of success in returning to a democracy.

Without intense and focused constructive effort from each of us, whether Republican or Democrat or independent, today's 21st Century Democracy of Dollars will leave us with a long-lasting national pandemic infecting us with a spiritual vacuum, perpetuating its authoritarian oligarchy devoid of fundamental values, constitutional principles and true representation of the interests of all Americans. In the long run that will be far more damaging to us than COVID-19. It will be worse for our future than if it were "stage IV" cancer.

First, Our Heroes: Their Lives Are Their Arguments

Trump's attempt to overturn the election of Joe Biden as our 46th President, and the coup d'état at the Capitol, failed because:

1. Elected state officials, primarily Republicans, in charge of assuring the accuracy of election results in a half dozen swing states — like

Georgia's Secretary of State Brad Raffensperger — refused to ignore the results of a fair and nonfraudulent election. After counting, and in many cases, auditing and recounting, the votes, despite Trump's pressure, no fraud was uncovered and the votes in each state were certified[65].

2. Federal and state judges, primarily Republican appointed judges, charged with opining whether the 60 plus lawsuits filed on behalf of Trump produced evidence of election fraud, refused to violate the courts' constitutional responsibilities as an institution governed by the rule of law, regardless of Trump's unfounded fraud claims or the fact he appointed conservative judges and expected their loyalty about all else[66]. As we pointed out earlier in this *Epilogue*, Trump and his supporters had the mistaken belief that the judges Trump appointed would be loyal to him and not to the Constitution and the rule of law. After the dismissal of the Texas fraud case by the Supreme Court, Trump called the Court "incompetent and weak."[67] To the contrary, the Court was strong, independent, and loyal to its Constitutional responsibilities.

3. Vice President Pence refused to bow to Trump's pressure. Trump demanded that, as chairperson of the joint assemblage of Congress meeting to ratify electoral college votes, he not accept votes certified by the states and send them back to the states so that the Republican state legislatures could override their electoral college votes.[68] During the insurgency, ten minutes after Vice President Pence was evacuated from the Senate chamber, Trump (aware of his evacuation) tweeted

"Mike Pence didn't have the courage to do what should have been done…" Videos of the insurgency indicate the rioters were reading Trump's tweets and were "hunting for Pence."[69] The truth: Pence had the courage to do what the Constitution required him to do.

4. Among the understaffed and overwhelmed Capitol security personnel — over 140 were injured and one killed during the insurrection — there were men and women like Eugene Goodman, a Capitol officer, who had the courage and presence of mind to divert insurgents waving weapons and shouting "hang Pence" and "kill Pelosi" away from the Vice President and Congressional members as they sought safety from the maddening rioters.

5. Business and labor successfully organized and operated a quiet, behind the scenes, highly effective, shadow campaign to preserve the integrity of the 2020 election. The campaign is discussed later in this *Epilogue*.

I do not know whether any of those brave men and women who worked to save our democracy read Schweitzer or were steeped in his philosophy, *my life will be my argument*. But I do know that during those dark days, they *pledged their lives and sacred honor* much as our Founding Fathers did when they adopted the Declaration of Independence. Their responses to Trump and the rioters he incited were lives lived with the utmost integrity and morality. They were men and women of principle, confirmations in the best way of Schweitzer's challenge.

Books will be written, and movies made of their heroics. Until then, I leave us with a few comments about one of those heroes, Capitol officer Eugene Goodman. Three lawmakers, two Democrats and one Republican, introduced a bill to award him a Congressional Gold Medal for his successfully luring the insurrectionists away from the rooms where the Vice President and Congressmen were during the January 6, 2021 Capitol insurrection. The Senate approved the bill with an affirmative vote and a standing ovation on February 12, 2021[70].

One of the bill's sponsors, Nancy Mace (S.C. Republican), said that Goodman, a Black man, "was the only thing standing between members of Congress and the violent mob, he quickly and selflessly redirected their fury upon himself so those members could escape. Thanks to his valor, we are here today. From the bottom of my heart, I cannot thank him enough for his bravery and for his dedication to the call of duty."[71]

These heroes should encourage each of us to be as brave in our giving a strong voice to the people, returning us to a Democracy of People.

But bravery has a price. In the battleground state of Michigan, Van Langevelde, the Republican attorney who joined with the two Democrat election officials to certify the Biden win, did not have his appointment renewed (the second Republican abstained from voting). At the time of the voting, he said, "We must not attempt to exercise power we don't have." He was replaced by a Republican activist. CNN reported that "A cluster of election officials around the country have lost or left their jobs in recent weeks, as the fallout from the tumultuous 2020 election season continues." For the many who voluntarily left, the political environment was too much[72].

A final takeaway on these heroes, from political commentator David Axelrod:

> "History will scorn the cowards who meekly complied with Trump's scheme to tarnish and overturn the election — and honor the many who showed courage and fidelity to the rule of law during this time of trial."[73]

Second, Voting. Will our state and federal governments promote or squelch our rights to vote?

We've pointed out that Madison and our Constitution's Framers never contemplated political parties nor the willful push by a political party — in today's 21st Century reality, the Republican Party representing a cross-section of about one-third of Americans — to perpetuate its control, not by championing useful ideas and healthy ideals, but by making it difficult for the rest of Americans to vote. Especially targeted by the Republican Party's extremists are the liberals, their elites, their poor and their minorities, who don't vote Republican. These "outsiders" are viewed as too socialistic or too un-American to have a right to an effective voice in our government.

Rather than recognizing that voter-inclusiveness is essential for a healthy and vibrant democracy, the Republican Party's focus has been on its perceived right to voter-exclusiveness and its right to stay in power, providing one-party government through voter suppression and voting district gerrymandering. In Chapter 6, I wrote:

> "As Paul Weyrich, co-founder of the conservative Heritage Foundation and the Moral Majority, put it in his 2007 speech, 'Now many of our Christians have what I call the 'goo-goo syndrome' – good government. They want everybody to vote. I don't want everybody to vote. Elections are not won by a majority of people. They never have been from the beginning of our country and they are not now. As a matter of fact, our leverage in the elections quite candidly goes up when the voting populace goes down.'"

Weyrich may be a co-founder of the Moral Majority; however, his views on voting are neither moral nor majoritarian.

The Pew Research Center, in "2020 Election reveals two broad voting coalitions fundamentally at odds," reported: "Overwhelming majorities of both Biden and Trump supporters said in October that a victory by the other candidate would lead to *lasting harm* to the nation." However, Pew added a caveat of hope:

"Majorities of both Trump (86%) and Biden (89%) supporters say that their preferred candidate, if elected, should focus on addressing the needs of all Americans, 'even if it means disappointing some of his supporters.' Only about one-in-ten in each camp (13% of Trump and 10% of Biden supporters) say their candidate should focus on the concerns of 'those who voted for him, without worrying too much about the concerns of those who didn't vote for him.'"[74]

Despite efforts in states controlled by Republicans to make voting by others more difficult in the 2020 presidential election, nearly 160 million Americans voted, the largest total ever, and highest percentage turnout of voters in more than a century. It was the ability of Americans to vote early and by mail that made the 2020 election high turnout special and inclusive. The 2020 turnout, 66.7% of eligible voters, was exceeded only in the election of 1900 when 73.7% of eligible voters cast their ballots[75].

Not restrained by limited voting hours and too few, and frequently too distant in minority areas, voting booths, early voting and voting by mail opened access to many Americans who otherwise would not, or could not, exercise their right to vote.

In "The voting experience in 2020," Pew Research Center reported that, in the 2020 election, 54% of Americans voted in person and 46% voted by mail-in or absentee ballots. Only 27% voted on election day. About 66.67% of the Trump supporters voted in person, as did 42% of the Biden voters. More White voters than Black voters voted by mail[76]. Mail-in voting also made it easier for Americans with disabilities to vote[77].

In their December 2020 New York Times article about the election, "Republicans Pushed to Restrict Voting. Millions of Americans Pushed Back," journalists Corasaniti and Rutenberg reported that "The expansion of voting options also created a fall 'election season' rather than a sole Election Day, a change that is likely to endure and force political campaigns to restructure fall operations with a greater emphasis on getting out the vote over a period of weeks." For example, in Arizona's largest county, Maricopa, more than 80% of the eligible voters voted – a record. Of the 2 million people in the county casting ballots, only 165,000 voted in person on election day. In Hawaii early voting increased by 111% over 2016, and the overall voter turnout was up by a third from the last presidential election.

However, Corasaniti and Rutenberg warned: "Though Mr. Trump and the [Republican] party have not managed to prove a single claim of fraud in the courts — where they and their allies have lost or withdrawn dozens of cases — Republicans at the state level are vowing to enact a new round of voting restrictions to prevent what they claim — without evidence — is widespread fraud."[78]

Disfranchising efforts began immediately after the November election. In preparation for Georgia's January 2021 Senatorial run-off election, ultimately won by Democrats, Georgia's controlling Republican Party set about reducing the numbers of places people vote, particularly among the poorer and Black communities. Georgia's Cobb County, with 760,000 residents and a large Black population, had its normal 11-voting-sites reduced to five. The expressed reason? A sudden shortage in the numbers of county staff personnel. After protests from the NAACP and other organizations, the Cobb County Elections Director increased the number of sites to 7[79].

Beyond reducing the number of places that the poor and Black can vote, Georgia Republicans quickly set out to "fix" the state's voting system by adopting new restrictions, including prohibiting voting on Sunday mornings — an attractive time for Blacks who like to vote immediately after church services. Pennsylvania Republicans also set out to revoke absentee ballot laws they installed a year ago. Wisconsin and Texas Republican-controlled state legislatures were on similar courses[80].

Iowa adopted voting changes that mandated closing election

places at 8 p.m. instead of 9 p.m., reduced early voting from 29 days to 20 days, and made it tougher to vote by absentee ballots. When signing the bill Iowa's governor insisted the changes protected "the integrity of every election."[81] Two states, Connecticut and Maryland, introduced bills to remove themselves from the interstate compact discussed in Chapter 2, which is an agreement among states to cast electoral college votes in sync with the popular majority vote[82].

In Florida, my home state? Having recently revised its election laws to facilitate mail-in voting, Florida had one of the best-working election systems in the 2020 election. However, its Republican-dominated legislature decided that automatic renewal of mail-in voting rights was too much of a good thing. Thus, state Republicans introduced bills to require all Floridians who want to vote by mail to re-register their choices each election cycle, putting Floridians and election officials to a lot of work to accomplish again what is already in place. Florida's Republicans also plan to eliminate ballot boxes, require tougher signature verification for mail-in ballots, prohibit counties from getting financial help from private organizations for "get out the vote" initiatives, and prohibit "ballot harvesting" — people turning in vote-by-mail ballots of persons who are not immediate family[83]. The ballot-harvesting Florida restriction is like a similar Arizona restriction, which the 9th Circuit Court of Appeals held unconstitutional because it is racially discriminatory. Arizona has appealed the decision to the Supreme Court[84].

In "Voting Laws Roundup 2021," the Brennan Center for Justice reported in February 2021 that 43 states introduced 253 bills in 2021 to restrict voting, more than 4 times the number of such bills introduced last year. On a positive note, 43 states introduced 704 bills to expand voting access. The restrictive bills "seek to (1) limit mail voting access; (2) impose stricter ID requirements; (3) slash voter registration opportunities; and (4) enable more aggressive voter roll purges." Arizona, Pennsylvania, Georgia and New Hampshire are the most active states in voter restriction. The expansive bills "focus on (1) mail voting; (2) early voting; (3) voter registration; and (4) voting rights restoration." New York, New Jersey, Mississippi, Missouri and Texas are the states most active in proposing voter expansion[85].

The Week Magazine, in its February 19, 2021 article, "Elections: Should it be easier or harder to vote?" points out that most of the restraints are under the guise of adopting voter restrictions to promote *ballot integrity*. "Republicans are keenly aware of their base of whiter, rural, mostly male voters is being steadily outnumbered by minorities, young progressives and educated suburban women" Quoting a Georgia election official: voting restrictions are necessary "'so that we at least have a shot at winning.'"[86] Responding to criticism, Georgia legislator, Barry Fleming, describes the voting law restrictions simply as "protecting the sanctity of the vote."[87]

The strong move by Republican-dominated states to restrain voting rights for all eligible people began in 2013 after the Supreme Court decided *Shelby County v. Holder*[88]. The case gutted the Voting Rights Act of 1965, which required states, primarily southern states, that had racially gerrymandered districts to obtain federal preclearance when changing voting restrictions that resulted in racial disenfranchisement. In a 5 to 4 decision, the court viewed the restraints as no longer being necessary because of the passage of time. Ironically, Section 4 of Article I of the Constitution provides that "The Times, Places and Manner of holding Elections for Senators and Representatives, shall be prescribed by each State by the Legislature thereof; but Congress may at any time by Law make or alter such Regulations, except as to the Places of choosing Senators."

To protect Blacks' voting rights, the ACLU's Voting Rights Project is monitoring the states and has developed sophisticated statistical methods for simulating redistricting plans, to minimize the efforts of legislators to draw maps that dilute Black votes. The practical problem? It can take years in the courts to challenge the maps. In the meantime, there are multiple elections. And the maps only deal with issues of racial gerrymandering, not other forms of voter restriction[89].

The soon-to-be-released 2020 census report will focus many states on redrawing their voting districts, in many cases gerrymandering to maintain legislative control. Quoting Michael Li of the Brennan Center, the Wall Street Journal reported: "'It's going to be a cycle unlike any other in that there will be more potential gerrymandering than ever before but also more pushback than ever before.'"[90] The New York Times reported that Republicans are considering redrawing districts in Atlanta suburbs to make one of them Republican. Republicans are also carving up Houston and Ohio districts to increase Republican representation. The Times concludes "Republicans hold total control of redistricting in 18 states, including Florida, North Carolina and Texas, which are growing in population and expected to gain seats after the 2020 census is tabulated." Some experts predict the Republicans could take control of the House in the 2022 election "solely on gains from newly drawn districts."[91] The Wall Street Journal added, "Democrats are set to go into the new Congress with 222 seats to Republicans' 211, with two races still in dispute [Republicans won the 2 seats]. The narrow majority has Republicans preparing to fight for favorable maps and the Democrats on the defense."[92]

Since the Republicans dominate so many state legislatures, at the local level their efforts to restrain voting rights will be difficult to overcome. At the Federal level, in 2019, the Democrats introduced H.R.1, the "For the People Act."[93] The law would require automatic voting registration in every state, 15 days of early voting, and unlimited absentee voting. The bill would also restore ex-felons voting rights and prohibit extreme gerrymandering. Unless the Senate rules are changed, the bill will be subject to the Senate filibuster rules. The filibuster rules require 60 votes for a bill to pass. McConnell blocked action on H.R. 1 when introduced to the Senate in 2019. Without changing the filibuster rules, Senate approval is unlikely. Although the Democrats control 51 Senate votes, and could change the filibuster rules, Democratic Senator Manchin from the Republican State of West Virginia has been opposed to the idea[94].

In its November 24, 2020 Opinion column, the Wall Street Journal pointed out that H.R.1 would be beneficial to all Americans, "The main objective of this bill is to make our politics less partisan, and more representative of every American. A true democracy, for example, doesn't let elected officials of any party pick their voters through gerrymandering like our current system allows." The Opinion column also pointed out that the bill would enhance ballot integrity because "It would ensure the protection of ballot integrity by prohibiting voter roll purges like those seen in Ohio and Georgia and expanding opportunities for mail-in voting — an effective and safe way to vote."[95]

However, after the 2021 election the Wall Street Journal's January 14, 2021 editorial, "Pelosi's Top Priority: Consolidating Power," came to a different conclusion: "Overall the bill is designed to auto-enroll likely Democratic voters, enhance Democratic turnout, with no concern for ballot integrity." The bill is also criticized as limiting free speech in that nonprofit corporations would be required to disclose donors who contribute more than $10,000; in addition, political ads on radio and TV require top donors to be named[96].

In its review of the Journal editorial, The Week Magazine commented somewhat tongue in cheek: adopting H.R. 1, making it easier to vote, would make voting available to every eligible voter, including "food-stamp recipients." Quoting Bill Scher in WashingtonMonthly.com, The Week Magazine continued: "'Both parties assume that making it easier to vote helps Democrats.' But 'that's hardly certain.'" The 2020 election produced an overall high-voter turnout, but no Democrat "blue wave."[97] Bloomberg Politics adds that "imposing voter ID requirements and reducing mail-in access could also [adversely] affect many of the older, rural and blue-collar voters that Republicans now depend on."[98] Some Republicans are also concerned that with the GOP now being known as the party of voter suppression — done in many cases to appease the Trump supporters within the party who still believe the election was stolen — Democrat efforts for the 2022 election will be accelerated[99].

In her Letters from an American column, Heather Cox Richardson reported "Sixty-eight percent of Americans approve the reform in the bill. Sixteen percent oppose it." Richardson also reported that seventy-four percent of Americans want nonpartisan redistricting. Sixty-eight percent want at least 15-day early voting, and fifty-eight percent want voting by mail. She adds, "Now, every House Democrat supports the bill, while Republican lawmakers oppose it."[100]

To the extent that H.R.1 applies to presidential elections it may be unconstitutional. Section 4 of Article I of the Constitution, granting Congress the right to pass regulations for the elections of Congress does not apply to presidential elections under Article II. Congressional power over presidential electors in Article II is limited to determining the time of electors' appointment. David Rivkin, Jr., a constitutional lawyer, thinks the application of H.R. 1 to presidential elections may be unconstitutional. Rivkin, who served in the White House Counsel's Office and Justice Department under Reagan and Bush, also favors states having the ability to "experiment with voting improvements."[101]

However, as can be surmised from our discussion, the voting suppression tactics advanced following the 2020 election fall far short of "experimentation" or "voting improvements." Furthermore, proposed laws in Pennsylvania and Arizona push politicizing elections to the extreme. Pennsylvania Republicans are attacking judicial independence, proposing gerrymandered districts instead of statewide judicial elections. Gerrymandering has allowed the Republicans to control the Pennsylvania State House of Representatives since 2011 and the State Senate since 1993, although the Democrats prevail in statewide elections.[102]

Arizona Republicans are proposing a bill to "allow the Legislature to override the will of a majority of Arizona voters and appoint members of the Electoral College to back the presidential candidate lawmakers want elected."[103] Is Arizona's approach constitutional? The Constitution is vague on the responsibilities of the electoral college, but the Supreme Court in *Chiafalo v. Washington*, discussed in Chapter 2, opined that the presidential electors "were understood to be instruments for expressing the will of those who selected them…. State election laws evolved … ensuring that a State's electors would vote the same way as its citizens." The Constitution's 12th Amendment, the Court continued, which required electoral voting by ballot created a "mechanism not for deliberation but for party-line voting." In a concurring opinion that agreed only with the case's results, Justices Thomas and Gorsuch disagreed with the majority reasoning, pointing out, "The Constitution does not address — expressly or by necessary implication — whether States have the power to require the Presidential electors vote for the candidates chosen by the people." Would the Supreme Court hold that Arizona's legislature has the right to cast Arizona's electoral votes contrary to the expressed will of Arizona voters? It is impossible for me to imagine such a result in a Democracy of People, either under Federal or State law. But Arizona is scary and contrary to the will of the people.

Beyond gerrymandering and voter restrictions, if elections, particularly the primaries, revert to their low participation levels, the result will not only favor Republican control of the House and the Senate, but extremist domination, as we pointed out in Chapter 6, and discuss in the next section of this *Epilogue*. Biden contemplates providing a pathway for immigrant admission to citizenship. He's advocating "common sense gun controls."[104] Although these steps are popular with most Americans, they are not with the far right. Although the Republicans are divided between those that want Trump gone and those who back him, blocking liberal ideas like gun control and citizenship paths for immigrants is a reason for the Republicans to set aside their differences and politic together against the Democrats' agenda.

Republican strategist Scott Reed said, "Biden is giving Republicans plenty of ammo. His continuing lurch to the left on domestic policy is creating a strong contrast for the midterm elections already." Senator Lindsey Graham added on Fox News, "My goal is to win in 2022 to stop the most radical agenda I have seen coming out of the Democratic presidency of

Joe Biden."[105]

Despite the uprising in Republican voter suppression movement, there is a ray of hope. The Republican State Leadership Committee recently launched a commission on election reform. The Committee's co-chair, John Merrill, said, "We want to find the best practices that are used in every state in the union and make sure those are available for legislative bodies in the 50 states to consider the options. We have a singular goal, and that is to make it easier to vote and harder to cheat — period."[106] The RSLC is the largest Republican organization focusing on state-level politics. Its objective is to elect state-level Republican officeholders. The Democratic counterpart is the Democratic Legislative Campaign Committee.

But the ray of hope needs our guidance. Only the continued, strong *Voice of the People*, like the voice expressed in the November 2020 election, will keep us on the road less traveled, leading to free and open voting by all eligible citizens.

Other divisive efforts to squelch voting are discussed in this book, particularly Chapters 2 and 6.

Third, The Non-Voters: Will They Take the Challenge and Vote in 2022 and Beyond?

About 160 million people voted in the 2020 presidential election. An all-time high in turnout and the second high in percentage voting. The total represented about 2/3s of the eligible voters, which means that about 80 million eligible voters did not show up at the polls. The Knight Foundation's *100 Million Project* provides us insight:

- 38% of non-voters lack confidence that elections reflect the will of the people. These non-voters are also more likely to believe elections are rigged or not counted accurately.

- Non-voters are also twice as likely as voters to not be news seekers, using media primarily for entertainment. Thus, they are less informed about issues and candidates.

- Non-voters are as likely to be Republican as they are Democrat.

- Young voters, as a group, are more politically disengaged than other non-voters.

When non-voters were asked why they hadn't registered to vote:

- 29% said they didn't care.

- 13% felt their vote wouldn't make a difference.

- 9% saw the system as being corrupt[107].

A 2020 study, *Lift Every Voice,* commissioned by The Brookings Institution and Harvard's Ash Center for Democratic Governance, critical of voter suppression and championing universal civic duty voting, points out that it is the primary responsibility of election officials "to allow citizens to embrace their duties, not to block their participation." The report questions:

> "In most non-presidential elections [*e.g.,* the 2022 mid-year election], turnout is typically below 50%, meaning that the winning party receives votes from roughly a quarter of eligible voters in a close election…. Do those leaders have true democratic legitimacy, since nonparticipants cannot be assumed to be giving their 'consent'? Indeed … many express skepticism about the workings of the system."[108]

The takeaway? The voter restraints and intensified gerrymandering being imposed by Republican-controlled states increase the likelihood of Republican control of Congress. Particularly, if the midterm election produces its typical low turnout. In Chapter 6, and this *Epilogue*, we remind ourselves that low voter turnout leads to extremist candidates. Extremists, voting for far, far right causes and not principles shared by political moderates, can easily dominate low turnout elections, particularly primaries.

The New York Times reported that following the January 6, 2021 attack on the Capitol, "tens of thousands of Republicans were calling in or logging on to switch their party affiliations." The Times estimated over 140,000 left the Republican Party and 79,000 left the Democratic Party since January 2021[109]. Gallup Polls since the 2020 election and its aftermath show an increasing percentage of Americans see themselves as Independent. The February 3-18, 2021 Gallup Poll indicated 26% consider themselves Republican, 32% Democrat and 41% Independent[110]. Sixty-two percent of Americans said that we need a third party because the Republicans and Democrats "do such a poor job representing the American people."[111] The exodus most likely will leave both parties more controlled by extremists, minimizing opportunities for constructive bipartisanship and not representing their middle-of-the road majorities, to the detriment of us all.

We repeat:

> Without intense and focused constructive effort from each of us, whether Republican or Democrat or independent, today's 21st Century Democracy of Dollars will leave us with a long-lasting national pandemic infecting us with a spiritual vacuum, perpetuating its authoritarian oligarchy devoid of fundamental values, constitutional principles and true representation of the interests of all Americans.

Fourth, Will We Listen to Cassandra?

Rush Limbaugh, conservative talk-radio pundit died February 17, 2021 at the age of seventy. According to Nielson Audio, his show was America's most listened to radio talk show with over 20 million listeners[112]. In the minds of many political analysts he shaped the message of the Republican Party and the political voice of Donald Trump. As Neil Young put it, Limbaugh "used his airwave to spew vitriol and hate, all the while pushing the Republican Party, with the help of Fox News, to the extremes where it now simmers."[113] Dennis Prager pondered in the Wall Street Journal that may be okay. After all, Limbaugh had the "left's number" and that's why they hated him[114]. The Wall Street Journal, in an editorial in memory of Limbaugh's death, wrote, "His real offense was to gain millions of weekly listeners by mocking the left's pieties."[115] Matthew Walther concluded that Limbaugh created modern politics and that all of us "live in the world Limbaugh helped to create." That world, at least in America, is contentious, poorly organized for the give and take of bipartisanship. Limbaugh thought the fruitful exchange of ideas between conservatives and liberals was never to be. He reasoned:

> "There cannot be a peaceful coexistence of two completely different theories of life, theories of government, theories of how we manage our affairs."[116]

As I read Limbaugh's tributes and criticisms, I could not help but think about the ancient Greek myth about Cassandra. The god Apollo fell in love with her, and as a lover's present, gave her the gift of prophecy. However, Cassandra rejected Apollo's affections. So, Apollo retaliated. He changed her gift of prophecy so that no one would believe her. For example, when she warned the Trojans not to bring the wooden horse into the city walls, her warnings were ignored. Writing about the story in *Willful Blindness*, Margaret Heffernan tells us,

> "The savage irony of Cassandra is that, as we read her prophecies, we know they are true but no one else does.... We learn that any situation can contain truths that we may not be able to see but that are, nevertheless, visible."

From a personal point of, Heffernan concludes, Cassandra also "embodies the baffled rage we all feel when no one else can see what we see."[117] We've pointed out in this *Epilogue* that the Republicans believe America will be getting into trouble if Democrats win elections, and the Democrats felt America will be getting into trouble if Republicans win elections. The irony of today's politics is that the Democrats are the Republicans' Cassandra and the Republicans are the Democrats' Cassandra, neither willing to believe, listen to, or learn from the other.

But a successful democracy does not work when it's a one-party system. For the truth of each political party to be discovered and implemented, it must be challenged, discussed and frequently compromised to be in balance with truth of the other political party. Success is not a winner-take-all proposition, which is why the Georgia election official we quoted earlier is wrong when she says that the voting restrictions being put in place in Georgia are necessary to give conservatives a chance. What should give conservatives — and liberals — a chance to win elections is the competition of ideas, not the imposition of voting restrictions that perpetuate control regardless of the support voters have for a political party's platform.

In chapter 6, I pointed out that our creator didn't make some of us liberals because being liberal is always right. Nor did our creator make some of us conservatives because conservatives are always right. Our creator relied on diversity, not only among all species, but of thought and human interaction, since diversity produces the best long-term results. With diversity of thought and interaction, listening and compromise are key ingredients.

In their *Lessons of History,* Pulitzer Prize winners Will and Ariel Durant, describe the importance of the diversity of thought and human interaction, not just regarding conservative and liberal politics, but regarding life itself:

> "So the conservative who resists change is as valuable as the radical who proposes it — perhaps much more valuable as roots are more vital than grafts. It is good that new ideas should be heard, for the sake of the few that can be used; but it is also good that new ideas should be compelled to go through the mill of

objection, opposition, and contumely; this is the trial heat which innovations must survive before being allowed to enter the human race. It is good that the old should resist the young, and that the young should prod the old; out of this tension, as out of the strife of the sexes and the classes, comes a creative tensile strength, a simulated development, a secret and basic unity and movement of the whole[118].

In *American Character*, Colin Woodard wrote about the "Epic Struggle Between Individual Liberty and the Common Good." Although today's political clash between Republicans and Democrats appears in many iterations — from confrontations about gun rights and immigration to COVID relief programs and Obamacare — that fundamental political clash is grounded in the "epic struggle" between individualism and the common good. This struggle is neither new nor 21st Century in origin. As we pointed out in the *Prologue* and Section 1 of this book, it has been with us since the beginning, from George Washington's first cabinet when Hamilton and Jefferson locked horns about the role of government. Those two competing definitions of freedom — individual liberty or common good — each have, as Woodard puts it, a "full spectrum of adherents, from radical revolutionaries to pragmatic centrists." Woodard continues:

"'When individual liberty and the common good come into conflict, with which principle will you side?' … Together they span the ideological distance between Thomas Jefferson, who imagined a self-regulating republic of independent producers led by enlightened gentlemen like himself, and Alexander Hamilton, who envisioned a vigorous national government staffed by the best and brightest, committed to promoting the public interest by building institutions and infrastructure, and strong enough to defend the

Constitution from enemies foreign and domestic."[119]

At the conservative fringes of the clash are libertarians who, as Ronald Reagan once said, see "government as not the solution to our problems; government is the problem;" and Ayn Rand extremists who would like all government to fade away. At the other end are social democrats who would build robust welfare programs, sarcastically critiqued by Rush Limbaugh: "Liberals measure compassion by how many people are given welfare;" and Marxist extremists who would cede all wealth and power to the state.

Sustaining our democracy requires us to balance individual liberty and the common good. Neither can dominate the other. Woodard perceptively observes, "Sacrifice one, and you are on the road to oligarchy or anarchy; lose the other, and the shadow of collectivist dictatorship looms. You simply can't have one without the other. The reasons for this go deeper than logic and philosophy. They're literally recorded in *Homo sapiens's* DNA."[120]

In addition to our DNA, the reasons also have something to do with geography. A close look at a map of the counties won by Biden and the counties won by Trump in the 2020 election illustrates two critical points — population and economic differences between red and blue counties also produce the Cassandra effect. The election map is awash with red counties: 2,497 counties generating 29% of our GDP are red counties won by Trump. In contrast, 477 counties contributing 70% of our GDP are blue counties won by Biden. The Biden counties are crowded population centers, with 67 million more people than the Trump counties. For the most part, Biden counties are clustered along the west and the east coast[121]. Of America's 2,974 counties only 77 counties flipped their presidential votes from the 2016 election. In 2020, 59 counties flipped to Biden and 18 flipped to Trump[122].

The red counties are where people live less shoulder-to-shoulder and are more likely to champion individual freedom. The blue counties are where people are crowded in urban areas and are more likely to require attention to programs that address their common good.

The economic inequality between crowded urban geographic areas with high GDP and less crowded rural areas with lower GDP is also a troubling source of our nation's political divide. The Fortune Magazine article, "Why the counties Joe Biden won represent 70% of US GDP," quotes Mark Muro, the author of the county GDP study: "'So, we now have this extreme political gridlock that aligns with this very deep economic divide.'" Absent a solution to reduce the political and economic divide, Fortune Magazine concludes, will lead America to an "existential crisis." Perhaps even a secession[123].

It should also be clear that, not only does a political philosophy of "one size fits all" not work, singling out either individual freedom or common good as the exclusive winning political philosophy is disastrous. Woodard warns us that both political parties are wrong in making such an assumption: "Human nature is not fundamentally individualistic or fundamentally collective. It is both." Quoting evolutionary biologist E.O. Wilson, Woodard continues, "'If individual selection were to dominate, societies would dissolve. If group selection were to dominate, human groups would come to resemble ant colonies.'" From an evolutionary point of view, selfish individuals may outperform altruistic individuals, but "groups of altruists beat groups of selfish individuals."[124]

We pointed out in Chapter 2 a complexity of American democracy not shared by European countries: America does not have a singular, common culture. We are a geographically vast and diverse country that houses eleven distinct nations, each with different geography, culture, priorities and fundamental values. Geographically, most of these 11 different nations, however, are aligned as red states; but even within the red states there are value differences — some are more libertarian than others. The nations that comprise the blue states, as we pointed out, have more people and economic power. These differing nations, red and blue, each have "a different answer as to where the balance point lies on the individualist-communitarian spectrum. Some have always been more inclined toward the common good, others to individual liberty."[125]

Thus, it should not be surprising that the needs of blue states with their urban dwellers are the Republican Party's Cassandra and the requirements of red states with their country dwellers are the Democrat's Cassandra.

Standing up to today's oligarchic Democracy of Dollars and returning us to a Democracy of People will not be accomplished in a society with a weak government that ignores or belittles either individual liberty or the common good or fails to protect us from oligarchic power. James Madison wrote in Federalist Papers #51, "It is of great importance in a republic not only to guard the society against the oppression of its rulers, but to guard one party of society against the injustice of the other part.... In a society under the forms of which the stronger faction can readily unite and oppose the weaker, anarchy may truly be said to reign as in the state of nature, where the weaker individual is not secured against the violence of the stronger."

Our political leanings and beliefs are certainly shaped by our upbringing and experiences as well as by our DNA. But to a large degree, perhaps not given enough attention in political philosophy, we are what Jim Marshall calls us, *Prisoners of Geography.* He writes, "The land on which we live has always shaped us. It has shaped the wars, the power, politics, and social development of peoples that now inhabit nearly every part of the earth.... The physical realities that underpin national and international politics are too often disregarded in both writing about history and in contemporary reporting of world affairs."[126] Geography underlies the "why" of much of human affairs. When it comes to problem-solving, and our shedding our Democracy of Dollars for a Democracy of People, we cannot be Cassandra-like nonbelievers and overlook that fact.

Texas is a big state, most of which resides under the Greater Appalachia banner of the 11 American nations. But its northern tip is in the Midlands nation. Its eastern borders are part of the

Deep South nation, and its southwest rests in the nation of El Norte. Except for El Norte Texans and Texans in large swatches of its major cities (San Antonio, Houston, Austin, Dallas) who voted primarily Democratic, Texas is a red state through and through.

Red states, like blue states, can suffer disasters, and in February 2021, one of the worst winter storms recorded in human history pummeled and battered Texas along with other parts of the South. Beyond freezing temperatures and heavy snows, millions of Texans lost power and water for several days. Untold numbers died from hypothermia or other storm-related causes. The Insurance Council of Texas said the storm would produce the "largest insurance claim in [Texas] history." People died in their homes, from house fires attributed to burning furniture to keep warm. Water pipes burst in homes and hospitals and roadways cracked. A lot of things went wrong for the Texans because of the storm; but the worst was the failure of its power grid. Strongly independent, Texas seceded from the national power grid, and ran its own power grid.

The Wall Street Journal reported, "A fundamental flaw in the freewheeling Texas electricity market left millions powerless and freezing in the dark this week during a historic cold snap." Why? The Journal says there's no law in Texas requiring electric utilities to deliver power during a storm. Texas utilities are only paid for power delivered, not power capacity banked for future emergencies. "Texas officials don't require plant owners to prepare for the worst by spending extra money to ensure they can continue operating through severe cold or heat."

Steeped in the principle that individual liberty has priority over the common good, the Texas idea has been that the potential for collecting extra revenues for peak power use during storms would motivate utilities to invest in the right kind of power generators and the grid. Obviously, the potential didn't provide enough motivation.

Opting out of participation in the federal grid, the Texas system neither receives nor delivers power outside its intrastate grid. The Journal says that was by design. When a cold snap knocked out 200 power plants in 2011, rather than rejoin the federal grid for backup power, or install mandatory regulatory standards from the lessons learned, or insist on systemic improvements to minimize blackouts, the Texas power grid operator, the Electric Reliability Council of Texas (ERCOT), came up with a set of non-enforceable best practices[127]. Calls from less libertarian Texans for ERCOT to prepare for future storms were treated as prognostics foisted by an unreliable Cassandra. The Texas Tribune reported that Texas regulators "have repeatedly ignored, dismissed or watered-down efforts to address weaknesses in the state's sprawling electric grid."[128]

Former governor turned energy secretary under Trump, Rick Perry, offered an "interesting perspective," published in the blog of Republican House Minority Leader Kevin Mc Carthy. McCarthy quoted Perry responding to the claim that "those watching on the left may see the situation in Texas as an opportunity to expand their top-down radical proposals." Perry's response:

> "'Texans would be without electricity for longer than three days to keep the federal government out of their business.'"

The subtitle to the Vanity Fair article about Perry's comments is "The former governor turned Trump energy secretary thinks people freezing to death should hold out a little longer."[129]

To the extent Perry's attitude has been shared by Texans, it may change. The Wall Street Journal reported that Texas's deregulated electric grid required "deregulated Texas residential consumers [to pay] $28 billion more for their power since 2004 than they would have paid at rates charged to the customers of the state's traditional utilities...."[130] And the New York Times reports about marathon legislative hearings, criminal investigation and demands for accountability in "Texans Demand Answers as They Grapple With Storm's Lingering Wrath."[131]

In "The Deadly Winter Storm In Texas Has Exposed The State's Deep Inequalities," Venessa Wong and Clarissa-Jan Lim wrote: "In a state that promotes a sense of independence and self-reliance, those with the least have been left to seek help on their own amid life-threatening circumstances."[132] Wealthy Texans, like Senator Ted Cruz, can avoid the ravages of the storm and power outage by flying off to balmy Cancun[133]. Or, if they can't go to Cancun, they can afford to camp out in hotels with backup power generators. But most Texans aren't that lucky. For the Texans who are unable to fend for themselves and are without heat, potable water or food, Perry's libertarian idea is not a problem-solver. For many, it was a death sentence[134]. As former Texas Congressman Beto O'Rourke put it, Texas politicians "like to spend more time on [Fox News] talking about the Green New Deal and wind turbines than they would in trying to help those who desperately need it."[135]

In Chapter 6, we commented: "Whether we have politically conservative or liberal leanings, our beliefs depend on how we value each of what psychologist Jonathan Haidt identified in 2013 as our six "moral foundations" in *The Righteous Mind.* The six foundations are care/harm, fairness/cheating, liberty/oppression, loyalty/betrayal, authority/subversion and sanctity/degradation. Democrats are more concerned about the moral foundation of care than are Republicans. Republicans prioritize the foundations of loyalty and authority more than Democrats.

Fortunately for the beleaguered Texans, President Biden declared Texas a major disaster, making available for Texans a wide range of "federal assistance to help those affected by the severe winter storm that pummeled the South ... killing more than 50 people and initially rendering millions without power, heat or potable water."[136]

Biden's focus was on caring, on the common good.

In his Sunday CNN interview, Republican Congressman Michael McCaul from Texas thought that was the right idea[137].

These four takeaways are but a few of the many lessons that will come to us from the 2020 election, the insurrection and the failed coup d'état. The four takeaways selected relate to issues that must be addressed if we are to invigorate our heretofore too-silent *Voice of the People* and meet the challenges we write about in this book.

We close our *Epilogue* with a compliment to corporate America.

Fifth, a Compliment to Corporate America for Its Successful Efforts in Saving Our Fragile Democracy

Democracy of Dollars is not a critique on corporate America. It is a critique on a broken political system, driven by dollars, that no longer produces the Democracy of People it was designed to create. It is the political system that's in need of course correction. Corporations are inanimate, intangible beings with neither personality nor independent will. It's those who run corporations, primarily boards of directors and CEOs, that give corporations personality and character. A surprising result of the 2020 election, the insurrection and attempted coup d'état, is that several corporations, reflecting the positive values of those who breathe life into their existence, also breathed some healthy life into our fragile democracy.

In a Wall Street Journal article, "How the Capitol Riot Thrust Big American Companies Deeper Into Politics," Emily Glazer and Chip Cutter wrote, "Corporate moves to decry the forces behind the Jan. 6 riot accelerate a broader movement in business to address social and political issues…. Companies like Marriott International, Inc. and Walmart, Inc. paused donations to dozens of Republican lawmakers who voted against certifying the Electoral College votes, with some others demanding refunds." Dow Inc. CEO Jim Fitterling wrote a memo to Dow employees explaining Dow's rationale for stopping contributions: "'Words are not enough. We are committed to action.'"[138]

As surprising and important as those statements of corporate ethics are, they were neither the most surprising nor significant for our Democracy of People. For a glimpse into that surprise, we turn to Molly Ball's Time Magazine article, "The Secret History of the Shadow Campaign That Saved the 2020 Election."[139] As the votes were being counted and Trump's protests to the legitimacy of the election sprouted wings, "a conspiracy unfolded behind the scenes, one that both curtailed the protests and coordinated resistance from CEOs." It was the result of an informal compact that initially formed between business and labor. After more than a year of hard work that began in the fall of 2019, the group released its November 3, 2020, election-day, Joint Press Release from the U.S. Chamber of Commerce, National Association of Evangelicals, AFL-CIO, and National African American Clergy calling for all votes to be counted. In part, the Press Release said:

> "Although we may not always agree on desired outcomes up and down the ballot, we are united in our call for American democratic process to proceed without violence, intimidation or any other tactic that makes us weaker as a nation. A free and fair election is one in which everyone eligible to cast a ballot can, all ballots are counted consistent with the law and the American people, through their votes, determine the outcome."[140]

The Press Release was not the culmination of the shadow campaign. It was simply the statement of the principles behind what was to come. The shadow partners did not aim to stop Trump from being elected. The group's goal was to shore up American institutions under attack and ensure an accurate election. In fact, several Trump supporters were participants in the group's bipartisan committees, convinced by the organizers that Trump, too, deserved a fair and accurate election. They pressured social media to be tough on misinformation. They put out public awareness campaigns across the nation. They monitored pressure points, like the Michigan vote count, to minimize the risk of an overturn based on the false claims that were being bandied across the media. Both Democrats and Republicans were recruited to participate in the effort.

Norm Eisen, Voter Protection Program's legal counsel, said, "The untold story of the election is the thousands of people of both parties who accomplished the triumph of American democracy at its very foundation."

Protect Democracy's Ian Basin added, "Every attempt to interfere with the proper outcomes of the election was defeated. But it's massively important for the country to understand that it didn't happen accidentally. The system didn't work magically. Democracy is not self-executing."

In the end, the plots to overturn the election were shut down. There were a lot of heroes who prevented the 2020 election from being overwhelmed by conspiracy theories and false news. But it was the unsung corporate heroes in the shadows, organized and led by the AFL-CIO and the U.S. Chamber of Commerce, that kept the election on a fair and honest course, who were the glue that made it happen. Molly Ball concludes her article, "Democracy won in the end. The will of the people prevailed. But it's crazy, in retrospect, that this is what it took to put on an election in the United States of America."[141]

We owe these quiet heroes more than our gratitude. We must take up their legacy and perpetuate their example. Like Schweizer, their lives were their arguments, as ours must also be.

"Democracy Doesn't Happen by Accident"

In his February 20, 2021 talk to the Munich Security Conference, President Biden warned that democracy is under attack worldwide. He said: "The challenges we face are different. We're at an inflection point.... New crises demand our attention. And we cannot focus only on competition among countries that threaten to divide the world, or only on global challenges that threaten to sink us together if we fail to cooperate. We must do both... We are in the midst of a fundamental debate about the future and direction of the world.

We're at an inflection point between those who argue that, given all the challenges we face — from the fourth industrial revolution to a global pandemic — that autocracy is the best way forward, they argue, and those who understand that democracy is essential — essential to meeting those challenges. … We must demonstrate that democracies can still deliver for our people in this changed world. That, in my view, is our galvanizing mission…. Democracy doesn't happen by accident. We have to defend it, fight for it, strengthen it, renew it."[142]

It's in the renewal, strengthening, and defense of democracy where you and I come in. It's where achieving a healthy balance between individual liberty and the common good must be achieved, and we must insist on it being accomplished.

No doubt we will meet resistance. Our insistence may be squelched by the Cassandra effect of those unwilling to imagine the frightening damage our fragile democracy is suffering. That's when we step up and crow like a rooster. It's when we bolster the Voice of the People until the result is achieved — because we never forget:

"Democracy doesn't happen by accident."

Epilogue Endnotes

1 Trump's campaign rhetoric, promising to protect Americans from the corruption of the *deep state*, is a source of his popularity. In February 2021, Florida Republican Representative Matt Goetz, criticizing Wyoming Republican Congresswoman Liz Cheney for voting with Democrats to impeach Trump, said he lists Cheney with people in the Democrat leadership who "want to return our government to its default setting of screwing the American people to their benefit." See DeBonis M and Kane M, "Senate Republicans move against 'nutty' House member in widening GOP rift" [*Washington Post* February 2, 2021]

2 Kessler G "Trump made 30,573 false or misleading claims as president. Nearly half came in his final year." [*Washington Post* January 23, 2021]

3 Vosoughi S, Roy D, and Aral S, "The spread of truth and false news online" [*359 Science 6380* March 9, 2018]

4 Farber D, "Rethinking Presidential Administration" [*Legal Planet* January 14, 2021]

5 Madison T, "Judicial Powers of the National Government," June 20, 1788 [*Founders Online*]

6 Higgins A, "Trump's Post-Election Tactics Put Him in Unsavory Company" [*New York Times* November 11, 2020, updated November 26, 2020]

7 Pompeo M, "The United States Responds to the Maduro Regime's Attempts To Corrupt Democratic Elections in Venezuela" [*U. S. Department of State* September 4, 2020]

8 Higgins A, *supra*, and Olsen R, "Myanmar's Military Stages Coup, Detains Aung San Suu Kai and Other Leaders" [*Forbes* January 31, 2021]

9 Frey W, "Biden-won counties are home to 67 million more Americans than Trump-won counties" [*Brookings* January 21, 2021]

10 Choi J, "Trump says he'll leave White House if Biden declared winner of Electoral College" [*The Hill* November 29, 2020]

11 Sullivan K and Agiesta J, "Biden's popular vote margin over Trump tops 7 million" [*CNN politics* December 4, 2020]

12 Cillizza C, "The titanic hypocrisy of the 'election fraud' crowd" [*CNN politics* December 8, 2020]

13 Butter M, *The Nature of Conspiracy Theories* (Suhrkamp Verlag Berlin 2018; Polity Press 2020) p. 20, 22

14 Wilstein M, "Trump Lawyer Calls for Supreme Court to "Step in and Do Something' to Help President Win" [*Daily Beast* November 5, 2020]

15 Long C and White E, "Trump thought courts were key to winning. Judges disagreed." [*Associated Press* December 8, 2020]

16 Guardian staff and agencies, "Trump's latest batch of election lawsuits fizzle as dozens of losses pile up" [*The Guardian* December 4, 2020]

17 Bade R, "Trump asks Pennsylvania House speaker for help in overturning election results, personally intervening in a third state" [*Washington Post* December 7, 2020]. However, several Pennsylvania Republican legislators wrote to their Congressional colleagues asking them to challenge the electoral college results.

18 See for example: Neidig H, "Federal judge rejects Michigan Republicans' efforts to decertify election results" [*The Hill* December 7, 2020]; and Choi J, "Georgia elections chief says special session to overturn election would be 'nullifying the will of the people'" [*The Hill* December 6, 2020]; and Ozimek T, "Arizona House Speaker Rejects Trump Campaign Call to Overturn Election"[*The Epic Times* December 5, 2020]. See also: Johnson K, "Attorney General Barr: Justice Dept. finds no evidence of fraud to alter election outcome" [*USA Today* December 1, 2020]. But see Chait J, "A Disturbing Number of Republicans Support Trump's Coup Attempt" [*Intelligence Report, New Yorker Magazine* November 17, 2020]

19 "Trump's failed attempt to overturn the election" [*The Week Magazine* December 4, 2020]

20 "Democracy Report 2020" [*V-Dem Institute* March 2020]

21 Ingram C, "The United States is backsliding into autocracy under Trump, scholars warn" [*Washington Post* November 23, 2020]

22 Trump D, "Remarks by President Trump at the Presentation of the Presidential Medal of Freedom to Dan Gable" [*White House* December 7, 2020]

23 Corasaniti N, Ember S, and Feuer A, "The Nation Reached 'Safe Harbor.' Here's What That Means." [*The New York Times* December 8, 2020]

24 Higgins T and Breuninger K, "Texas sues four battleground states in Supreme Court over 'unlawful election results' in 2020 presidential race" [*CNBC* December 8, 2020]

25 The states: Missouri, Alabama, Arkansas, Florida, Indiana, Kansas. Louisiana. Mississippi, Montana, Nebraska, North Dakota, Oklahoma, South Carolina, South Dakota, Tennessee, Utah and West Virginia.

26 State of Texas v. Commonwealth of Pennsylvania, State of Georgia, State of Michigan, and State of Wisconsin "On Motion for Leave to File Bill of Complaint" [*Office of the Missouri Attorney General* December 9, 2020]

27 Zhao C, "Republicans Rally Around Texas Election Lawsuit as AG's Rail Against the 'Circus' [*Newsweek* December 8, 2020]

28 Quinn M, "GOP lawmaker soliciting fellow Republicans to back Texas effort challenging election results [*CBS NEWS* November 10, 2020]

29 Brufke J and Wong S, "100 House Republicans sign brief backing Texas lawsuit challenging election results" [*The Hill* December 10, 2020]

30 Totenberg N, "Trump Asks Supreme Court To Let Him Join Widely Scorned Texas Election Law Suit" [*NPR WBEZ Chicago* November 9, 2020]

31 Wilson K, "Moody signs brief in support of Texas lawsuit" [*Times/Herald* December 10, 2020]

32 Gordon JS, "The 12th Amendment's Dangerous Defect" [*Wall Street Journal* February 23, 2021]

33 Editorial Board, "Trump's coup might not work. But he may pave the way for the next failed candidate" [*Washington Post* November 18, 2020]

34 Shepherd K, "Armed protestors alleging voter fraud surrounding the home of Michigan's secretary of state" [*Washington Post* December 7, 2020]

35 Mogelson L, "Among the Insurrectionists" [*The New Yorker* January 25, 2021]

36 Ramachandran S, Berzon A, and Ballhaus R "Jan. 6 Rally Funded by Top Trump Donors, Helped by Alex Jones, Organizers Say" [*Wall Street Journal* February 1, 2021]. See also Papenfuss M "Trump Campaign Paid $2.7 Million To People, Firms That Planned Rally Sparking Capital Riot" [*Huff Post* January 22, 2021]

37 Magelson L, "Among the Insurrectionists" [*The New Yorker* January 25, 2021]

38 Peiser J, "GOP Rep. Madison Cawthorn told a crowd before Capitol riots it had 'fight in it.' Now he says. 'I don't regret it.' [*Washington Post* February 5, 2021]

39 "It Was an Attempted Coup: The Cline Center's Coup D'État Project Categorizes the January 6, 2021 Assault on the US Capitol" [*Cline Center for Advanced Social Research, University of Illinois* January 27, 2021]. See also United States House of Representatives, In the Senate of the United States Sitting as a Court of Impeachment, "Trial Memorandum of the United States House of Representatives in the Impeachment Trial of President Donald J. Trump" [*United States House of Representatives* February 2, 2021]

40 WSJ Editors, "Why Democrats Want a Trump Trial" [*Wall Street Journal* February 9, 2021]

41 Ball M, "Breaking Point" [*Time Magazine* February 18, 2021]

42 Wong S and Lillis M, "Five big takeaways on the Capitol security hearings" [*The Hill* February 23, 2021]

43 Shabad R, "Capitol Police chief warns extremists 'want to blow up the Capitol' when Biden addresses Congress" [*NBC News* February 25, 2021]. See also Lang JL, "As fractures emerge among Proud Boys, experts warn of a shift toward extremist violence" [*Washington Post* February 26, 2021]. See also Simon M, Sidner S, and Rappard

A-M, "Proud Boys leader has no sympathy for lawmakers targeted by Capitol riot" [*CNN politics* February 25, 2021]

44 O'Donnell T, "Lindsey Graham: Impeachment could 'destroy' GOP [*yahoo! News* January 17, 2021]

45 Sprunt B, "7 GOP Senators Voted to Convict Trump. Only 1 Faces Voters Next Year" [*NPR* February 15, 2021]

46 Higgins T "GOP senators who voted to convict Trump are now facing backlash in their home states" [*CNBC* February 14, 2021]

47 McConnell M, "Acquittal Vindicated the Constitution, Not Trump" [*Wall Street Journal* February 15, 2021]. But see Lam C, "McConnell's Trump impeachment outrage passes the buck and he knows it" [*Think* February 17, 2021]

48 Hulse C and Fandos N, "McConnell, Denouncing Trump After Voting to Acquit, Says His Hands Were Tied" [*New York Times* February 13, 2021]

49 Hughes S, "McConnell Doesn't Care About Trump Brand in 2022, He Just Wants Electable Candidates" [*Wall Street Journal* February 15, 2021]

50 Leary A and Wise L, "Trump's Statement Criticizes McConnell, Calling Him a 'Political Hack'" [*Wall Street Journal* February 16, 2021]

51 Field J, "Mitch McConnell 'absolutely' would support Trump if GOP nominee in 2024" [*Fox News* February 26, 2021]

52 "Pelosi says independent commission will examine Capitol riot" [*PBS News Hour* February 15, 2021]. See also, Yen H, "Bipartisan support grows for 9/11-style inquiry into Capitol riot after Trump acquittal" [*Fox29* February 15, 2021]. See also Feuer A and Hong N, "As Impeachment Ends, Federal Inquiry Looms as Reminder of Trump's Role in Riot" [*New York Times* February 13, 2021]

53 Mihm K, Apkon A and Venkatachalam S, "Litigation Tracker: Pending Criminal and Civil Cases Against Donald Trump" [*Just Security* March 1, 2021]. See also Bump P, "Once Impeachment is over, the threat to Trump shifts to real courtrooms" [*Washington Post* February 12, 2021]; and Associated Press, "Impeachment Isn't the Final Word on Capitol Riot for Trump" [*US News* February 15, 2021]; and Rubin J, "Could Trump be disqualified through other

means?" [*Washington Post* February 15, 2021]; and Mangan D, "Former President Trump faces serious criminal, civil investigations after White House" [*CNBC* February 16, 2021]

54 Goldiner D, "NAACP sues Trump under anti-Ku Klux Klan Act for intimidation and incitement of Capitol riot" [*Daily News* February 16, 2021]

55 AP, "Congressman Eric Swalwell files lawsuit against Trump over Capitol insurrection" [*ABC 7 News* March 5, 2021]

56 Valentino-DeVries J, Ashford G, Lu D, Lutz E, Matthews AL, and Yourish K, "Arrested in Capitol Riot: Organized Militants and a Horde of Radicals" [*New York Times* February 4, 2021]

57 Tillman Z, "The Capitol Rioters Are Starting To Face Much More Serious Charges For the Insurrection" [*BuzzFeed News* February 19, 2021]. See also "Program on Extremism" [*George Washington University* February 18, 2021]

58 Harrington R, Hall M, Gould S, Haroun AQ, Shamsian J, and Ardrey T, "More than 310 people have been charged in the Capitol insurrection. This searchable table shows them all." [*Insider* March 1, 2021]. See also Lynch SN and Hosenball M, "U.S. says more than 300 people charged to date over Capitol riots [*Reuters* February 26, 2021]

59 McDonald C and Hymes C, "'Duped' and 'egged on': Capitol rioters use Trump as an excuse in court" [*CBS News* February 16, 2021]

60 Weiner R and Hsu SS, "Capitol riot defendants facing jail time have regrets. Judges aren't buying it." [*Washington Post* February 26, 2021]

61 "The Influence of the Nuremberg Trial on International Criminal Law" [Robert H. Jackson Center]

62 Trump D, "Protecting American Monuments, and Statutes and Combating Recent Criminal Violence" Executive Order 13933 [*Federal Register* June 26, 2020]

63 Benner K, Feuer A and Goldman A, "F.B.I. Finds Contact Between Proud Boys Member and Trump Associate Before Riot" [*New York Times* March 5, 2021]. See also Valentino-DeVries J, Lu D, Lutz E and Matthews AL, "A Small Group of Militants' Outsize

Role in the Capitol Attack" [*New York Times* February 21, 2021]. See also Broadwater L and Rosenberg M, "Republican Ties to Extremist Groups Are Under Scrutiny" [*New York Times* updated February 5, 2021]. See also Feuer A, "Oath Keeper Plotting Before Capitol Riot Awaited 'Direction' From Trump, Prosecutors Say" [New York Times February 11, 2021]

64 Olorunnipa T and Lee MYH "Trump's lie that the election was stolen has cost $519 million (and counting) as taxpayers fund enhanced security, legal fees, property repairs and more" [*Washington Post* February 6, 2021]. See also, Cochrane E and Broadwater L, "Capitol Riot Costs Will Exceed $30 Million, Official Tells Congress" [*New York Times* February 24, 2021]

65 Lipton E, "Trump Call to Georgia Official Might Violate State and Federal Law" [*New York Times* January 3, 2021]. See also, Sullivan A and Martina M, "In recorded call, Trump pressures Georgi official to 'find' votes to overturn election" [*Reuters* January 3, 2021]

66 Biskupic J, "The Supreme Court's clear message to President Trump: Stop" [*CNN politics* December 12, 2020]. See also "'The last wall:' How dozens of judges across the political spectrum rejected Trump's efforts to overturn the election" [*Washington Post* December 12, 2020]

67 Zhong A, "Trump Says Supreme Court 'Incompetent and Weak' Over Election Fraud" [*Epoch Times* December 26, 2020]

68 Mangan D and Breuninger K, "Mike Pence rejects Trump's call to overturn Biden election" [*CNBC* January 6, 2021]

69 "Trump publicly attacked Pence during the Capitol riot knowing Pence was in trouble, GOP senator suggests." [*The Week* February 11, 2021]

70 Carney J, "Senate passes bill to award Capitol Police officer Congressional Gold Medal" [*The Hill* February 12, 2021]

71 Yancey-Bragg N, "'Hero' Capitol officer who led rioters away from Senate may get a Congressional Gold Medal" [*USA Today* January 15, 2021]. See also Kristian B, "Would the Capitol mob have killed Mike Pence?" [*The Week* February 11, 2021]

72 Schouten F and Mena K, "high-profile elections officials leave posts after a tumultuous 2020" [*CNN politics* February 19, 2021]

73 Axelrod D, "David Axelrod: History will scorn the cowards who fear Trump [*CNN Opinion* December 11, 2020]

74 Deane C and Gramlich J, "2020 Election reveals two broad voting coalitions fundamentally at odds" *[Fact Tank Pew Research Center* November 6, 2020]

75 Lindsay J, "The 2020 Election by the Numbers" [*Council on Foreign Relations* December 15, 2020]

76 "The voting experience in 2020" [*Pew Research Center* November 20, 2020]

77 Abrams A, "Mail Voting Boosted Turnout for Voters With Disabilities. Will Lawmakers Let It Continue? [*Time Magazine* February 18, 2021]

78 Corasaniti N and Rutenberg J, "Republicans Pushed to Restrict Voting. Millions of Americans Pushed Back" [*New York Times* December 6, 2020]. See also Wines M, "After Record Turnout, Republicans Are Trying to Make It Harder to Vote" [*New York Times* January 30, 2021].

79 Timm JC, "Cobb County in Georgia adds 2 more early voting sites after outcry from voting rights advocates" [*NBC News* December 9, 2020]. See also Mansoor S, "After Georgia Flips Blue, Voting Rights Advocates Brace for New Voting Restrictions" [*Time Magazine* January 14, 2021]

80 Tanfani J and Lewis S, "As Trump pushes baseless fraud claims, Republicans pledge tougher voting rules" [*Reuters* December 21, 2020]. See also Gardner A, "State GOP lawmakers propose flurry of voting restrictions to placate Trump supporters, springing fear of backlash" [*Washington Post* February 19, 2021]

81 LeBlanc P, "Iowa governor signs controversial law shortening early and Election Day voting" [*CNN politics* March 8, 2021]

82 "Voting Laws Roundup 2021" [*Brennan Center for Justice* February 8, 2021]

83 Klas ME, "Florida Republicans push limits on vote by mail" [*Tampa Bay Times* February 16, 2021]; and Stracqualursi V, "Florida GOP Gov. DeSantis proposes voting restrictions for state lawmakers to pass this session" [*CNN politics* February 19, 2021]

84 Morales-Doyle S, "The Supreme Court Case Challenging Voting Restrictions in Arizona Explained" [*Brennan Center for Justice* February 25, 2021]

85 "Voting Laws Roundup 2021" [*Brennan Center for Justice* February 8, 2021]; and "Voting Laws Roundup Appendix: February 2021" [*Brennan Center for Justice* February 24, 2021]. See also "State Voting Bills Tracker 2021" [*Brennan Center for Justice* Updated February 24, 2021]

86 Controversy of the Week, "Elections: Should it be easier or harder to vote?" [*The Week Magazine* February 19, 2021]

87 Anderson J, "Challenges to Black voting rights harks back to Jim Crow era" [*USA Today* March 5, 2021]

88 Shelby County v. Holder, 570 U. S. 529 (2013)

89 Hardy M, "Drawing the Line" [*ACLU Magazine* Winter 2021]

90 Andrews N, "Lawmakers Prepare for Battles Over Congressional Redistricting" [*Wall Street Journal* December 28, 2020]

91 Epstein RJ and Corasaniti N, "The Gerrymander Battle Looms, as G.O.P. Looks to Press Its Advantage" [*New York Times* February 1, 2021]

92 Andrews N, "Lawmakers Prepare for Battles Over Congressional Redistricting" [*Wall Street Journal* December 28, 2020]. See also, Wilson R, "Legislatures across country plan sweeping election reform push" [*The Hill* December 10, 2020]

93 Sozan M, "Momentum Grows for Bold Democracy Reform" [*Center for American Progress* February 10, 2021]

94 Park S, "Sen. Manchin holds key to Biden's progressive agenda: [*FOX Business* February 18, 2021]

95 WSJ Opinion, "H.R.1 Will Make America More Democratic" [*Wall Street Journal* November 24, 2020]

96 The Editorial Board, "Pelosi's Top Priority: Consolidating Power" [*Wall Street Journal* January 14, 2021]

97 See Controversy of the Week, *supra*, EN #86

98 Beckwith RT, "Republicans Efforts to Restrict Voting Risk

Backfiring on Party" [*Bloomberg* February 16, 2021]

99 Gardner A, "State GOP lawmakers propose flurry of voting restrictions to placate Trump supporters, springing fear of backlash" [*Washington Post* February 19, 2021]. See also Rosenfeld S, "Republicans Trying to Restrict Voting May See Their Schemes Backfire" [*The National Memo* March 5, 2021]

100 Richardson HC, "February 25, 2021" [*Letters from an American* February 25, 2021]

101 Rivkin DB and Snead J, "An Unconstitutional Voting 'Reform'" [*Wall Street Journal* February 17, 2021]

102 Corasaniti N, "Pennsylvania G.O.P.'s Push for More Power Over Judiciary Raises Alarms" [*New York Times* February 15, 2021]

103 Cooper JJ, "GOP Bills Target Arizona Voting Laws After Trump's Loss" [*US News* January 29, 2021]

104 Brownstein R, "On immigration, Biden seeks a new approach to an old deadlock" [*CNN* politics January 26, 2021]; and Carvajal N, "Biden calls on Congress to 'enact common sense gun law reforms' on third anniversary of Parkland shooting" [*CNN politics* February 14, 2021]

105 Leary A, "Biden Agenda Seeking to Unify in Opposition After Impeachment" [*Wall Street Journal* February 14, 2021]

106 "For Better Elections, Copy the Neighbors" [*Wall Street Journal* February 17, 2021]

107 "The Hundred Million Project" [*Knight Foundation* February 18, 2020]/

108 "Lift Every Voice: The Urgency of Universal Civic Duty Voting" [*Brookings* July 20, 2020]

109 Corasaniti N, Karni A and Paz IG, "'There's Nothing Left': Why Thousands of Republicans Are Leaving the Party" [*New York Times* February 10, 2021]. See also, Reid T, "Exclusive: Dozens of former Bush officials leave Republican Party, calling it 'Trump cult'" [*Reuters* February 1, 2021]

110 "Party Affiliation" [*Gallup News:* trends since 2004, updated through February 18, 2021]

111 Brown EN, "Americans Reject Republicans *and* Democrats in Record Numbers" [*Reason Roundup* March 3, 2021]

112 "Radio Host Shaped Conservative Views" [*Wall Street Journal* February 19, 2021]

113 Young NJ, "Rush Limbaugh taught Republicans to rage" [*The Week Magazine* February 18, 2021]

114 Prager D, "The Left Hated Rush Limbaugh Because He Had Their Number" [*Wall Street Journal* February 19, 2021]

115 "Rush Limbaugh" [*Wall Street Journal* February 19, 2021]

116 Walther M, "How Rush Limbaugh created modern politics" [*The Week Magazine* February 17, 2021]

117 Heffernan M, *Willful Blindness* (Bloomsbury USA 2011) p. 201

118 Durant W and Durant A, *The Lessons of History* (Simon & Schuster Paperbacks 1968) p. 36

119 Woodard C, *American Character* (Penguin Books 2016) p. 7

120 Woodard, *supra,* p 9

121 Haensel B, "Why the counties Joe Biden won represent 70% of US GDP" [*Fortune* November 12, 2020]

122 "2020 US Presidential Election Map By County & Vote Share" [*Brilliant Maps* December 3, 2020]

123 Haensel B, *supra.*

124 Woodard, *supra,* p 11

125 Woodard, *supra,* p 23

126 Marshall T, *Prisoners of Geography* (Scribner 2015) p 1

127 Blunt K and Gold R, "The Texas Freeze: Why the Power Grid Failed" [*Wall Street Journal* February 19, 2021]

128 Oxner R, Ferman M and Aguilar J, "Catastrophic Texas power outages prompt finger pointing and blame shifting at legislative hearings" [*The Texas Tribune* February 25, 2021]

129 Levin B, "Rick Perry Suggests Texans Voluntarily Go Without Heat to Fend Off Scourge of Socialism." [*Vanity Fair* February 18,

2021]

130 McGinty T and Patterson S, "Texas Electric Bills Were $28 Billion Higher Under Deregulation" [*Wall Street Journal* February 24, 2021]

131 Rojas R, "Texans Demand Answers as They Grapple With Storm's Lingering Wrath" [*New York Times* February 26, 2021]

132 Wong V and Lim C-J, "The Deadly Winter Storm In Texas Has Exposed the State's Deep Inequalities" [*Buzz-Feed* February 18, 2021]

133 Easley J, "Cruz takes hits at home for leaving during crisis" [*The Hill* February 18, 2021]

134 McDonnell G, del Rio N, Fausset R, and Diaz J, "Extreme Cold Killed Texans in Their Bedrooms, Vehicles and Backyards" [*New York Times* February 19, 2021]

135 Sargent G, "Opinion: The latest GOP nonsense on Texas shows us the future Republicans want" [*Washington Post* February 18, 2021]

136 Martin B, Iati M, Wang AB, and Bellware K, "Biden declares major disaster in Texas as focus shifts to who is responsible for the winter weather crisis" [*Washington Post* February 20, 2021]

137 Bowden J, "Texas GOP congressman: Federal disaster aid will help homeowners with high utility bills" [*The Hill* February 21, 2021]

138 Glazer E and Cutter C, "How the Capitol Riot Thrust Big American Companies Deeper Into Politics" [*Wall Street Journal* January 16, 2021]

139 Ball M, "The Secret History of the Shadow Campaign That Saved the 2020 Election" [*Time Magazine* February 4, 2021]

140 Press Release "AFL-CIO, Chamber of Commerce, National Faith Leaders Call for Votes to Be Counted" [*AFL-CIO* November 3, 2020]

141 Ball M, "The Secret History of the Shadow Campaign That Saved the 2020 Election" [*Time Magazine* February 4, 2021]

142 "Remarks by President Biden at the 2021 Virtual Munich Security Conference" [*The White House* February 21, 2021]

Index

Definitions Appendix

Primary Definitions Source: Black's Law Dictionary, Fifth Pocket Edition, Bryan A. Garner, Editor in Chief, Thomson Reuters (2016). Definitions from Black's Law Dictionary identified: [BLD].

Administrative Law: The law governing the organization and operation of administrative agencies (including executive and independent agencies) and the relations of administrative agencies with the legislature, the executive, the judiciary, and the public. [BLD]

Amicus curiae: [Latin "friend of the court."] Someone who is not a party to a lawsuit but who petitions the court or is requested by the court to file a brief in the action because that person has a strong interest in the subject matter. – Often shortened to *amicus.* [BLD]

Amicus brief: A brief, usually at the appellate level, prepared and filed by an amicus curiae with the court's permission. [BLD]

Answer: A defendant's first pleading that addresses the merits of a case, usually by denying the plaintiffs allegations. [BLD]

Baker Factors: Court-designed tests to determine if an issue before the court is a political question:[1] a textually demonstrable constitutional commitment of the issue to a coordinate political department; or [2] a lack of judicially discoverable and manageable standards for resolving it; or [3] the impossibility of deciding without an initial policy determination of a kind clearly for nonjudicial discretion; or [4] the impossibility of a court's undertaking independent resolution without expressing lack of the respect due coordinate branches of government; or [5] an unusual need for unquestioning adherence to a political decision already made; or [6] the potentiality of embarrassment from multifarious pronouncements by various departments on one question. [Baker v. Carr decision]

Brief: A written statement setting out the legal contentions of a party in litigation, especially on appeal; a document prepared by counsel as the basis for arguing a case, consisting of legal and factual arguments and the authorities in support of them. [BLD]

Cabinet: The advisory council to an executive officer, especially the President. [BLD]

Checks and balances: The theory of governmental power and functions whereby each branch of government has the ability to counter the actions of any other branch, so no single branch can control the entire government [BLD]

Common law: 1. The body of law derived from judicial decisions, rather than from statutes or constitutions; caselaw. 2. The body of law based on the English legal system, as distinct from a civil law system; the general Anglo-American system of legal concepts, together with the techniques of applying them, that form the basis of the law in jurisdictions where the system applies. [BLD]

Complaint: The initial pleading that starts a civil action and states the basis for the court's jurisdiction, the basis for the plaintiff's claim, and the demand for relief. [BLD]

Dictum: A statement of opinion or belief considered authoritative because of the dignity of the person making it. *Judicial dictum:* An opinion of the court on a question that is directly involved, briefed and argued by counsel, and even passed on by the court, but that is not essential to the decision and therefore not binding even if it may later be accorded some weight. [BLD]

Executive Order: An order issued by or on behalf of the President, usually intended to direct or instruct the actions of executive agencies or government officials or to set policies for the executive branch to follow. [BLD]

Framers: The individuals (referred to frequently as "Founders") who negotiated, designed, and wrote our federal Constitution, adopted in 1789.

Habeas corpus: [Law Latin "that you have the body."] A writ employed to bring a person before a court, most frequently to ensure that a person's imprisonment or detention is not legal. In addition to being used to test the legality of an arrest or commitment, the writ may be used to obtain judicial review of (1) the regularity of the extradition process, (2) the right to or amount of bail, or (3) the jurisdiction of the court that has imposed a criminal sentence. [BLD]

Interlocutory appeal: An appeal that occurs before the trial court's final ruling on the entire case. Some interlocutory appeals involve legal points necessary to the determination of the case, while others involve collateral orders that are wholly separate from the merits of the action. [BLD]

Judicial review: A court's power to review the actions of other branches of government; especially, the courts' power to invalidate legislative and executive actions as being unconstitutional. [BLD]

Lobby: 1. To talk with or curry favor with a legislator, usually repeatedly, or frequently, in an attempt to influence the legislator's vote. 2 To support or oppose (a measure) by working to influence a legislator's vote. 3. To try to influence (a political decision maker). [BLD]

Lobbying activities: Lobbying contacts and efforts in support of such contacts, including preparation and planning activities, research and other background work that is intended, at the time it is performed, for use in contacts, and coordination with the lobbying activities of others. [Lobbying Disclosure Act]

Mandamus: A writ issued by a court to compel performance of a particular act by a lower court or governmental officer or body, usually to correct a prior action or failure to act. [BLD]

Motion: A written or oral application requesting a court to make a specific ruling or order. [BLD]

Natural law: 1. A physical law of nature. 2. A philosophical system of legal and moral principles purportedly deriving from a universalized conception of human nature or divine justice rather than from legislative or judicial action; moral law embodied in principles of right and wrong. [BLD]

Pleading: A formal document in which a party to a litigation proceeding (especially a civil lawsuit) sets forth or responds to allegations, claims, denials, or defenses. [BLD]

Police Power: The inherent and plenary power of a sovereign power to make all laws necessary and proper to preserve public security, order, health, morality, and justice. [BLD]

Political question: A question that a court will not consider because it involves the exercise of discretionary power by the executive or legislative branch of government. [BLD]

Redress: 1. Relief, remedy. 2. A means of seeking relief or remedy. [BLD]

Redressability: The "standing" requirement that the plaintiff's claims or injuries must be redressable by a federal court under constitutional authority granted to them as Article III courts.

Ripeness: 1. The state of a dispute that has reached, but has not passed, the point when the facts have developed sufficiently to permit an intelligent and useful decision to be made. 2. The requirement that this state must exist before a court will decide a controversy. [BLD]

Separation of powers: 1. The division of governmental authority into three separate branches of government – legislative, executive, judicial – each with specific duties on which neither of the other branches can encroach. 2. The doctrine that such a division of governmental authority is the most desirable form of government because it establishes checks and balances designed to protect the people against tyranny. [BLD]

Standing: A plaintiff's right to make a legal claim and seek a judicial remedy, based on the plaintiff showing the court that (1) the plaintiff suffered an injury in fact, (2) the injury is fairly traceable to the defendant, and (3) the injury is likely redressable by a favorable judicial decision. [Juliana v. United States, 9th Circuit Court of Appeals decision]

Stare decisis: [Latin 'to stand by things decided'] The doctrine of precedent, under which a court must follow earlier judicial decisions when the same points arise again in litigation. [BLD]

Writ: A court's written order, in the name of the state or other competent legal authority, commanding the addressee to do or refrain from doing some specified act. [BLD]

References and Resources

Cases

Abrams v. United States, 250 U.S. 616 (1919}

Baker v. Carr, 369 U.S. 186 (1962)

Bostock v. Clayton County, Georgia, 590 U.S. ____ (2020)

Boynton v. State, 64 So. 2nd 536 (Florida 1953)

Brown v. Board of Education, 347 U.S. 483 (1954)

Buttfield v. Stranahan, 192 U.S. 470 (1904)

Chiafalo et al v. Washington, 591 U.S. ____ (2020)

Citizens United v. FEC, 558 U.S. 310 (2010)

Concerned Citizens of Nebraska v. United States Nuclear Regulatory Commission, 970 F. 2d 421 (8th Cir. 1992)

Damien Guedes, et al. v. Bureau of Alcohol, Tobacco, Firearms and Explosives et al, 589 U.S. ____ (March 2020)

District of Columbia v. Heller, 554 U.S. 570 (2008)

Endo v. the United States, 323 U.S. 283 (1944).

Gasper v. Louisiana Stadium and Expo. Dist., 418 F. Supp. 716 (E.D. La. 1976)

Gundy v. the United States, #17-6086, 586 U.S. ____ (2019)

Griswold v. Connecticut, 381 U.S. 479 (1965)

Hollingsworth v. Perry, 570 U.S. 693 (2013)

In re Abbott, #20-50264, 5th Circuit Court of Appeals (April 2020)

INS v. Chadha, 462 U.S. 919 (1983)

Jacobson v. Massachusetts, 197 U.S. 11 (1905)

Jones v. Securities and Exchange Commission, 298 U.S. 1 (1936)

Juliana v. United States, Docket # 18-36082, Court of Appeals, 9th Circuit (2020)

J. W. Hampton, Jr. v. United States, 296 U. S. 394 (1928)

League of United Latin America v. Gregory A, Doc. #19-50215 (5th Circuit 2020)

Lochner v. State of New York, 198 U.S. 45 (1905)

Marbury v. Madison, 5 U.S 137 (1803)

McCulloch v. Maryland, 17 U.S. 316 (1819)

Ohio Valley Water Co. v. Ben Avon Borough, 253 U.S. 287 (1920)

Planned Parenthood of Southeastern Pa. v. Casey, 505 U.S. 833 (1992)

Plessy v. Ferguson, 163 U.S. 537 (1896)

Poe v. Ulman, 367 U.S. 497 (1961)

Roe v. Wade, 410 U.S. 113 (1973)

Rucho v. Common Cause, 139 S. Ct. 2484 (2019)

Schechter v. United States, 295 U.S. 495 (1935)

Seila Law v. Consumer Financial Protection Bureau, #19-7, 140 S. Ct. 2183 (2020)

Trop v. Dulles, 356 U.S. 86 (1958)

United States v. Bollman et al, #14,622, Circuit Court District of Columbia (1807)

United States v. Carolene Products, 304 U.S. 144 (1938)

United States v. Richardson, 418 U.S. 166 (1974)

United States v. Robel, 389 U.S. 258 (1967)

Wayman v. Southard, 10 Wheat. 1 (U.S. 1825)

Youngstown Sheet and Tube Co. v. Sawyer, 343 U.S. 579 (1952)

Laws

Ethic in Government Act, 5 U.S.C. Appendix §§101-505

Ethics Reform Act of 1989, 18 U.S.C. §207 (Amends Ethic in Government Act)

Lobbying Disclosure Act, 2 U.S.C. 1602

National Emergency Act, 50 U.S.C. 1601

Standards of Ethical Conduct for Employees of the Executive Branch, U.S Office of Government Ethics, 5 C.F.R Part 2635, amended at 81 FR 81641 (January 1, 2017)

Texts

Allen D, "The Road from Serfdom," in *The American Crisis* by the writers of The Atlantic (Simon and Schuster 2020)

Barnett RE, *The Ninth Amendment: It Means What It Says* (University of Texas School of Law 2006)

Bickel AM, *The Least Dangerous Branch* (2nd edition, Yale Press 1986), quoted in Friedman, *The Will of the People*

Blumm MC and Wood MC, *The Public Trust Doctrine in Environmental and Natural Resources Law* (2nd Edition, Carolina Academic Press 2015)

Bork RH, The *Tempting of America* (Free Press 1990)

Cole D, *Engines of Liberty* (Basic Books 2016-17)

Cousins N, *Albert Schweitzer in Lambaréné* (Harper & Brothers 1960)

Cox A, *The Warren Court* (Harvard University Press 1968)

De Tocqueville A, Reeve H and Spencer JC, *Democracy in America* (J & HG Langley 1835)

Douglas WO, *The Right of the People* (Pyramid Books 1961)

Dorsen N, *The Evolving Constitution,* The James Madison Lectures (Wesleyan University Press 1987)

Elliot J, *The Debate in the Several State Conventions on the*

Adoption of the Federal Constitution, (2nd Edition 1836), reprinted in Barnett, Randy, *Rights Retained by the People: The History and Meaning of the Ninth Amendment*, 2 volumes (University Publishing Association 1993)

Farber DA, *Retained by the People* (Basic Books 2007)

Fink HP and Tushnet MV, *Federal Jurisdiction: Policy and Practice* (Michie 1987)

Friedman B, *The Will of the People* (Farrar, Straus and Giroux 2009)

Frost B-P and Sikkenga J, Editors, *History of American Political Thought* (2nd Edition, Lexington Books 2019)

Garner B, Editor in Chief, *Black's Law Dictionary* (Thomson Reuters 2016)

Gorsuch N, *A Republic, If You Can Keep It* (Crown Forum 2019)

Haidt J, *The Righteous Mind* (Vintage 2013)

Hamilton A, *The Papers of Alexander Hamilton*, referenced in Suzanna Sherry, "The Founders' Unwritten Constitution," vol 54, 4 (University of Chicago Law Review 1987), <https://chicagounbound.uchicago.edu/cgi/viewcontent.cgi?article=4538&context=uclrev>

Hartmann T, *The Hidden History of the Supreme Court and the Betrayal of America* (Berrett-Koehler Publishers 2019)

Hartmann T, *The Hidden History of the War on Voting* (Berrett-Koehler Publishers 2020)

Holmes OW, *The Common Law* (1st edition 1881; Barnes & Noble edition 2004)

Howard RM and Randazzo KA, editors, *Routledge Handbook of Judicial Behavior* (Routledge 2017)

Jacobs R, *Crash Landing – Surviving a Business Crisis* (Glenbridge Publishing 1991)

Jacobs R, *Wonderlust* (Glenbridge Publishing 2014)

Jay J, Madison J, and Hamilton A, *The Unabridged Federalist Papers and Anti-Federalist Papers*, (ReadaClassic 2010)

Jefferson T, *Jefferson Writings* (The Library of America 1984)

Jefferson T, *First Inaugural Address*, The Papers of Thomas Jefferson, Vol 33 (Princeton University Press 2006)

Lincoln A, *Fragment on the Constitution and the Union*, Collected Works of Abraham Lincoln, vol 4 (1st edition 1809-1865; University of Michigan Digital Library Production Services 2001) <https://quod.lib.umich.edu/l/lincoln/lincoln4/1:264?rgn=div1;view=toc>

Mapp AJ, *Thomas Jefferson, A Strange Case of Mistaken Identity* (Madison Books 1987)

Rakove JN, *Original Meanings* (Vintage Books 1997)

Riesman D, et al, *The Lonely Crowd* (2nd Edition, Yale University Press 2001)

Rossum RA, *Antonin Scalia's Jurisprudence: Text and Tradition* (University Press of Kansas 2016)

Rudenstine D, *The Age of Deference,* (Oxford University Press 2016)

Scalia A and Gutmann A, *A Matter of Interpretation: Federal Courts and the Law* (Princeton University Press 1998)

Shane PM, *Madison's Nightmare: How Executive Power Threatens American Democracy* (University of Chicago Press 2016)

Stibbe A, *Ecolinguistics* (Routledge 2015)

Stone C, *Should Trees Have Standing? Toward Legal Rights for Natural Objects* (3rd Edition, Oxford University Press 2010)

Tucker G, *View of the Constitution of the United States,* in *Blackstone's Commentaries: with Notes of Reference, to the Constitution and Laws, of the Federal Government of the United States; and the Commonwealth of Virginia* (1st edition, Birch and Small 1803) 140, 154, in Kurt T. Lash , "Inkblot: The Ninth Amendment as Textual Justification for Judicial Enforcement of the Right to Privacy " (Chicago Unbound 2017)

Washington G, *Farwell Address, September 19, 1796,* The World's Great Speakers (Dover Publications 1999)

Weale A, *The Will of the People - A Modern Myth* (Polity 2018)

Will G, *The Conservative Sensibility* (Hachette Books 2019)

Woodard C, *American Nations: A History of the Eleven Rival Regional Cultures of North America* (Penguin Books 2012)

Polls

"Americans Are United Against Partisan Gerrymandering" (*Brennan Center for Justice* March 2019) <https://www.brennancenter.org/our-work/research-reports/americans-are-united-against-partisan-gerrymandering>

"Americans Struggle with Truth, Accuracy and Accountability" (*Pew Research Center* July 2019) <https://www.pewresearch.org/politics/2019/07/22/americans-struggles-with-truth-accuracy-and-accountability/>

Associated Press NORC, "Growing Dissatisfaction With Direction of Country" (July 2020) <https://apnorc.org/projects/growing-dissatisfaction-with-direction-of-country/>

Associated Press NORC, "Only 23% of Americans have high levels of trust in what Trump is saying about the coronavirus" (*Market Watch* April 2020) <https://www.marketwatch.com/story/poll-shows-only-23-of-americans-have-high-levels-of-trust-in-what-trump-is-saying-to-the-public-2020-04-23>

Barnes R, "Polls show trust is Supreme Court, but there is growing interest in fixed terms and other changes" (*The Washington Post* Oct 2019) <https://www.washingtonpost.com/politics/courts_law/polls-show-trust-in-supreme-court-but-there-is-growing-interest-in-fixed-terms-and-other-changes/2019/10/24/dcbbcba4-f64c-11e9-8cf0-4cc99f74d127_story.html>

"Confidence in Institutions" (*Pew Research Center* 2019) <https://news.gallup.com/poll/1597/confidence-institutions.aspx>

"Congress and the Public" (*Gallup News* June 2020) <https://news.gallup.com/poll/1600/congress-public.aspx>

"Environment" (*Gallup News* 2020) <https://news.gallup.com/poll/1615/environment.aspx>

"Few Americans Express Positive Views of Trump's Conduct in

Office" (*Pew Research Center* March 2020) <https://www.pewresearch.org/politics/2020/03/05/few-americans-express-positive-views-of-trumps-conduct-in-office/>

"For Most Trump Voters, 'Very Warm' Feelings for Him Endured" *(Pew Research Center* 2018) <https://www.pewresearch.org/politics/2018/08/09/for-most-trump-voters-very-warm-feelings-for-him-endured/#in-march-2018-modest-gender-gap-in-views-of-trump-among-supporters>

Franklin CH, "Public Views of the Supreme Court" (*Marquette University Law School* October 2019) <https://law.marquette.edu/poll/wp-content/uploads/2019/10/MULawPollSupremeCourtReportOct2019.pdf>

Funk C and Kennedy B, "How Americans see climate change and environment in 7 charts" (*Pew Research Center* April 21, 2020), <https://www.pewresearch.org/fact-tank/2020/04/21/how-americans-see-climate-change-and-the-environment-in-7-charts/>

Hartig H, "Before Ginsburg's death, a majority of Americans viewed the Supreme Court as 'middle of the road,'" (*Pew Research Center* September 25, 2020), <https://www.pewresearch.org/fact-tank/2020/09/25/before-ginsburgs-death-a-majority-of-americans-viewed-the-supreme-court-as-middle-of-the-road/?utm_source=Pew+Research+Center&utm_campaign=64a7e8a2e5-Weekly_2020_09_26&utm_medium=email&utm_term=0_3e953b9b70>

"In Views of U.S. Democracy, Widening Partisan Divides Over Freedom to Peacefully Protects: Majority of "Americans say significant changes are needed in the 'fundamental design and structure of American government'" (*Pew Research Center* September 2, 2020) <https://www.pewresearch.org/politics/2020/09/02/in-views-of-u-s-democracy-widening-partisan-divides-over-freedom-to-peacefully-protest/>

Kennedy B, "U.S. concern about climate change is rising, but mainly among Democrats" (*Pew Research Center* April 18, 2020) <https://www.pewresearch.org/fact-tank/2020/04/16/u-s-concern-about-climate-change-is-rising-but-mainly-among-democrats/>

Livini E, "Americans trust the Supreme Court more than other

government branches" (*Justice League* October 25, 2019)
<https://qz.com/1735709/americans-trust-supreme-court-more-than-other-government-branches/>

McCarthy J, "64% of Americans Want Stricter Laws on Gun Sales" (*Gallup News* November 19, 2019)
<https://news.gallup.com/poll/268016/americans-stricter-laws-gun-sales.aspx>

McCarthy J, "Approval of Supreme Court Highest Since 2009" (*Gallup News* August 2020)
<https://news.gallup.com/poll/316817/approval-supreme-court-highest-2009.aspx>

Montanard D, "Poll: Majority Want to Keep Abortion Legal, But They Also Want Restrictions" (*NPR* June 2019)
<https://www.npr.org/2019/06/07/730183531/poll-majority-want-to-keep-abortion-legal-but-they-also-want-restrictions>

Neuman S, "Much of the World Doesn't Trust President Trump, Pew Survey Finds" (*NPR* January 8, 2020)
<https://www.npr.org/2020/01/08/794466129/much-of-the-world-doesnt-trust-president-trump-pew-survey-finds>

"7 facts about guns in the U.S." (*Pew Research Center* October 2019) <https://www.pewresearch.org/fact-tank/2019/10/22/facts-about-guns-in-united-states/>

"Party Affiliation" (*Gallup News* Updated February 18, 2021) https://news.gallup.com/poll/15370/party-affiliation.aspx

Raine L, Keeter S and Perrin A, "Trust and Distrust in America, a 4-part series" (*Pew Research Center* July 2019)
<https://www.pewresearch.org/politics/2019/07/22/trust-and-distrust-in-america/>

"Trust in Institutions" (*Pew Research Center* August 2020)
<https://www.pewresearch.org/topics/trust-in-government/>

"Trust in Government 1958-2015" (*Pew Research Center* November 2015)
<https://www.pewresearch.org/politics/2015/11/23/1-trust-in-government-1958-2015/>

"Trust in Government 1958-2019" (*Pew Research Center* April 2019) <https://www.pewresearch.org/politics/2019/04/11/public-trust-in-government-1958-2019/>

Wike R, Poushter J, Fetterolf J and Schumacher S, "Trump Ratings Remain Low Around the Globe, While Views of U.S. Stay Mostly Favorable" (*Pew Research Center* January 2020) <https://www.pewresearch.org/global/2020/01/08/trump-ratings-remain-low-around-globe-while-views-of-u-s-stay-mostly-favorable/>

U.S. Government Sources

"Constitutionality of Excluding Aliens from the Census for Apportionment and Redistricting Purposes" (*Congressional Research Service* April 13, 2012) <https://www.everycrsreport.com/files/20120413_R41048_e4eb1c36 9b633cea52b254c5a305e6111eb5d795.pdf>

"Emergency Authorities Under the National Emergencies Act, Stafford Act, and Public Health Act" (*Congressional Research Service* July 14, 2020) <https://fas.org/sgp/crs/natsec/R46379.pdf>

"Executive Orders" (*Federal Register* N.D.) <https://www.federalregister.gov/presidential-documents/executive-orders>

Gorsuch N, "Confirmation Hearing on the Nomination of Hon. Neil M. Gorsuch to be an Associate Justice of the Supreme Court of the United States" (*U.S. Government Publishing Office* March 2017) <https://www.congress.gov/115/chrg/CHRG-115shrg28638/CHRG-115shrg28638.htm>

"High-Income Nonfilers Owing Billions of Dollars Are Not Being Worked By The Internal Revenue Service," Internal Revenue Service" (*Treasury Inspector General for Tax Administration (Office of Audit)* May 2020) <https://www.treasury.gov/tigta/auditreports/2020reports/202030015_oa_highlights.html>

Kagan E, "The Nomination of Elena Kagan to be an Associate Justice of the Supreme Court of the United States" (*U.S. Government Publishing Office* June 28-30 & July 1, 2010) <https://www.congress.gov/111/chrg/shrg67622/CHRG-111shrg67622.htm>

Obama B, "Executive Order 13490 – Ethics Commitment by Executive Branch Personnel" (*Obama White House Archives* January

2009) <https://obamawhitehouse.archives.gov/the-press-office/ethics-commitments-executive-branch-personnel>

"The Court and Constitutional Interpretation" (The Supreme Court N.D.) <https://www.supremecourt.gov/about/constitutional.aspx>

"The Executive Branch" (*The White House* N.D.) <http://www.whitehouse.gov/about-the-white-house/the-executive-branch>

The Vacancies Act: A Legal Overview (*Congressional Research Service,* updated May 28, 2020) https://fas.org/sgp/crs/misc/R44997.pdf

Trump D, "Executive Order, Accelerating the Nation's Economic Recovery From the COVID-19 Emergency by Expediting Infrastructure Investments and Other Activities" (June 4, 2020) <https://www.federalregister.gov/documents/2020/06/09/2020-12584/accelerating-the-nations-economic-recovery-from-the-COVID-19-emergency-by-expediting-infrastructure>

Trump D, "Executive Order, Ethics Commitments by Executive Branch Appointees" (January 2017) <https://www.whitehouse.gov/presidential-actions/executive-order-ethics-commitments-executive-branch-appointees/>

Trump D, "Executive Order, Safe Policing for Safe Communities" (June 2020) <https://apps.npr.org/documents/document.html?id=6948245-Trump-Policing-Executive-Order>

Trump D, "Executive Order, Memorandum on Excluding Illegal Aliens From the Apportionment Base Following the 2020 Census" (July 2020) <https://www.whitehouse.gov/presidential-actions/memorandum-excluding-illegal-aliens-apportionment-base-following-2020-census/>

Other References and Resources

"2018 Primary Election Turnout and Reforms" (*Bipartisan Policy Center* November 2018) <https://bipartisanpolicy.org/wp-content/uploads/2019/03/2018-Primary-Election-Turnout-and-Reforms.pdf>
American College of Obstetricians and Gynecologists, "Joint

Statement on Abortion Access During the COVID-19 Outbreak"
(*ACOG* May 18, 2020), <https://www.acog.org/news/news-
releases/2020/03/joint-statement-on-abortion-access-during-the-
covid-19-outbreak>

"AG Nessel Joins Coalition Urging President Trump to Maintain
Environmental Protections during Review of Infrastructure Projects"
(*Department of Attorney General, Michigan* June 30, 2020)
<https://www.michigan.gov/ag/0,4534,7-359--533267--,00.html>

"A Guide to Emergency Powers and Their Use," (*Brennan Center for
Justice at New York University School of Law* September 4, 2019)
<https://web.archive.org/web/20200416140257/https://www.brennanc
enter.org/sites/default/files/2019-
10/2019_10_15_EmergencyPowersFULL.pdf>

Allison B, and Harkins S, "Fixed Fortunes: Biggest corporate
political interests spend billions, get trillions" (*Sunlight Foundation*
November 17, 2014),
<https://sunlightfoundation.com/2014/11/17/fixed-fortunes-biggest-
corporate-political-interests-spend-billions-get-trillions/>

American Civil Liberties Union (ACLU), "The case against the death
penalty" (N.D.) <https://www.aclu.org/other/case-against-death-
penalty>

"Attorney Generals Letter to President Trump Regarding Executive
Order 13927" (June 29, 2020)
<https://www.marylandattorneygeneral.gov/news
%20documents/062920_Letter_to_President.pdf>

Axelrod T, "Federal Judge Shoots down Texas Proclamation
Allowing One Ballot Drop-off Location per County" (*The Hill*
October 9, 2020) <https://thehill.com/homenews/state-watch/520460-
federal-judge-shoots-down-texas-proclamation-allowing-one-ballot-
drop>

Bagley N, "Most of Government Is Unconstitutional" (*New York
Times* June 21, 2019)
<https://www.nytimes.com/2019/06/21/opinion/sunday/gundy-united-
states.html>

Barnett RE, "A Ninth Amendment for Today's Constitution," Volume
26, 419 (*Valparaiso University Law Review* 1991)
<http://www.bu.edu/rbarnett/26val419.htm>

Barnett RE, "The Ninth Amendment Means What it Says," Volume 85, 1-82 (*Texas L. Review* November 2006) <https://scholarship.law.georgetown.edu/cgi/viewcontent.cgi?article=1850&context=facpub>

"Barrett takes her Supreme Court seat" [*The Week Magazine* November 6, 2020]

Benen S, "Scalia rejects privacy rights" (*MSNBC reporting on Fox News Sunday* July 30, 2012) <http://www.msnbc.com/rachel-maddow-show/scalia-rejects-privacy-rights>

Beyer D, "House Democrats Propose Supreme Court Term Limits, Appointments Schedule, Without Constitutional Amendment" (*Don Beyer Press Release* September 25, 2020) <https://beyer.house.gov/news/documentsingle.aspx?DocumentID=4925>

Borràs S, "Colonizing the atmosphere: a common concern without climate justice law?" Volume 26, 1, Journal of Political Ecology (*The University of Arizona* 2019) <https://journals.uair.arizona.edu/index.php/JPE/article/view/21817>

Brannon VC and Cole JP, "Chevron Deference: A Primer" (*Congressional Research Service* September 2017) <https://fas.org/sgp/crs/misc/R44954.pdf>

Bump P, "New data makes it clear: Nonvoters handed Trump the presidency" (*The Washington Post* August 9, 2018) <https://www.washingtonpost.com/news/politics/wp/2018/08/09/new-data-makes-it-clear-nonvoters-handed-trump-the-presidency/>

Caplan L, "The Embattled First Amendment," The American Scholar (*Phi Beta Kappa* Spring 2015) <https://theamericanscholar.org/the-embattled-first-amendment/#.X1YCvS2z2VM>

Chabot CK, "The Lost History of Delegation at the Founding" (*SSRN* August 3, 2020) <https://papers.ssrn.com/sol3/papers.cfm?abstract_id=3654564>

Charles G-U and Fuentes-Rohwer LE, "Dirty Thinking About Law and Democracy in Rucho v. Common Cause" (*American Constitution Society* 2019) <https://www.acslaw.org/analysis/acs-supreme-court-review/dirty-thinking-about-law-and-democracy-in-rucho-v-common-cause/>

Chung A, "Democrats prepare bill limiting U.S. Supreme Court justices term to 18 years" (*Reuters* September 24, 2020) <https://www.reuters.com/article/us-usa-court-termlimits/democrats-prepare-bill-limiting-u-s-supreme-court-justice-terms-to-18-years-idUSKCN26F3L3>

Cohen A, "The Most Powerful Dissent in American History" (*The Atlantic Magazine* August 2013), <https://www.theatlantic.com/national/archive/2013/08/the-most-powerful-dissent-in-american-history/278503/>

Conniff R, "Wisconsin Supreme Court takes voter purge case" (*Wisconsin Examiner* June 1, 2020) <https://wisconsinexaminer.com/brief/wisconsin-supreme-court-takes-voter-purge-case/>

"Constitution Daily, Executive Orders 101," NCC Staff (*National Constitution Center* January 23, 2017) <https://constitutioncenter.org/blog/executive-orders-101-what-are-they-and-how-do-presidents-use-them/>

Cost J, "James Madison's Lessons on Free Speech" (*National Review* September 4, 2017) <https://www.nationalreview.com/2017/09/james-madison-free-speech-rights-must-be-absolute-nearly/>

Dahl RA, "Decision-Making in a Democracy: The Supreme Court as National Decision Maker," Volume 6, 279 (*Journal of Public Law* 1957) <http://epstein.wustl.edu/research/DahlDecisionMaking.pdf>

Damante B, "At Least 15 Trump Officials Do Not Hold Their Positions Lawfully" (*Just Security* September 17, 2020) https://www.justsecurity.org/72456/at-least-15-trump-officials-do-not-hold-their-positions-lawfully/

Davison L and Versprille A, "For now, millionaires face little chance of IRS audit" (*Bloomberg and Tampa Bay Times* June 29, 2020) <https://www.bloomberg.com/news/articles/2020-06-29/corporate-audits-fell-71-as-coronavirus-pandemic-crippled-irs>

Deese K, "Texas governor orders only one mail ballot drop-off location allowed per county" (*The Hill* October 1, 2020) <https://thehill.com/homenews/state-watch/519183-texas-governor-orders-only-one-mail-ballot-drop-off-location-allowed-per>

Deiter RC, "Smart on Crime" (*Death Penalty Information Center* October 2009)

<https://files.deathpenaltyinfo.org/documents/pdf/CostsRptFinal.f156
0295688.pdf>

"Delegation of Legislative Power," Legal Information Institute
(*Cornell Law School* N.D.)
<https://www.law.cornell.edu/constitution-conan/article-1/section-
1/delegation-of-legislative-power>

Drutman L, "About half of retiring senators and a third of retiring
House members register as lobbyists" (*VOX* January 15, 2016)
<https://www.vox.com/2016/1/15/10775788/revolving-door-
lobbying>

Duffin E, "Voter turnout rate in presidential primary elections in
the United States in 2020, by state" (*Statista* August 14, 2020)
<https://www.statista.com/statistics/1102189/voter-turnout-us-
presidential-primaries-state/>

Durkee A, "Postal Service Reversing DeJoy's Changes, But Says
It Can't Reinstall All Sorting Machines" (*Forbes* September 24,
2020) <https://www.forbes.com/sites/alisondurkee/2020/09/24/postal-
service-reversing-dejoy-changes-but-cant-reinstall-all-sorting-
machines/#47fbc7266eea>

Ebling A, "IRS Fails to Pursue High-Income Nonfilers Who Owe
$46 Billion in Back Taxes, Watchdog Says" (*Forbes* June 2, 2020)
<https://www.forbes.com/sites/ashleaebeling/2020/06/02/irs-fails-to-
pursue-high-income-nonfilers-who-owe-46-billion-in-back-taxes-
watchdog-says/#7c7addc04535>

Fallon RH, "Foreword: Implementing the Constitution," Volume
111, 56 (*Harvard Law Review* November 1997)
<https://heinonline.org/HOL/LandingPage?
handle=hein.journals/hlr111&div=15&id=&page=>

Farber D, "Constitutional Rights in a Pandemic" (*Legal Planet*
July 15, 2020) <https://legal-planet.org/2020/07/15/constitutional-
rights-in-a-pandemic/>

Farias C, "Comments on Ferguson? Not My Job, Says Justice
Stephen Breyer" (*The New Republic* March 13, 2015)
<https://newrepublic.com/article/121294/stephen-breyer-dodges-
noah-feldmans-question-about-ferguson>

"Federal Government to Resume Capital Punishment After
Nearly Two Decade Lapse" (*Department of Justice Press Release*

July 25, 2019) <https://www.justice.gov/opa/pr/federal-government-resume-capital-punishment-after-nearly-two-decade-lapse>

"Federal Manager's Daily Report, Misuse of Position Most Common Ethics Violation, Says OGE" (*FEDweek* July 16, 2019) <https://www.fedweek.com/federal-managers-daily-report/misuse-of-position-most-common-ethics-violation-says-oge/>

Fichtner J, Heemskerk EM and Garcia-Bernardo J, "Hidden power of the Big Three? Passive index funds, re-concentration of corporate ownership, and new financial risk," Volume 19 Cambridge Core, Special. Issue 2 (*Cambridge University Press* June 2017) <https://www.cambridge.org/core/journals/business-and-politics/article/hidden-power-of-the-big-three-passive-index-funds-reconcentration-of-corporate-ownership-and-new-financial-risk/30AD689509AAD62F5B677E916C28C4B6>

"Founders Online, From James Madison to George Hay, 23 August 1823" (*National Archives* N.D.) <https://founders.archives.gov/documents/Madison/04-03-02-0109>

French D, "Polarization Prevailed, Again" [*Time Magazine* November 16, 2020] Online titled "It's Clear That America is Deeply Polarized. No Election Can Overcome That" (*Time Magazine* November 4, 2020) <https://time.com/5907318/polarization-2020-election/>

Guadiano N, and others, "Trump threatens to cut federal funds from schools that don't open" (*Politico* July 8, 2020) < https://www.politico.com/news/2020/07/08/trump-schools-reopening-federal-funding-352311 >

Green JE, "Mike Pence calls supreme court justice John Roberts a "disappointment" (*The Guardian* August 6, 2020) <https://www.theguardian.com/us-news/2020/aug/06/mike-pence-supreme-court-disappointment-justice-john-roberts>

Gross S, "What is the Trump administration's track record on the environment?" Policy 2020 (*Brookings Institute* August 4, 2020) <https://www.brookings.edu/policy2020/votervital/what-is-the-trump-administrations-track-record-on-the-environment/>

Grove TL, "The Supreme Court's Legitimacy Dilemma," Volume 132, 2240 (*Harvard L. Review* June 1, 2019) <https://harvardlawreview.org/2019/06/the-supreme-courts-legitimacy-dilemma/>

Haberman M, Karni A and Hakim D, "N.R.A. Gets Results on Gun Laws in One Phone Call With Trump" (*New York Times* August 20, 2019) <https://www.nytimes.com/2019/08/20/us/politics/trump-gun-control-nra.html>

Harris M, "The Return of Federal Executions" (*Slate* July 16, 2020) <https://slate.com/news-and-politics/2020/07/federal-executions-return-supreme-court-daniel-lee.html>

Hartmann T, "The Second Amendment Was Ratified to Preserve Slavery" (*Truthout* January 13, 2013) <https://truthout.org/articles/the-second-amendment-was-ratified-to-preserve-slavery/>

Hasen RL, "Race or Party, Race as Party, or Party All the Time: Three Uneasy Approaches to Conjoined Polarization in Redistricting and Voting Cases," Volume 59, 5 (*William & Mary Law Review* April 15, 2018) <https://scholarship.law.wm.edu/cgi/viewcontent.cgi?referer=https://www.google.com/&httpsredir=1&article=3754&context=wmlr>

Hasen RL, "The Gerrymandering Decision Drags the Supreme Court Further Into the Mud" (*New York Times* July 27, 2019) <https://www.nytimes.com/2019/06/27/opinion/gerrymandering-rucho-supreme-court.html>

Hatcher B, "Notes for the Next Constitution (or maybe the one after that)" (*Hermetica* 2016, revised 3-15-20) <https://www.hermetica.info/Constitution.html>

History.com Editors, "Executive Order" (*History channel* August 21, 2018) <https://www.history.com/topics/us-government/executive-order>

History.com Editors, "Japanese Internment Camps" (*History channel* February 21, 2020) <https://www.history.com/topics/world-war-ii/japanese-american-relocation>

Holmes OW, "Privilege, Malice and Intent," Volume 8, 1 (*Harvard Law Review* April 25, 1894) <https://www.jstor.org/stable/i256826>

"Is Lobbying Good or Bad?" (*RepresentUs* 2020) <https://represent.us/action/is-lobbying-good-or-bad/>

Jay P, "Three Investment Banks Control More Wealth Than GDP China – and Threaten Our Existence" (*theAnalysis.news* January 22,

2020) <https://theanalysis.news/commentary/the-lords-of-finance-own-the-media-arms-and-big-oil-and-threaten-our-existence-paul-jay-theanalysis/>

Johnson L, "Gerrymandering: Why only 2 percent of Americans feel elections work properly" (*The Hill* May 22, 2019) <https://thehill.com/opinion/campaign/445119-gerrymandering-why-only-2-percent-of-americans-feel-elections-work-properly>

Kagan E, "Presidential Administration," Vol. 114, 2245 (*Harvard L. Review* 2000-2001) <https://harvardlawreview.org/wp-content/uploads/pdfs/vol114_kagan.pdf>

Kelly M, "The Purpose of Dissenting Opinions in the Supreme Court" (*ThoughtCo* July 12, 2019) <https://www.thoughtco.com/the-purpose-of-dissenting-opinions-104784>

Kirschenbaum J, "Gerrymandering and Racial Justice in Wisconsin" (*Brennan Center for Justice at New York University School of Law* September 1, 2020) <https://www.brennancenter.org/our-work/analysis-opinion/gerrymandering-and-racial-justice-wisconsin>

Kolhatkar S, "Billionaires, Not Voters, Are Deciding Elections" (*Truthdig* November 9, 2018) <https://www.truthdig.com/articles/billionaires-not-voters-are-deciding-elections/>

Kravitz D, "Former Trump Officials Are Supposed to Avoid Lobbying. Except 33 Haven't" (*Pro Politico* February 14, 2019) <https://www.propublica.org/article/the-lobbying-swamp-is-flourishing-in-trumps-washington>

Lash KT, "Inkblot: The Ninth Amendment as Textual. Justification for Judicial Enforcement of the Right to Privacy," Vol. 80, The University of Chicago Law Review Dialogue, 219 (*Richmond School of Law, UR Scholarship Repository* 2013) <https://scholarship.richmond.edu/cgi/viewcontent.cgi?article=2451&context=law-faculty-publications>

Lavelle M, McKenna P, Hasemyer D and Kuznetz N, "Trump's Move to Suspend Enforcement of Environmental Laws is a Lifeline to the Oil Industry" (*Inside Climate News* March 27, 2020) <https://insideclimatenews.org/news/27032020/coronavirus-COVID-19-EPA-API-environmental-enforcement>

Lazarus J, McKay A, and Herbel L, "Who walks through the

revolving door? Examining the lobbying activity of former members of Congress" (*Journal Interest Groups & Advocacy*, *Springer* January 14, 2016) <https://link.springer.com/article/10.1057/iga.2015.16>

"Legal Change: Lessons from America's Social Movements" (*Brennan Center for Justice at New York University School of Law* September 29, 2015), <https://www.brennancenter.org/our-work/research-reports/legal-change-lessons-americas-social-movements>

Leuchtenburg W, "When Franklin Roosevelt Clashed With the Supreme Court and Lost" (*Smithsonian Magazine* May 2005) <https://www.smithsonianmag.com/history/when-franklin-roosevelt-clashed-with-the-supreme-court-and-lost-78497994/>

Lipton E, "Courts Thwart Administration's Efforts to Rescind Obama-Era Environmental Regulations" (*New York Times* October 6, 2017) <https://www.nytimes.com/2017/10/06/climate/trump-administration-environmental-regulations.html>

Lipton E and Protess B, "Banks' Lobbyists Help in Drafting Financial Bills" (*New York Times* May 23, 2013) <https://dealbook.nytimes.com/2013/05/23/banks-lobbyists-help-in-drafting-financial-bills/>

"List of national emergencies in the United States" (*Wikipedia* March 2020) <https://en.wikipedia.org/wiki/List_of_national_emergencies_in_the_United_States>

"Lobbying Registrations Report" (*ProPublica* 2020 - updated daily) <https://projects.propublica.org/represent/lobbying>

"Lobbyists in (and out of) the Trump Administration," Open Secrets (*Center for Responsive Politics* 2020) <https://www.opensecrets.org/trump/lobbyists>

Madison J, "1787: Madison's Notes of Debates in the Federal Convention" (*Online Library of Liberty* 1787) <https://oll.libertyfund.org/pages/1787-madison-s-notes-of-debates-in-the-federal-convention>

Madison J, "Parties" [1792] National Gazette

Magleby DB, "The Necessity of Political Parties and the Importance of Compromise," Vol. 54, no. 4 (*BYU Studies Quarterly* 2015) <https://byustudies.byu.edu/content/necessity-political-parties-and-

importance-compromise>

Maskell J, "Post-Employment, "Revolving Door," Laws for Federal Personnel" (*Congressional Research Service* 2014) <https://fas.org/sgp/crs/misc/R42728.pdf>

McConnell MW, "The Originalist Case for Brown v. Board of Education," University of Chicago Law School, Chicago Unbound Journal Articles, Vol. 19, 2 (*Harvard Journal of Law & Policy* 1995) <https://chicagounbound.uchicago.edu/cgi/viewcontent.cgi?article=12612&context=journal_articles>

McGrath T, "The US is now involved in 134 wars or none, depending on your definition of 'war'" (*Global Post* September 16, 2014) <https://www.pri.org/stories/2014-09-16/us-now-involved-134-wars-or-none-depending-your-definition-war>

Meyer T and Kahn D, "Dozens of Trump veterans cash out on K. St. despite 'drain the swamp' vow" (*Politico* July 8, 2020) <https://www.politico.com/news/2020/07/08/trump-administration-veteranslobbying-348273>

Mindock C, "Trump stokes fears Democrats will 'take your guns away', after flip flopping on gun control support" (*Independent.co.uk* September 16, 2019) <https://www.independent.co.uk/news/world/americas/us-politics/trump-gun-control-twitter-today-reform-checks-democrats-legislation-a9107336.html>

Molla R, "Voter turnout is estimated to be the highest in 120 years" (*Vox* November 4, 2020) <https://www.vox.com/2020/11/4/21549010/voter-turnout-record-estimate-election-2020>

Mora D, "Update: We Found a 'Staggering'*281 Lobbyists Who've Worked in the Trump Administration"* (Columbia Journalism Investigations reporting in ProPublica October 15, 2019) <https://www.propublica.org/article/we-found-a-staggering-281-lobbyists-whove-worked-in-the-trump-administration>

Moreno JE, "Wisconsin appeals court overturns order to purge more than 200,000 voters from rolls" (*The Hill* February 28, 2020) <https://thehill.com/regulation/court-battles/485190-wisconsin-court-overturns-plan-to-purge-more-than-200000-voters-from>

Morris P, "182 of those sent to death row actually were innocent" [*National Geographic* March 2021]

Morshedi M, "Marbury v. Madison (February 24, 1803)" (*Subscript Law* July 12, 2019) <https://www.subscriptlaw.com/blog/marbury-v-madison>

Mortenson JD & Bagley N, "There's No Historical Justification for One of the Most Dangerous Ideas in American Law" (*The Atlantic Magazine* May 28, 2020) <https://www.theatlantic.com/ideas/archive/2020/05/nondelegation-doctrine-orliginalism/612013/>

Mortenson JD & Bagley N, "Delegation at the Founding," University of Michigan Public Law Research Paper # 658 (*SSRN* September 1, 2020) <https://papers.ssrn.com/sol3/papers.cfm?abstract_id=3512154>

"Mr. Lincoln and the Supreme Court," New York Time Archive (*New York Times* March 9, 1861) <https://www.nytimes.com/1861/03/09/archives/mr-lincoln-and-the-supreme-court.html>

Mufson S, "Scott Pruitt's likely successor has long lobbying history on issues before the EPA" (*Washington Post* July 5, 2018) <https://www.washingtonpost.com/business/economy/epas-acting-administrator-has-long-lobbying-record-on-issues-before-the-agency/2018/07/05/a591cd40-6a6b-11e8-bea7-c8eb28bc52b1_story.html>

Neidig H, "Court blocks Trump order to exclude undocumented immigrants from census" (*The Hill* September 10, 2020) <https://thehill.com/regulation/515937-court-strikes-down-trumps-order-to-exclude-undocumented-from-census>

Neidig H, "Supreme Court rules states can remove 'faithless electors'" (*The Hill* July 6, 2020) <https://thehill.com/regulation/court-battles/505984-supreme-court-rules-states-can-remove-faithless-electors>

Neuman S, "Much of the World Doesn't Trust President Trump, Pew Survey Finds" (*NPR* January 8, 2020) <https://www.npr.org/2020/01/08/794466129/much-of-the-world-doesnt-trust-president-trump-pew-survey-finds>

Noll BD and Revesz RL, "Regulatory Rollbacks Have Changed the

Nature of Presidential Power" (*The Regulatory Review* March 16, 2020) <https://www.theregreview.org/2020/03/16/davis-noll-revesz-regulatory-rollbacks-changed-nature-presidential-power/>

Oppenheimer R, "The Supreme Court and Administrative Law," JSTOR, vol. 37, no. 1 (*Columbia Law Review* 1937) 1–42 www.jstor.org/stable/1116949>

Our Children's Trust Press Release, "9th Circuit Denies En Banc Review for *Juliana v United States*; Youth Plaintiffs Will Take Their Case to Supreme Court" [*Our Children's Trust* February 10, 2021]

"Overruled: The Untold Story of the Trump Administration" (*EarthJustice* July 2020, updated August 31, 2020) <https://earthjustice.org/features/environmental-lawsuits-trump-administration>

Perkins VL, "The War-Making Power: Congress vs. President," Vol 4 (*Brigham Young University Studies* 1961) 25-42 <https://www.jstor.org/stable/43040056?read-now=1&refreqid=excelsior%3A1d14e39fbc68b08573265f026bf70e1f&seq=9#page_scan_tab_contents>

Pilon R, "Rethinking Judicial Restraint" (*Cato Institute* 1991) <https://www.cato.org/publications/commentary/rethinking-judicial-restraint?mod=article_inline>

Pilon R, "Proper Judging Means Principled Engagement, Not Judicial Deference" (*Cato at Liberty* July 10, 2018) <https://www.cato.org/blog/proper-judging-means-principled-engagement-not-judicial-deference>

Popovich N, Ripka LA and Pierre-Louis K, "The Trump Administration Is Reversing 100 Environmental Rules. Here's the Full List" (*New York Times* July 15, 2020) <https://www.nytimes.com/interactive/2020/climate/trump-environment-rollbacks.html>

Posner R, "Appeal and Consent" (*New Republic* August 1999) cited in Segal and Chapman, *Routledge Handbook of Judicial Behavior*

Pusey, Merlo, "F.D.R. Vs. The Supreme Court," Vol 9, 3 (*American Heritage Magazine* April 1958) <https://www.americanheritage.com/fdr-vs-supreme-court>

Randolph E, "Draft Sketch of Constitution" (*ConSource, Inc.* July 26,

1787) <https://www.consource.org/document/draft-sketch-of-constitution-by-edmund-randolph-1787-7-26/>

Rios D, Blattmachr JG and Gans MM, "Chapter 1" in *Deference: When the Court Must Yield to the Government's Interpretation*, Circular 230 Deskbook (*Practicing Law Institute* 2006) <https://www.thecre.com/oira/wp-content/uploads/2015/03/ABA-Deference.pdf>

Roosevelt F, "Campaign Address at Madison Square Garden, New York City: We Have Only Just Begun to Fight" (October 31, 1936), in Rosenblum, *Public Papers of FDR*, volume 5, reported by Friedman, The Will of the People

Roosevelt T, "Eighth Annual Message" (December 8, 1908) <https://www.presidency.ucsb.edu/documents/eighth-annual-message-4>

Rosane O, "Trump Announces Final Rollback of Law That Gives Communities a Say in Fossil Fuel Project" (*EcoWatch* July 16, 2020) https://www.ecowatch.com/trump-nepa-rollback-2646418035.html?rebelltitem=1#rebelltitem1

"Roundup: Trump-Era Agency Policy in the Courts, Institute for Policy Integrity" (*New York University School of Law* October 27, 2020) <https://policyintegrity.org/trump-court-roundup>

Russell K, "Judge Gorsuch on separation of powers and federalism" (*SCOTUS Blog* March 15, 2017) <https://www.scotusblog.com/2017/03/judge-gorsuch-separation-powers-federalism/>

Schmidt M, "Donald Trump takes aim at Wisconsin Supreme Court justice Brian Hagedorn over election ruling," (*Wisconsin State Journal* December 29, 2020) <https://madison.com/wsj/news/local/govt-and-politics/donald-trump-takes-aim-at-wisconsin-supreme-court-justice-brian-hagedorn-over-election-ruling/article_c818b2f3-680e-5225-8c89-2a018924abb8.html>

Schultz D, "Carolene Products Footnote Four," (*The First Amendment Encyclopedia* 2009) <https://www.mtsu.edu/first-amendment/article/5/carolene-products-footnote-four>

Schweitzer A, "Nobel Lecture" (*Nobel Prize* November 4, 1954) <https://www.nobelprize.org/prizes/peace/1952/schweitzer/lecture/>

Sheeler A and Irby K, "California has spent $43 million suing the Trump administration. It's paying off, officials say" (*The Sacramento Bee* August 10, 2020) <https://www.sacbee.com/news/politics-government/capitol-alert/article244692807.html>

Shepard S, "Supreme Court tees up census case over whether Trump can exclude undocumented immigrants" (*Politico* October 16, 2020), <https://www.politico.com/news/2020/10/16/supreme-court-undocumented-immigrants-census-429969>

Sherry S, "A Summary of Why We Need More Judicial Activism" (*Vanderbilt Law School* Spring 2019) <https://law.vanderbilt.edu/news/a-summary-of-why-we-need-more-judicial-activism/>

Sherry S, "The Founders' Unwritten Constitution," Vol 54, 4 (*University of Chicago Law Review* Fall 1987) <https://chicagounbound.uchicago.edu/cgi/viewcontent.cgi?article=4538&context=uclrev>

Short K, "Like Roosters" (*Thoreau Farm* March 15, 2015) <https://thoreaufarm.org/2015/03/like-roosters/>

Slodysko B, "Trump frees former aides from ethics pledge, lobbying ban" (*Associated Press* January 20, 2021) https://apnews.com/article/donald-trump-lobbying-e911209abab83899eadd18b5776f6095

Sobel L, Ramaswamy A, Frederiksen B and Salganicoff A, "State Action to Limit Abortion Access During the COVID-19 Pandemic" (*Kaiser Family Foundation* August 10, 2020) <https://www.kff.org/coronavirus-COVID-19/issue-brief/state-action-to-limit-abortion-access-during-the-COVID-19-pandemic/>

Souter D, "Text of Justice David Souter's speech," Harvard 359th Commencement Remarks (May 27, 2010) <https://news.harvard.edu/gazette/story/2010/05/text-of-justice-david-souters-speech/>

"Spotlight on the Swamp Report, Has lobbyist influence been reduced and the revolving door slowed?" (*Issue One Action* June 2020) <https://www.spotlightontheswamp.org>

Straus JR, "Ethics Pledges and Other Executive Branch Appointee Restrictions Since 1993: Historical Perspective, Current Practices, and Options for Change" (*Congressional Research Service* September

29, 2017) <https://fas.org/sgp/crs/misc/R44974.pdf>

Stein J, "Citing an economic emergency, Trump directs agencies across government to waive federal regulations" (*The Washington Post* June 5, 2020) <https://www.washingtonpost.com/climate-environment/citing-an-economic-emergency-trump-directs-agencies-across-government-to-waive-federal-regulations/2020/06/05/6a23546c-a0fc-11ea-b5c9-570a91917d8d_story.html>

Stein J, "Trump signs order to waive environmental reviews for key projects" (*Washington Post* June 4, 2020) <https://www.washingtonpost.com/climate-environment/2020/06/04/trump-sign-order-waive-environmental-reviews-key-projects/>

Stoddard M, "Measures in Nebraska Legislature would change electoral college vote allocation, require voter ID" (*Omaha World-Herald* February 14, 2021) https://omaha.com/news/state-and-regional/govt-and-politics/measures-in-nebraska-legislature-would-change-electoral-vote-allocation-require-voter-id/article_030ee848-5111-11eb-9b35-9f1298cdb3d5.html

Summers L, "The IRS is leaving billions on the table. Here's how it can collect that money." (*Washington Post* June 22, 2020) <https://www.washingtonpost.com/opinions/2020/06/22/how-irs-could-fix-tax-gap/>

Swann S, *"D.C. swamp has gotten swampier under Trump, report finds"* (*UPI* June 19, 2020) <https://www.upi.com/Top_News/Voices/2020/06/19/DC-swamp-has-gotten-swampier-under-Trump-report-finds/1051592570936/>

Thayer JB, "The Origin and Scope of the American Doctrine of Constitutional Law," (*Harvard Law Review* October 1893) <https://www.jstor.org/stable/1322284>

"The American Presidency Project" (*University of California Santa Barbara* August 26, 2020 - periodically updated) <https://www.presidency.ucsb.edu/statistics/data/executive-orders>

The Week Staff, "How to rig elections, the legal way (*The Week Magazine* May 22, 2016) <https://theweek.com/articles/625095/how-rig-elections-legal-way>

"Tracking deregulation in the Trump era" (*Brookings* August 28,

2020), <https://www.brookings.edu/interactives/tracking-deregulation-in-the-trump-era/>

"Trump's Corporate Cabinet" (*Public Citizen* as of July 15, 2020) <https://www.citizen.org/article/corporatecabinet/>

"Trump imposes lifetime ban on some lobbying, five years on others" (*CNBC* January 27, 2017) <https://www.cnbc.com/2017/01/29/trump-imposes-lifetime-ban-on-some-lobbying-five-years-for-others.html>

"US Supreme Court blocks census citizenship question for now" (*BBC News* June 28, 2019) <https://www.bbc.com/news/world-us-canada-48791272>

Volcovici V, "Nine U.S. states sue EPA for easing environmental enforcement amid pandemic" (*Reuters* May 13, 2020) <https://www.reuters.com/article/us-health-coronavirus-epa/nine-u-s-states-sue-epa-for-easing-environmental-enforcement-amid-pandemic-idUSKBN22P36U>

Wachtler S, "Judging the Ninth Amendment," Vol. 59, 4 (*Fordham Law Review* 1991) <https://ir.lawnet.fordham.edu/cgi/viewcontent.cgi?article=2907&context=flr>

Walker C, "Attacking Auer and Chevron Deference: A Literature Review," Volume 16, 103 (*The Georgetown Journal of Public Policy* 2018) <https://www.law.georgetown.edu/public-policy-journal/wp-content/uploads/sites/23/2018/05/16-1-Attacking-Auer-and-Chevron-Deference.pdf>

"War Powers Act" (*Encyclopaedia Britannica* October 31, 2020) <https://www.britannica.com/topic/War-Powers-Act>

Washington G, "Transcript of President George Washington's Farewell Address (1796) [ourdocuments.gov https://www.ourdocuments.gov/doc.php?flash=false&doc=15&page=transcript]

Wegman J, "The Electoral College Will Destroy America" (*New York Times* September 8, 2020) <https://www.nytimes.com/2020/09/08/opinion/electoral-college-trump-biden.html>

Weyrich P, "I don't want everybody to vote" (*pflaw.org* June 8, 2007). <https://www.youtube.com/watch?v=8GBAsFwPglw>

Wilson R, "Five things we learned from this year's primaries" (*The Hill* September 4, 2020) <https://thehill.com/homenews/campaign/515028-five-things-we-learned-from-this-years-primaries?userid=254096>

Wiley LF and Valdeck SI, "COVID-19 Reinforces the Argument for "Regular" Judicial Review – Not Suspension of Civil Liberties – In Times of Crisis" (*Harvard Law Review Blog* April 9, 2020) <https://blog.harvardlawreview.org/COVID-19-reinforces-the-argument-for-regular-judicial-review-not-suspension-of-civil-liberties-in-times-of-crisis/>

Wiley LF and Valdeck SI, "Coronavirus, Civil Liberties, and the Courts: The Case Against 'Suspending' Judicial Review," Volume 33, 9 (*Harvard Law Review Forum* July 2020) <https://harvardlawreview.org/wp-content/uploads/2020/07/179-198_Online.pdf>

Will G, "The fourth branch is on its way to replacing Congress" (*The Washington Post* September 11, 2020) <https://www.washingtonpost.com/opinions/the-fourth-branch-of-government-is-on-its-way-to-evicting-congress/2020/09/10/f790b512-f39d-11ea-bc45-e5d48ab44b9f_story.html>

Wurman I, "Nondelegation at the Founding," SSRN, Volume 130, (*Yale Law Review* 2020) <https://papers.ssrn.com/sol3/papers.cfm?abstract_id=3559867>

Appendix

Appendix A: Chapter 5 – Juliana v. United States Chronology of Actions

1. The *Juliana* complaint, brought by 21 youths, was filed in September 2015 against the federal government (the Obama Administration), alleging that, through the government's affirmative actions that cause climate change, the federal government violated the youth's constitutional rights to life, liberty, and property, and also failed to protect essential "public trust resources," which include the air we breathe and the water we drink.

2. Initially, the fossil fuel industry intervened as defendants with the federal government who together filed motions for the trial court to dismiss the youths' lawsuit in 2016.

3. The denial of the motions by the court was followed by the fossil fuel industry withdrawing from the case in June 2017, during the Trump Administration. The trial judge set the trial date for February 5, 2018.

4. In 2017 the federal government (the Trump Administration) filed a 'writ of mandamus' with the 9th Circuit Court of Appeals. A petition for a writ of mandamus is an appeal to Court of Appeals for it to compel the trial court to do its bidding – in this case to order the trial court to block discovery or enter a judgment in favor of the government. The youths filed their answer along with eight amicus ("friends of the court") briefs supporting the youths' claims. Amicus briefs are supporting briefs filed with the court by interested persons who are not parties in the litigation. The writ was rejected by the 9th Circuit Court of Appeals on March 7, 2018, with the trial date reset for October 29, 2018.

5. The government then filed for a protective order to block

discovery and for summary judgment and judgment on the pleadings and followed these filings with a second petition for a writ of mandamus filed with the 9th Circuit Court of Appeals on July 5, 2018. The government's motions and writ were rejected.

6. The government then appealed to the Supreme Court, which, on July 30, 2018, unanimously rejected the government's appeal.

7. In October 2018, shortly before the scheduled trial, the government filed another motion with the trial court to block discovery and its third writ of mandamus with the 9th Circuit Court of Appeals.

8. Following denial by the trial court and the Court of Appeals, the government then filed its second writ of mandamus with the Supreme Court, which was denied on November 2, 2018. The Supreme Court ruled the government's writ was premature, but the Court also noted that the "breadth" of the youth plaintiffs' claims "is striking … and the justiciability of those claims presents substantial grounds for difference of opinion."

9. The denial was followed by another government writ of mandamus filed with the 9th Circuit Court of Appeals, which, considering the Supreme Court's comments above, was partially granted November 8, 2018.

10. On November 21, 2018, following the recommendation of the Court of Appeals, the trial court reluctantly referred the *Juliana* case to the 9th Circuit Court of Appeals to determine if the case should go to trial. The 9th Circuit Court of Appeals had requested it to so because of the concerns expressed by the Supreme Court (# 8 above). As a result, no new trial date was set.

11. On January 7, 2019, in response to the trial court's referral, the Court of Appeals granted the government's motion to file an interlocutory appeal. An interlocutory appeal is a discretionary appeal filed by a party in litigation – in the *Juliana* case, by the government – asking the Court of Appeals to resolve controlling issues of law where there are

grounds for differences in opinions and such an appeal may advance the ultimate termination of the litigation.

12. Fifteen additional amicus [friends of the court] briefs, filed by members of Congress, religious groups, legal scholars, businesses, historians, and others, including 32,000 youths under the age of 25, indicating broad support for the youth plaintiffs in *Juliana*, urged the Court approve the trial. Amicus briefs filed with a court in support of a party in litigation – in this case, in support of the 21 youths – are briefs filed by persons who are not parties to the litigation, but who have a strong interest in the subject matter of the litigation.

13. On January 17, 2020, in a 2 to 1 decision favoring the government, the 9th Circuit Court of Appeals recognized the gravity and truthfulness of the evidence supporting the youths' claims and the role of the government in causing harm. While it found the government had violated the constitutional rights of the youths, the majority opinion said that, contrary to the trial court's findings, under constitutional Separation of Powers Doctrine, the remedies must come from the legislative and executive Branches and not from the judicial branch. The third judge dissented and confirmed the children's constitutional claims, writing "our nation is crumbling – at our government's own hand – into a wasteland."

14. On March 2, 2020, the youth plaintiffs filed a petition before the 9th Circuit Court of Appeals, to rehear the case before a panel of all 11 judges.

15. On March 12, 2020, 24 members of Congress, and experts in constitutional and environmental law joined with leading women's, children's and environmental groups filed ten more amicus briefs.

16. On February 10, 2021, the request to the 9th Circuit Court of Appeals was denied without opinion. The youth plaintiffs plan an appeal to the Supreme Court and are approaching the Biden administration to join in their efforts to obtain constitutional rights protection,

Appendix B: Chapter 7 – President's Cabinet Members

(As of July 2020)
- Alex Azar, Secretary of Health & Human Services
- Andrew Wheeler, Administrator of Environmental Protection Agency
- Ben Carson, Secretary of Housing and Urban Development
- Betsy DeVos, Secretary of Education
- Chad Wolf, Acting Secretary of Homeland Security
- Dan Brouillette, Secretary of Energy
- David Bernhardt, Secretary of Interior
- Elaine Chao, Secretary of Transportation
- Eugene Scalia, Secretary of Labor
- Gina Haspel, Director of Central Intelligence
- John Ratcliffe, Director of National Intelligence
- Jovita Carranza, Administrator of Small Business Administration
- Mark Esper, Secretary of Defense
- Mark Meadows, Chief of Staff
- Mike Pence, Vice President
- Mike Pompeo, Secretary of State
- Robert Lighthizer, U.S. Trade Representative
- Robert Wilkie, Secretary of Veterans Affairs
- Russell Vought, Acting Director of Management and Budget
- Sonny Perdue, Secretary of Agriculture
- Steven Mnuchin, Secretary of the Treasury
- Wilbur Ross, Secretary of Commerce
- William Barr, Attorney General

Appendix C: Chapter 7 – Executive Branch Agencies' Employees

(Source: Executive Branch White House website: https://www.whitehouse.gov/about-the-white-house/the-executive-branch/)

Excluding the Department of Defense, as of June 2020:

1. Department of Agriculture, 100,000 employees, 17 sub-agencies, $95 billion budget

2. Department of Commerce, 38,000 employees, $6.5 billion budget

3. Department of Education,4,200 employees, $68.6 billion budget

4. Department of Energy, 100,000 employees, $23 billion budget

5. Department of Health and Human Services, 11 operating divisions, 65,000 employees, $700 billion budget

6. Department of Homeland Security, 216,000 employees, 22 executive branch agencies, budget unstated on Executive Branch| White House website

7. Department of Housing and Urban Development, 9,000 employees, $40 billion budget

8. Department of the Interior, 70,000 employees, 200,000 volunteers and $16 million budget

9. Department of Justice, 40 component organizations, $25 billion budget. Number of employees unstated on Executive Branch website

10. Department of Labor, 15,000 employees, $50 billion budget

11. Department of State, 30,000 employees, $35 billion budget

12. Department of Transportation, 55,000 employees, $70 billion budget

13. Department of the Treasury, 100,000 employees, $13 billion budget

14. Department of Veterans Affairs, 235,000 employees, $90 budget

Appendix D: Chapter 7 – Presidents' Executive Orders

Source: "The American Presidency Project" UC Santa Barbara
https://www.presidency.ucsb.edu/statistics/data/executive-orders

As of November 3, 2020:

- George Washington   8
- John Adams   1
- Thomas Jefferson   4
- James Madison   1
- James Monroe   1
- John Q. Adams   3
- Andrew Jackson   12
- Martin Van Buren   10
- William H. Harrison   0
- John Tyler   17
- James Polk   18
- Zachary Taylor   5
- Millard Fillmore   12
- Franklin Pierce   35
- James Buchanan   16
- Abraham Lincoln   48
- Andrew Johnson   79
- Ulysses S. Grant   217
- Rutherford B. Hayes   92
- James Garfield   6
- Chester Arthur   96
- Grover Cleveland   13
- Benjamin Harrison   43
- Grover Cleveland   140
- William McKinley   185
- Theodore Roosevelt   1,081
- William Howard Taft   522
- Woodrow Wilson   1,803
- Warren Harding   522
- Calvin Coolidge   1,203
- Herbert Hoover   968
- Franklin D Roosevelt   3,721
- Harry S. Truman   907
- Dwight D. Eisenhower   484
- John F. Kennedy   214
- Lyndon B. Johnson   325
- Richard Nixon   346

- Gerald R. Ford   169
- Jimmy Carter   320
- Ronald Reagan   381
- George Bush   168
- William Clinton   364
- George W. Bush   291
- Barack Obama   276
- Donald J. Trump   220

Appendix E: Chapter 7 – Executive Order 13770

Ethics Commitments by Executive Branch Appointees

By the authority vested in me as President of the United States by the Constitution and the laws of the United States of America, including section 301 of title 3, United States Code, and sections 3301 and 7301 of title 5, United States Code, it is hereby ordered as follows:

Section 1. *Ethics Pledge.* Every appointee in every executive agency appointed on or after January 20, 2017, shall sign, and upon signing shall be contractually committed to, the following pledge upon becoming an appointee:

"As a condition, and in consideration, of my employment in the United States Government in an appointee position invested with the public trust, I commit myself to the following obligations, which I understand are binding on me and are enforceable under law:

"1. I will not, within 5 years after the termination of my employment as an appointee in any executive agency in which I am appointed to serve, engage in lobbying activities with respect to that agency.

"2. If, upon my departure from the Government, I am covered by the post-employment restrictions on communicating with employees of my former executive agency set forth in section 207(c) of title 18, United States Code, I agree that I will abide by those restrictions.

"3. In addition to abiding by the limitations of paragraphs 1 and 2, I also agree, upon leaving Government service, not to engage in lobbying activities with respect to any covered executive branch official or non- career Senior Executive Service appointee for the remainder of the Administration.

"4. I will not, at any time after the termination of my employment in the United States Government, engage in any activity on behalf of any foreign government or foreign political party which, were it undertaken on January 20, 2017, would require me to register under the Foreign Agents Registration Act of 1938, as amended.

"5. I will not accept gifts from registered lobbyists or lobbying organizations for the duration of my service as an appointee.

"6. I will not for a period of 2 years from the date of my appointment participate in any particular matter involving specific parties that is directly and substantially related to my former employer or former clients, including regulations and contracts.

"7. If I was a registered lobbyist within the 2 years before the date of my appointment, in addition to abiding by the limitations of paragraph 6, I will not for a period of 2 years after the date of my appointment participate in any particular matter on which I lobbied within the 2 years before the date of my appointment or participate in the specific issue area in which that particular matter falls.

"8. I agree that any hiring or other employment decisions I make will be based on the candidate's qualifications, competence, and experience.

"9. I acknowledge that the Executive Order entitled 'Ethics Commitments by Executive Branch Appointees,' issued by the President on January 28, 2017, which I have read before signing this document, defines certain terms applicable to the foregoing obligations and sets forth the methods for enforcing them. I expressly accept the provisions of that Executive Order as a part of this agreement and as binding on me. I understand that the obligations of this pledge are in addition to any statutory or other legal restrictions applicable to me by virtue of Government service."

Sec. 2. *Definitions.* As used herein and in the pledge set forth in section 1 of this order:

(a) "Administration" means all terms of office of the incumbent President serving at the time of the appointment of an appointee covered by this order.

(b) "Appointee" means every full-time, non-career Presidential or Vice- Presidential appointee, non-career appointee in the Senior Executive Service (or other SES-type system), and appointee to a position that has been excepted from the competitive service by reason of being of a confidential or policy- making character (Schedule C and other positions excepted under comparable criteria) in an executive agency. It does not include any person appointed as a member of the Senior Foreign Service or solely as a uniformed service commissioned officer.

(c) "Covered executive branch official" shall have the definition set forth in the Lobbying Disclosure Act.

(d) "Directly and substantially related to my former employer or former clients" shall mean matters in which the appointee's former employer or a former client is a party or represents a party.

(e) "Executive agency" and "agency" mean "executive agency" as defined in section 105 of title 5, United States Code, except that the terms shall include the Executive Office of the President, the United States Postal Service, and the Postal Regulatory Commission, and excludes the Government Ac- countability Office. As used in paragraph 1 of the pledge, "executive agency" means the entire agency in which the appointee is appointed to serve, except that:

(1) with respect to those appointees to whom such designations are applicable under section 207(h) of title 18, United States Code, the term means an agency or bureau designated by the Director of the Office of Government Ethics under section 207(h) as a separate department or agency at the time the appointee ceased to serve in that department or agency; and

(2) an appointee who is detailed from one executive agency to another for more than 60 days in any calendar year shall be deemed to be an officer or employee of both agencies during the period such person is detailed.

(f) "Foreign Agents Registration Act of 1938, as amended" means sections 611 through 621 of title 22, United States Code.

(g) "Foreign government" means the "government of a foreign country," as defined in section 1(e) of the Foreign Agents Registration Act of 1938, as amended, 22 U.S.C. 611(e).

(h) "Foreign political party" has the same meaning as that term has in section 1(f) of the Foreign Agents Registration Act of 1938, as amended, 22 U.S.C. 611(f).

(i) "Former client" is any person for whom the appointee served personally as agent, attorney, or consultant within the 2 years prior to the date of his or her appointment, , but excluding instances where the service provided was limited to a speech or similar appearance. It does not include clients of the appointee's former employer to whom the appointee did not personally provide services.

(j) "Former employer" is any person for whom the appointee has within the 2 years prior to the date of his or her appointment served as an employee, officer, director, trustee, or general partner, except that "former employer" does not include any executive agency or other entity of the Federal Government, State or local government, the District of Columbia, Native

(k) "Gift"

(1) shall have the definition set forth in section 2635.203(b) of title 5, Code of Federal Regulations;

(2) shall include gifts that are solicited or accepted indirectly as defined at section 2635.203(f) of title 5, Code of Federal Regulations; and

(3) shall exclude those items excluded by sections 2635.204(b), (c), (e)(1) & (3), (j), (k), and (l) of title 5, Code of Federal Regulations.

(l) "Government official" means any employee of the executive branch.

(m) "Lobbied" shall mean to have acted as a registered lobbyist.

(n) "Lobbying activities" has the same meaning as that term has in the Lobbying Disclosure Act, except that the term does not include communicating or appearing with regard to: a judicial proceeding; a criminal or civil law enforcement inquiry, investigation, or proceeding; or any agency process for rulemaking, adjudication, or licensing, as defined in and governed by the Administrative Procedure Act, as amended, 5 U.S.C. 551 *et seq.*

(o) "Lobbying Disclosure Act" means sections 1601 *et seq.* of title 2, United States Code.

(p) "Lobbyist" shall have the definition set forth in the Lobbying Disclosure Act.

(q) "On behalf of another" means on behalf of a person or entity other than the individual signing the pledge or his or her spouse, child, or parent.

(r) "Particular matter" shall have the same meaning as set forth in section 207 of title 18, United States Code, and section 2635.402(b)(3) of title 5, Code of Federal Regulations.

(s) "Particular matter involving specific parties" shall have the same meaning as set forth in section 2641.201(h) of title 5, Code of Federal Regulations, except that it shall also include any meeting or other communication relating to the performance of one's official duties with a former employer or former client, unless the communication applies to a particular matter of general applicability and participation in the meeting or other event is open to all interested parties.

(t) "Participate" means to participate personally and substantially.

(u) "Pledge" means the ethics pledge set forth in section 1 of this order.

(v) "Post-employment restrictions" shall include the provisions and exceptions in section 207(c) of title 18, United States Code, and the implementing regulations.

(w) "Registered lobbyist or lobbying organization" shall mean a lobbyist or an organization filing a registration pursuant to section 1603(a) of title 2, United States Code, and in the case of an organization filing such a registration, "registered lobbyist" shall include each of the lobbyists identified therein.

(x) Terms that are used herein and in the pledge, and also used in section 207 of title 18, United States Code, shall be given the same meaning as they have in section 207 and any implementing regulations issued or to be issued by the Office of Government Ethics, except to the extent those terms are otherwise defined in this order.

(y) All references to provisions of law and regulations shall refer to such provisions as in effect on January 20, 2017.

Sec. 3. *Waiver.* (a) The President or his designee may grant to any person a waiver of any restrictions contained in the pledge signed by such person. (b) A waiver shall take effect when the certification is signed by the President or his designee.

(c) A copy of the waiver certification shall be furnished to the person covered by the waiver and provided to the head of the agency in which that person is or was appointed to serve.

Sec. 4. *Administration.* (a) The head of every executive agency shall establish for that agency such rules or procedures (conforming as nearly as practicable to the agency's general ethics rules and procedures, including those relating to designated agency ethics officers) as are necessary or appropriate:

(1) to ensure that every appointee in the agency signs the pledge upon assuming the appointed office or otherwise becoming an appointee; and

(2) to ensure compliance with this order within the agency.

(b) With respect to the Executive Office of the President, the duties set forth in section 4(a) shall be the responsibility of the Counsel to the President or such other official or officials to whom the President delegates those duties.

(c) The Director of the Office of Government Ethics shall:

(1) ensure that the pledge and a copy of this Executive Order are made available for use by agencies in fulfilling their duties under section 4(a);

(2) in consultation with the Attorney General or Counsel to the President, when appropriate, assist designated agency ethics officers in providing advice to current or former appointees regarding the application of the pledge; and

(3) adopt such rules or procedures (conforming as nearly as practicable to its generally applicable rules and procedures) as are necessary or appropriate:

(i) to carry out the foregoing responsibilities;

(ii) to apply the lobbyist gift ban set forth in paragraph 5 of the pledge to all executive branch employees;

(iii) to authorize limited exceptions to the lobbyist gift ban for circumstances that do not implicate the purposes of the ban;

(iv) to make clear that no person shall have violated the lobbyist gift ban if the person properly disposes of a gift as provided by section 2635.206 of title 5, Code of Federal Regulations;

(v) to ensure that existing rules and procedures for Government employ- ees engaged in negotiations for future employment with private businesses that are affected by their official actions do not affect the integrity of the Government's programs and operations; and

(vi) to ensure, in consultation with the Director of the Office of Personnel Management, that the requirement set forth in paragraph 8 of the pledge is honored by every employee of the executive branch;

(d) An appointee who has signed the pledge is not required to sign

the pledge again upon appointment or detail to a different office, except that a person who has ceased to be an appointee, due to termination of employment in the executive branch or otherwise, shall sign the pledge prior to thereafter assuming office as an appointee.

(e) All pledges signed by appointees, and all waiver certifications with respect thereto, shall be filed with the head of the appointee's agency for permanent retention in the appointee's official personnel folder or equivalent folder.

Sec. 5. *Enforcement.* (a) The contractual, fiduciary, and ethical commitments in the pledge provided for herein are solely enforceable by the United States by any legally available means, including any or all of the following: debarment proceedings within any affected executive agency or civil judicial proceedings for declaratory, injunctive, or monetary relief.

(b) Any former appointee who is determined, after notice and hearing, by the duly designated authority within any agency, to have violated his or her pledge may be barred from engaging in lobbying activities with respect to that agency for up to 5 years in addition to the 5-year time period covered by the pledge. The head of every executive agency shall, in consultation with the Director of the Office of Government Ethics, establish procedures to implement this subsection, which shall include (but not be limited to) providing for factfinding and investigation of possible violations of this order and for referrals to the Attorney General for his or her consideration pursuant to subsection (c).

(c) The Attorney General or his or her designee is authorized:

(1) upon receiving information regarding the possible breach of any commitment in a signed pledge, to request any appropriate Federal investigative authority to conduct such investigations as may be appropriate; and

(2) upon determining that there is a reasonable basis to believe that a breach of a commitment has occurred or will occur or continue, if not enjoined, to commence a civil action on behalf of the United States against the former officer or employee in any United States District Court with jurisdiction to consider the matter.

(d) In such civil action, the Attorney General or his or her designee is authorized to request any and all relief authorized by law, including but not limited to:

(1) such temporary restraining orders and preliminary and permanent injunctions as may be appropriate to restrain future,

recurring, or continuing conduct by the former officer or employee in breach of the commitments in the pledge he or she signed; and

(2) establishment of a constructive trust for the benefit of the United States, requiring an accounting and payment to the United States Treasury of all money and other things of value received by, or payable to, the former officer or employee arising out of any breach or attempted breach of the pledge signed by the former officer or employee.

Sec. 6. *General Provisions.* (a) This order supersedes Executive Order 13490 of January 21, 2009 (Ethics Commitments by Executive Branch Personnel), and therefore Executive Order 13490 is hereby revoked. No other prior Executive Orders are repealed by this order. To the extent that this order is inconsistent with any provision of any prior Executive Order, this order shall control.

(b) If any provision of this order or the application of such provision is held to be invalid, the remainder of this order and other dissimilar applications of such provision shall not be affected.

(c) The pledge and this order are not intended to, and do not, create any right or benefit, substantive or procedural, enforceable at law or in equity by any party (other than by the United States) against the United States, its departments, agencies, or entities, its officers, employees, or agents, or any other person.

(d) The definitions set forth in this order are solely applicable to the terms of this order and are not otherwise intended to impair or affect existing law.

(e) Nothing in this order shall be construed to impair or otherwise affect:

(1) the authority granted by law to an executive department, agency, or the head thereof; or relating to budgetary, administrative, or legislative proposals.

(f) This order shall be implemented consistent with applicable law and subject to the availability of appropriations.

Appendix F: Chapter 5 - Our Children's Trust: Congressional Resolution Introduced

Children's Fundamental Climate Rights and Recovery Resolution

Introduced by Senator Jeff Merkley & Representatives Jan Schakowsky, Pramila Jayapal and Bobby L. Rush September 23, 2020, https://www.ourchildrenstrust.org/congressionalresolution?utm_term=0_4094e87487-ec94ce2b46-110459049

S. Con. Res.___ / H. Con. Res. ___

Experts agree that human-caused climate change is adversely impacting our children. Renewed United States leadership is needed to immediately recognize that the climate crisis is affecting children's fundamental rights and to demand a plan.

THE CLIMATE CRISIS DISPROPORTIONATELY IMPACTS OUR CHILDREN

There is an overwhelming scientific consensus that the present rate of global heating and ocean acidification is a result of the buildup of atmospheric greenhouse gas emissions, primarily carbon dioxide (CO_2) emissions, largely from the combustion of fossil fuels. Our current climate crisis disproportionately affects the health, economic opportunity, and fundamental rights of children.

Congress must act now to protect our children's rights, their health, and our planet.

CHILDREN'S FUNDAMENTAL RIGHTS ARE AT STAKE

Children are uniquely vulnerable to human-caused climate change. Today's children were born into a climate system that is hazardous to their health and well-being. A climate system capable of sustaining human life is fundamental to a free and ordered society and is preservative of other fundamental rights, including the rights to life, liberty, and property. Our Nation's children have called upon government leaders to take science-based and equitable action to address this crisis and ensure climate justice for their generation, future generations, and vulnerable communities, including communities of color, low-income communities, and indigenous peoples.

THE TIME TO ACT IS NOW

Scientists state that global atmospheric CO_2 concentrations must be reduced from over 415 parts per million (ppm) to below 350 ppm by 2100 to restore the planet's energy balance and stabilize our climate system. Experts have found technically and economically feasible pathways to place all sectors of our economy on a path to reach 350 ppm. Congress must demand a climate recovery plan that puts the United States on a trajectory consistent with reaching this target to uphold children's rights.

THIS RESOLUTION RECOGNIZES CHILDREN'S RIGHTS & DEMANDS A CLIMATE PLAN

The resolution calls on Congress to:

- support the youth climate movement and children across our Nation, including children from frontline and vulnerable communities seeking climate justice;

- protect children's fundamental rights to life, liberty, and property, and equal protection of the laws, which includes a climate system capable of sustaining human life; and

- demand a national, comprehensive, science-based, and just climate recovery plan prepared by the executive branch.

About the Author

Richard Jacobs graduated from the University of Wisconsin in 1954, with a degree in business. He earned Phi Beta Kappa and other honors. After military service and a career in the life insurance business, he graduated from Stetson University College of Law in 1967, *Magna Cum Laude*, first in his class. He was admitted to practice in June 1967, after achieving the high score on the March 1967 Florida Bar examination. As a practicing lawyer, he attained an Av rating and was included in Best Lawyers in America. After more than five decades practicing business law, he "mostly retired" in 2013; and, in 2014, wrote *Wonderlust*, the stories of the lessons learned in his trekking the seven continents. In 2020 he became a member of Stetson University College of Law's Hall of Fame.

His civic activities have included his being chairman and trustee of his community hospital and arts center and serving as a trustee of his law school and other educational institutions. Motivated by the lessons learned in his travels, he also devoted his attention to environmental, sea-level rise, and global warming issues, as a writer, speaker, and a lawyer, working particularly close with Our Children's Trust and Stetson College of Law. *Democracy of Dollars* grew out of his experiences in being thwarted in problem-solving environmental issues by government inaction when action is needed.

A lawyer by training, a photographer by passion, he has been fortunate to have trekked and photo'd on the seven continents — and those experiences have shaped his life and understanding the nature of our responsibilities for the care of each other and our earth, the only home we will ever have.

CPSIA information can be obtained
at www.ICGtesting.com
Printed in the USA
FSHW021710090521
81285FS